This book is dedicated to the
memory of John McShane

The Child as Psychologist

An introduction to the development of social cognition

Edited by

Mark Bennett

HARVESTER WHEATSHEAF

New York   London   Toronto   Sydney   Tokyo   Singapore

First published 1993 by
Harvester Wheatsheaf
Campus 400, Maylands Avenue
Hemel Hempstead
Hertfordshire, HP2 7EZ
A division of
Simon & Schuster International Group

Typeset in 10/12pt Ehrhardt
by Photoprint, 9–11 Alexandra Lane, Torquay, Devon

Printed and bound in Great Britain by
BPCC Wheatons Ltd, Exeter

British Library Cataloguing in Publication Data

A catalogue record for this book is available from the British Library

ISBN 0–7450–1233–7 (hbk)
ISBN 0–7450–1234–5 (pbk)

1 2 3 4 5   96 95 94 93

Contents

Notes on the contributors

Mark Bennett, Department of Psychology, University of Dundee, Dundee DD1 4HN.

Julie Dickinson, Department of Occupational Psychology, Birkbeck College, University of London, Malet Street, London WC1.

Nicholas Emler, Department of Experimental Psychology, University of Oxford, South Parks Road, Oxford OX1 3UD.

Paul L. Harris, Department of Experimental Psychology, University of Oxford, South Parks Road, Oxford OX1 3UD.

Judith A. Hudson, Department of Psychology, Rutgers University, Tillett Hall, Kilmer Campus, New Brunswick, NJ 08903, USA.

Sue Leekam, Institute of Social and Applied Psychology, University of Kent, Canterbury CT2 7NZ.

Paul Light, Department of Psychology, University of Southampton, Southampton SO9 5NH.

Mark Meerum Terwogt, Faculty of Psychology, Free University of Amsterdam, Van der Boechorststraat 1, 1081 BT Amsterdam, The Netherlands.

Judith G. Smetana, Graduate School of Education and Human Development, University of Rochester, Rochester, NY 14627, USA.

Nicola Yuill, School of Cognitive and Computing Sciences, University of Sussex, Falmer, Brighton BN1 9QN.

Preface and acknowledgements

The developmental study of social cognition has been flourishing for at least a decade. It is odd, then, that with so much having been written, so little has been specifically addressed to an undergraduate audience. This book is intended for intermediate and advanced undergraduates, though it is likely to be useful to postgraduates, too. It is concerned primarily to introduce some of the major literature within the developmental social cognition field.

Whilst I wanted to convey something of the achievements of this field, I was keen to avoid creating the impression that this is too 'comfortable' an area of research. To this end I invited Paul Light to write a concluding chapter which would present a critique both of the individual chapters and of the field more generally. Whilst his critique is necessarily personal, I think it touches on issues which many researchers will recognize as important, even if they disagree with him. At the very least, I hope it will serve as a useful basis for discussion.

Thanks are extended to the MIT Press for allowing me to reproduce Figure 4.1 from Henry Wellman's (1990) book *The Child's Theory of Mind*. I am also pleased to have the opportunity of thanking Farrell Burnett at Harvester Wheatsheaf for her enthusiastic and constructive support of this project, and for never allowing me to lose sight of deadlines. Finally, for her discussion of so many issues which arose in the preparation of this book, I would like to express special thanks to Sue Leekam, who has been as good a colleague as one could wish to have.

Mark Bennett
Dundee, Scotland
August 1992

Chapter 1

Introduction
Mark Bennett

The child and psychologist have at least one significant common goal: the understanding of human action. Both are in the business of trying to *interpret*, *predict* and sometimes even *control* what people do. In the case of the psychologist this is perfectly clear, but a moment's reflection will tell us that children, too, are frequently preoccupied with what others do. All of us at some point have witnessed children's zealous attempts at psychological understanding: 'Why are you doing that?', 'Why are you sad?', 'Do you like me?', and so on, apparently *ad infinitum*.

But what exactly do children understand about human action? Where does this understanding come from? And how does it develop? This is what this book is about. This chapter, however, has a stage-setting function and takes up two main themes. First, we will look at the origins and development of the tradition of viewing ordinary people as psychologists or scientists. Second, we will consider the sorts of constructs, or conceptual 'tools', that the everyday psychologist uses in getting to grips with human action – desire, belief, emotion, personality, social rules, etc. Children's understanding of these constructs will be considered in detail in the following chapters. In the penultimate chapter, consideration will be given to the child as sociologist. Finally, the closing chapter will provide a critical commentary on the contents of this book, and on the field in general.

1.1 Viewing the layperson as psychologist or scientist

1.1.1 Historical background

Likening ordinary people to psychologists, or scientists, has a considerable history in psychology (e.g. in the study of personality: Kelly, 1955; in social

1

psychology: Heider, 1958; Kelley, 1967; Ross, 1977; Wegner and Vallacher, 1977; in developmental psychology: Kassin, 1981; Miller, 1985; Ross, 1981). The general idea behind this view is that the person in the street is engaged in the process of constructing a theory, of sorts, about the everyday actions of self and other. In making sense of what we observe, we evolve a body of knowledge made up of interrelated propositions about action that enables us to account for what we observe. Inevitably, we will often be wrong, and so, like scientists, we may have to revise our theories. And by modifying or enhancing our theories, we may be in a better position to manage the everyday world.

Why is it that so many psychologists should have been preoccupied with the ordinary person's construction of the world? After all, the cynic might say: 'I don't care what my neighbour thinks about human behaviour; I want the *facts*'. Well, as Asch (1952) noted:

> We act and choose on the basis of what we see, feel and believe. . . . When we are mistaken about things, we act in terms of our erroneous notions, not in terms of things as they are. To understand human action it is therefore essential to understand the conscious mode in which things appear to us. (pp. 64–5)

In short, then, what Asch is suggesting is that if psychologists are to understand human behaviour, they must look at people's everyday constructions of the world.

The sociologist Schutz (1932) was an early advocate of this general position. Commenting upon the *nature* of such knowledge, he maintained that:

> All our knowledge . . . , in common-sense as in scientific thinking, involves constructs. . . . Strictly speaking, there are no such things as facts, pure and simple. All facts are from the outset facts selected from a universal context by the activities of our minds. . . . This does not mean that, in daily life or in science, we are unable to grasp the reality of the world. It just means that we grasp merely certain aspects of it, namely those which are relevant to us. (p. 5)

What Schutz highlights, then, is the 'conceptually driven' nature of our everyday understanding – that it is guided not by intrinsic properties of the world, but by our prior conceptual apparatus. This position was developed by the philosopher Hanson (1958), who made the case that *all* observation, scientific or lay, is *theory-dependent*: only when theories are in place are we able to discern distinct and meaningful 'facts' from the rich flow of events we observe. Consider the commonplace matter of recognizing that what you are now looking at is a page of a book. To recognize it *as such* requires that you understand something of the nature of pages and books as classes of object distinct from other objects. In short, Hanson made the case that 'raw' observation does not exist. Hanson's general sort of position has a substantial history in Western thought, going back at least as far as Kant. Following in this tradition, the basic assumption made by most researchers who have been concerned with everyday psychology is that our perception and knowledge are the result of a *constructive* process, based both on information from the world and on our mental actions upon the world.

1.1.2 George Kelly's Personal Construct Theory

Within psychology, the earliest attempt to cast people as 'everyday scientists' was probably that of George Kelly. Kelly initiated his work in the 1930s and eventually published his classic work *The Psychology of Personal Constructs* in 1955. Fundamental to his position was the conviction that there is no absolute or pre-given reality, only *interpretations* of what passes for reality. And those interpretations depend upon individuals' constructs. For Kelly, constructs are bipolar concepts which enable us to categorize information from the world. For example, we might categorize information in terms of constructs such as *warm–cold*, *heavy–light*, *easy–difficult*, *like me–not like me*, etc.

Kelly was insistent that constructs are not just a way of describing the world; rather, they provide a basis for prediction. So, let us assume that one of your salient constructs is *kind–mean*. In identifying a person as 'kind' you are not just labelling her, you are making an implicit prediction about her future behaviour – a prediction which will guide the manner in which you interact with her. Constructs serve the practical function of orientating us to the world in more or less useful ways. According to Kelly, each individual will evolve a somewhat different system of constructs from any other individual – and the unique structure and organization of our construct systems constitute what we refer to as 'personality'.

It is important to note that Kelly saw our constructs as forming *systems*. Thus, he drew attention to the fact that the constructs we use in everyday life are not isolated and disconnected from one another, but are interconnected and constitute a coherent body of knowledge. In short, construct systems may be viewed as implicit 'theories' about the world.

1.1.3 Fritz Heider's study of 'naive psychology'

Just a few years after the publication of Kelly's book, the Gestalt psychologist Heider (1958) published his now-celebrated work *The Psychology of Inter-personal Relations*. This book is perhaps the most widely acknowledged attempt to formulate an explicit statement about the nature of *naive psychology*. As Heider put it: 'there exists a system hidden in our thinking about interpersonal relations, and that system can be uncovered' (1958, p. 14). Thus, his aim was to look at ordinary people's everyday understanding of human behaviour. Unlike Kelly, Heider was not especially interested in the naive psychologies of *particular* individuals, but in the naive psychology commonly held within our culture. What interested him was the fact that within our culture we all subscribe to essentially the same version of everyday psychology – for example, that human behaviour often reflects inner determinants such as abilities, wants, emotions, personalities, etc., rather than, say, witchcraft or the spirit forces of our ancestors. (For a discussion of the everyday psychologies of *other* cultures, see Heelas and Lock, 1981.)

Of course, it is important that we *do* subscribe to a common psychology, since doing so provides an orientating context in which we can understand, and be understood by, others. Imagine a world in which your version of everyday psychology was fundamentally at odds with that of your friends – without a shared 'code' for making sense of behaviour, social life would hardly be possible. Forguson and Gopnik (1988) express it well when they say:

> It is difficult to overestimate the extent to which our commitment to commonsense psychology is implicated in our everyday lives as adults. Our ability to make cooperative plans; our deeply ingrained practice of praising, blaming, excusing, and justifying behaviour; our ability to predict what others will do under various conditions; our ability to influence others' behaviour, all depend on attributing beliefs, expectations, knowledge, wants, fears, wishes, motives, strategies, and the like to others . . . (p. 227)

In looking at this body of shared knowledge, Heider's approach was to examine the psychological concepts – and their relations – expressed in ordinary language, in novels, plays, everyday conversation, and so on. He suggested, on the basis of his analysis, that the fundamental concepts of naive psychology (emphasized in the following passage) are relatively few:

> People have an awareness of their surroundings and the events in it (the *life space*), they attain this awareness through *perception* and other processes, they are *affected* by their personal and impersonal environment, they *cause* changes in the environment, they are able to (*can*) and *try* to cause these changes, they have wishes (*wants*) and *sentiments*, they stand in . . . relation to other entities (*belonging*) and they are accountable to certain standards (*ought*). (p. 17)

Heider discusses each of these concepts, and their relationships to one another, at length.

Heider's approach to the study of the naive psychologist is founded on three key assumptions. First, he was emphatic that to understand a person's behaviour necessitates attention to the way they construe their social world. Regardless of the truth or falsity of a person's beliefs, 'If a person believes that the lines in his palm foretell his future, this belief must be taken into account in explaining certain of his expectations and actions' (p. 5). Second, he argued that people are motivated in their everyday perception by the needs for prediction and control. For example, we often try to establish in advance how others might judge our intended behaviour, so that we can either evolve a different plan of action or come up with ways of averting whatever unfavourable reactions might occur. Finally, Heider was of the opinion that the perception of objects and people is not essentially different. In the perception of both we are concerned primarily with establishing the invariant or dispositional characteristics that incline an entity to behave in a particular way.

Thus, rather than being absorbed by superficial information – such as a person's reddened, perspiring face, her flared nostrils, clenched fists and shouting – we are much more likely to attempt to establish whether she is, by disposition, 'hot-headed'. In terms of future interaction, dispositional information will prove more helpful than information about facial hue and nostril diameter. Better to know about underlying causes than superficial behaviours.

For Heider, then, the central task of the naive psychologist is to establish causes for behaviour. He divided causes into two basic classes: the personal and the environmental. Personal causes are those which reside within the individual, the most important being motivation and ability. Environmental causes are those which lie outside the individual and may be subdivided into the physical environment and other people. This distinction between personal and environmental causes (and its variants – see Kruglanski, 1975, 1989) has been a central one in much of cognitive social psychology, and quite understandably: it obviously makes a difference to know, for example, that someone drove into your car because they hit a patch of ice (environmental cause) rather than because they weren't paying attention (personal cause).

Heider's (1958) work (which I have been able only to touch on here) can rightly be identified as a 'landmark publication' (Hewstone, 1989, p. 12), stimulating as it did immense interest in how ordinary people go about making sense of action. His ideas were to fashion the thinking of many scholars, and played a central role in stimulating research on attribution.

1.1.4 Attribution theory and social cognition

Despite the breadth and richness of Heider's ideas, one particular aspect of his work was to be pursued at length: that concerned with the everyday perception of the *causes* of behaviour. This work was picked up by Jones and Davis (1965) in their *Correspondent Inference Theory*, and by Kelley (1967, 1972) in his *Covariation and Causal Schemata Theories*. (See Hewstone, 1989, for a good review.) Jones and Davis's theory attempted to account for the way perceivers make inferences about others' intentions and dispositions. Kelley's theories were concerned with the processes by which a perceiver assigns causes to events, and decides whether observed actions are due to personal or environmental causes (or some interaction between the two). These theories in turn generated a prodigious literature in the field of *attribution theory*, particularly during the 1970s (Pleban and Richardson, 1979). Indeed, Heider himself commented that 'keeping up with the literature on attribution is difficult'! (1976, p. 14).

The central focus of attention for attribution theory has been the processes by which ordinary perceivers go about assigning causes to the events they observe. This work has proved useful in various applied contexts, leading to insights into the cognitive bases of depression, addiction, marital distress and other real-world problems. Valuable though this work has been – and still is – many new lines of related research emerged in social psychology during the 1970s and 1980s. A glance at social psychology journals will reveal a very considerable range of research themes under the *social cognition* umbrella: attention (Bargh, 1982; McArthur, 1981), person prototypes (Cantor and Mischel, 1979), person memory (Hastie, 1988), schema (Fiske and Linville, 1980; Taylor and Crocker, 1981), heuristics (Tversky and Kahneman, 1974) and biases (Nisbett and Ross, 1980). Since the early 1980s, then, much research in social psychology has been concerned with the *processes* and *structures* hypothesized to underlie everyday understanding of the social world.

This expansion of research themes is important in so far as it reflects an acknowledgement of the sheer complexity of everyday social perception. In this sense it is faithful to the spirit of Heider's early work. In another respect, though, it is quite *different* from Heider's work in that much of today's research is explicitly cognitive, looking at the processes hypothesized to underlie our understanding of the social world. Thus, more recent work has drawn on developments in cognitive psychology to look at processes of social perception, attention, memory, inference, etc., and many researchers are now guided in their work by cognitive models. As a consequence, they often rely on experiments involving methods very different from those used by Heider. For example, where Heider relied upon an analysis of ordinary language as a basis for understanding naive psychology, many researchers now use techniques such as reaction time as a way of mapping cognitive representations. In this sense, much current research has moved beyond Heider's work in that it attempts to look at processes of which people have little, if any, conscious awareness – such as how information about people is organized in memory. Nevertheless, in the most general sense the research goal remains the same: to understand ordinary perceivers' construction of, or theories about, the social world.

Such was the proliferation of social cognition research in the 1980s that Markus and Zajonc (1985) remarked that 'the cognitive approach is now clearly the dominant approach among social psychologists, having virtually no competitors . . . ' (p. 137). Ostrom (1984) went so far as to speak of 'the sovereignty of social cognition' (p. 28). Although the late 1980s and the 1990s have seen the emergence of alternatives to the social cognition position (see, for example, Potter and Wetherell, 1987; Valenti and Good, 1991; Zebrowitz, 1990), it is probably fair to say that this approach continues to enjoy a dominant position in social psychology, particularly in North America.

Despite all that has been done on social cognition within social psychology, remarkably little has found its way into developmental psychology. If we cast an eye over the last twenty years, the only social–psychological work which has been explored developmentally by more than a few researchers is attribution theory. This research was conducted mostly in the 1970s and was primarily concerned with the processes by which children assign causes to behaviour (e.g. DiVitto and McArthur, 1978; Karniol and Ross, 1976, 1979; Kassin, 1981; Kassin and Gibbons, 1981, Sedlak, 1979; Shultz and Butkowsky, 1977; Shultz, Butkowsky, Pearce and Shanfield, 1975). Apart from attributionally orientated research, there have been various smaller-scale efforts to draw on relevant social-psychological work (e.g. social representations: Duveen and Lloyd, 1990). Overall, however, social-psychological theory has been much-neglected by developmentalists.

1.2 Social cognition in developmental psychology: a thumbnail sketch

As I have noted, little social cognition research has been imported from social to developmental psychology. This does not mean, however, that developmental psychology has been uninterested in social cognition, only that its concerns within this general area have been rather different from those of social psychology. Later in this section reference will be made to the sorts of interests that developmentalists have had, but we begin by providing a historical context.

1.2.1 Piaget's early work on egocentrism and morality

The earliest work on children's understanding of the social world was undertaken by Piaget (1929, 1932). His interest lay primarily in egocentrism and morality. On the one hand, then, he was interested in young children's (apparent) inability to distinguish the perspective of self from that of other people. On the other, he was concerned with the shift from a morality based on a view of rules as fixed and unchanging to a morality which sees rules as providing a basis for cooperation and mutuality between people. In looking at these phenomena, Piaget gave attention to a broad range of related phenomena such as understanding of intentionality, punishment and justice. In addition, he was concerned with the likely 'motor' underlying cognitive development – social interaction. Specifically, Piaget suggested that differences of opinion between children may be crucial: such conflicts may facilitate cognitive development by prompting children to integrate their points of view with those of others.

1.2.2 The growth of social cognition research in the 1960s and 1970s

Notwithstanding Piaget's early work on the child's understanding of social phenomena, developmental psychology's interest in social cognition did not start to gain momentum until the late 1960s and early 1970s – much the same time as social psychology's. Before this, where developmental psychology was interested in cognition it focused upon the child's understanding of the physical and logical worlds, looking at matters such as seriation, class inclusion and conservation. Where it addressed social phenomena, it was concerned with socialization – that is: 'the process whereby a person's behaviour is modified to conform to the expectations held by members of the group to which he or she belongs' (Secord and Backman, 1974, p. 462).

These earlier research interests attracted criticism which was to be important in clearing the way for a concerted look at the development of social cognition. In particular, many researchers provided evidence which showed how children's performances on logical tasks frequently reflected their attempts to make 'human sense' of the experimental situation (Donaldson, 1979). Thus, it was found that children often acted not as logicians but as everyday psychologists, trying to read the social context and the experimenter's probable intentions. And with regard to work on socialization, there was a growing feeling that the child needed to be viewed as more than a 'cultural bucket', passively filling up with what adults presented as social reality. Research in many areas of developmental psychology (e.g. language acquisition: McNiell, 1970) indicated that children are *actively* involved in constructing a view of reality; they do not just passively adopt what adults provide.

With these sorts of considerations floating around, developmental psychology was clearly poised for a sustained look at children's understanding of the social world. And sustained it has been: for the last decade, research in this area has been one of the central interests of the discipline, and there are no signs that it is abating.

Much of the early work on social cognition, in the 1960s, focused precisely on those areas which Piaget had originally mapped out thirty years previously. Thus, there were extensive programmes of research on role-taking (e.g. Feffer, 1970; Feffer and Gourevitch, 1960) and moral judgement (e.g. Kohlberg, 1963). However, inspired by Piaget's stage approach to cognitive development, many other researchers, too, examined children's understanding of phenomena as diverse as sex roles (Emerich, Goldman, Kirsch and Sharabany, 1977; Kohlberg, 1966), identity (DeVries, 1969), altruism (Bar-Tal, Raviv and Sharabany, 1977), economic concepts (Berti and Bombi, 1988) and society (Furth, 1978). Furthermore, Piaget's ideas about the role of social interaction in cognitive development were extensively explored by the 'Genevan School' (e.g. Doise and Mugny, 1979; Doise, Mugny and Perret-Clermont, 1975, 1976).

But Piaget's influence upon the field at this time was not reflected simply in prevailing research interests: he also shaped many developmentalists' views about the very nature of cognitive development. Specifically, Piaget's *structural* view of cognition was widely accepted and used as a foundation for a great deal of research. This view assumed that within a given *stage* of cognitive development, all aspects of thought were interrelated by virtue of the *cognitive structures* taken to define that stage. For example, it was believed that a child in the pre-operational stage would be illogical in its thinking about any phenomenon that one cared to mention, since the same underlying cognitive structures would be involved in all thought. Within a stage, then, the *form* that thought takes was assumed to be independent of the *content* of what was being thought about. Cognition was seen to be *content-independent*. This was a very appealing position, suggesting a view of cognitive development as coherent and highly orderly.

Despite its obvious appeal, Piagetian theory was not to guide all early research on social cognition. Much research – then as now – was essentially descriptive, attempting to provide detailed accounts of what children of different ages could and could not understand in social life. Some research was guided by other theoretical positions, such as that of Werner (1957), which drew attention to how, with age, cognition becomes increasingly differentiated and integrated (e.g. Montemayor and Eisen, 1977; Scarlett, Press and Crockett, 1971).

1.2.3 The decline of Piaget's influence upon social cognition research

Towards the end of the 1970s Piaget's theory came to exert less influence than it had a decade earlier. Various problems were identified. For example, a basic problem was that much empirical evidence contradicted the idea that cognition was content-independent to the extent that Piaget maintained: competencies in one area of knowledge would not always be paralleled by competencies in another (Carey, 1985), despite being formally identical. For example, a child who can conserve number may take many months before passing other tests of concrete-operational thought, such as conservation of volume, or class inclusion (Tomlinson-Keasey *et al.*, 1979). Although Piaget had discussed this problem [*décalage*], new disquiet was expressed about it in the late 1970s. It was also argued – contrary to Piaget – that cognitive development is not marked by the sorts of sudden transitions one might expect from a stage account; instead, it is more gradual and continuous (e.g. Brainerd, 1978). (For a full discussion of these and related issues, see Flavell, 1985.) It is probably accurate to say that little contemporary research in social cognition is directly guided by a Piagetian formulation.

The decline of Piagetian theory has not been matched by the rise of a specific alternative. Much current work, however, can be seen as taking place within the *cognitive science* or *information-processing* framework (e.g. Ackerman, Jackson and Sherrill, 1991; Lawrence, 1991; Martin and Halverson, 1981; Nelson, 1985). From these positions:

> the human mind is conceived of as a complex cognitive system, analogous in some ways to a digital computer. Like a computer, the system manipulates or processes

information coming in from the environment or already stored within the system. It processes information in a variety of ways: encoding, recoding, or decoding it; comparing and combining it with other information; storing it in memory or retrieving it from memory; bringing it into or out of focal attention or conscious awareness, and so on. (Flavell, 1985, p. 75)

A basic aim of this approach is to provide detailed descriptions of how information is processed and represented by children of different ages. The key question is: 'What's going on in the child's cognitive system?' The answers provided are framed in terms of concepts such as attention, schema, memory and representation – concepts with which you will probably be familiar, from courses on cognitive psychology.

These approaches contrast with Piaget's in a number of ways. For example, whereas Piaget assumed that the same cognitive structures underpinned understanding of all aspects of the world, many information-processing theorists and cognitive scientists take it that the cognitive system is made up of a number of relatively autonomous 'modules' which are responsible for dealing with particular aspects of the world, or 'domains' (such as number, language and interpersonal relations). On this view, it is not surprising that children may demonstrate some degree of sophistication in one area yet seem quite naive in another: task performance within a domain of knowledge is seen to be subserved by independent and specialized procedures and systems of representation.

A second difference that should be noted is that information-processing and cognitive science approaches, unlike Piagetian theory, did not emerge to address developmental issues in particular. More recently, however, specifically developmental approaches have been advanced, with researchers focusing upon how, with age, either increased *knowledge* (Chi *et al.*, 1982) or information-processing *capacity* (e.g. Case, 1985) is responsible for children's improved performance on cognitive tasks.

A final difference I shall mention here is that the information-processing and cognitive science approaches, unlike Piagetian theory, are not specific theories offering testable predictions. Rather, they provide useful frameworks for understanding the means by which children deal with social information. (For further discussion, see McShane, 1991.)

1.2.4 Summary

Piaget's early work on egocentrism and morality played a vital role in guiding later work, in terms of both its substantive and its theoretical orientation. However, research interests quickly went beyond egocentrism and morality, addressing a diverse range of social phenomena. Although Piagetian theory was taken as a basis for much of this research, its grip started to loosen towards the end of the 1970s. Since then, no single theory has had the impact that had been enjoyed by Piaget's. Increasingly, however, the information-processing and cognitive science positions have provided a theoretical context for research.

1.3 The conceptual tools of the everyday psychologist

1.3.1 Background

In making sense of action, the everyday psychologist draws upon a considerable range of constructs, or conceptual 'tools'. To illustrate the point, consider the following case, reported in *The Independent* (2 July 1991): A young Indian man, Vivekananda, leaves his house early one evening to see a movie. On his way he is kidnapped at gunpoint. He is forced to dress in clothes and jewellery appropriate to a wedding and then finds that he is to be married to a young woman he has never met. Signatures are forced from him, and the ceremony is photographed as further proof that a wedding has taken place. Before the movie has even finished, Vivekananda is a married man. Apparently, it was easier for the bride's father to pay for this type of marriage than for a conventional one involving a dowry.

As adults, we effortlessly make sense of this event. We understand, for example, the *motivations* of the various parties concerned: of the young man to escape his captors, of the kidnappers to make money, and of the father to avoid bankruptcy. We are also likely to be alert to their different *emotions*: anger on the part of the bridegroom, resignation or despair on the part of the bride, and satisfaction in the case of father and kidnappers. We might also muse on the father's ruthless *personality*. And over and above this, we draw on taken-for-granted knowledge about the institution of marriage (e.g. that its obligations will greatly change the lives of the hapless young couple) and the nature of the wedding ceremony (eg. that it involves following a set of social conventions concerned with such things as dress, making vows, giving signatures, and in India, the giving of a dowry). In short, understanding this event depends upon an understanding of a substantial range of constructs – desires, beliefs, dispositions, social conventions, moral rules, roles, and so on.

Although we have been able to identify a broad range of constructs, it is helpful to see them as falling into two general classes: the *psychological* and the *social*. Psychological, or mentalistic, constructs are those which may be viewed as properties of the individual – desires, emotions, personality, etc. Social constructs, however, may be seen as properties of the group or society to which we belong – social rules, roles, etc. Here, what we are thinking about are 'sources of social behaviour that lie outside the individual' (Pepitone, 1981, p. 983). (It should be noted that the psychological/social distinction is not without its problems – see, for example, Valsiner, 1991.)

At what age do children understand such constructs? How do they acquire them? Do they emerge at roughly the same time as one another? And having emerged, do they immediately correspond to the adult version, or must they gradually be refined over a period of years? Clearly, the social world of the young child might look rather different from that of the adult, and the following chapters will provide some sense of possible differences. But what is needed here is a closer look at the system of constructs which forms the basis of everyday psychology. If we are to understand the process of social-cognitive development, we should be clear about what exactly it is that needs to be understood by the child. To try to discover this, we begin by looking at everyday mentalistic constructs – that is, those constructs which may be best viewed as psychological properties of the individuals. Then we come on to consider some of the social constructs that are implicated in everyday understanding.

1.3.2 Everyday mentalistic psychology

Wellman (1990), like many before him (e.g. Davidson, 1980; Papineau, 1977), maintains that at the heart of everyday thinking about action lie two vital constructs: desire and belief. These fit together in what he calls 'everyday mentalistic psychology'. Stated at its simplest, this holds that what people do results from their *believing* that certain actions will bring about ends that they *desire*. I go to the bar because I desire a drink and believe this to be the right place to get one. I visit my friend's house because I believe she is at home and I would like to see her. And so on. So, just about every time you ask someone to explain their 'reason' for acting in a particular way, you will be seeking information about either their desire or their belief (or both).

Wellman suggests that in everyday psychology our beliefs and desires are accepted as the causes of what we do: we might say that we visited a friend because we wanted to, or that despite wanting to see her, we stayed at home because we believed she was away for the weekend. With such examples in mind, we are able to summarize the essence of everyday psychology very simply: 'Beliefs and desires provide . . . the internal mental causes for overt actions' (Wellman, 1990, p. 105).

Everyday psychology, however, goes much further than this. To begin with, it will be apparent that the everyday psychologist has some idea about what *causes* desires and beliefs. Clearly, it will often matter to us *why* someone believes what they do. Wellman proposes that in everyday psychology, beliefs are typically taken to result from *perception* – seeing, hearing, touching, and so on. We believe what we do because of information from our perceptual senses. And what causes desires? Wellman suggests that everyday psychology acknowledges two basic causes: our *physiology* (hunger, thirst, etc.) and our *basic emotions* (love, hate, fear, etc.). So: I want food because I am hungry, and I want to see my friend because I love or have affection for her.

Just as desires and beliefs are caused by other factors, and are themselves seen to cause action, action is viewed as causing certain *re*actions, typically *emotions*. For example, if we want to see a friend, and then do so, we are likely to be satisfied or happy; if we are thwarted, we are dissatisfied or unhappy. Similarly, if we believe that our friend is at home and find that she isn't, we may be surprised or disappointed.

Our interest in emotions as everyday psychologists is plain to see from the fact that we frequently want to know more than just *what* someone did (action) and *why* (desires and beliefs): we also want to know how they *felt*. Others' emotions provide us with important cues about how to behave towards them – for example, whether to comfort or avoid them. They also give us insights into the strength of others' desires and beliefs: someone who reacts with joy at seeing you is likely to desire your company more than someone who struggles to raise a smile. Emotion, then, is one of the basic constructs of everyday psychology.

The version of everyday psychology described so far has been represented by Wellman in schematic form in Figure 1.1. Although this is a simplification of the version employed by the typical adult, it is worth noting that a person armed with this particular 'theory' of action could probably manage quite well. Following Wellman, though, let us see in what sense it *is* a simplification.

While desires and beliefs may be at the heart of everyday psychology, Wellman suggests that there are various other central constructs, perhaps most importantly *thinking* and *intention*. The importance of the concept of thinking is that it takes us beyond the view – implied above – of the mind as a

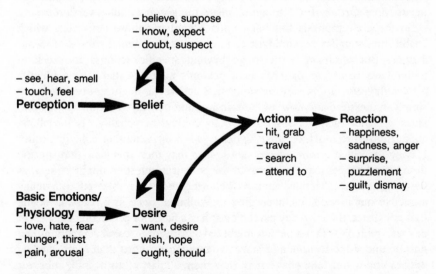

Figure 1.1 Simplified scheme for depicting belief–desire reasoning.
Source: Wellman [1990]

passive repository of beliefs. Thinking may be viewed as an *active* process, and the mind may now be seen as engaged in all sorts of directive processes: attending to information, interpreting, storing and recalling it. And with this elaborated version of everyday psychology, we can say that beliefs can arise in the absence of direct perceptual inputs and may result from *inference*: if you know that Paul is heavier than Peter, and that Peter is heavier than Philip, you don't need perceptual information to establish that Paul is the heaviest member of this trio. Thus, under the earlier scheme, beliefs were taken to result purely from perceptual inputs; but now we can say that they can also arise from the activity of the mind itself.

The other important additional concept is *intention*, a concept which provides us with a more subtle view of the cause of action than is implied by desire alone. You may desire, for example, to travel to Antarctica, but never actually intend to do so. Intentions may be viewed as mediating between desire and action; they 'function to actualise (some but not all) desires' (Wellman, 1990, p. 110). That is, they translate our wants into strategic courses of action which will help us satisfy those wants. Intentions, then, clearly imply cognitive activity, such as planning.

The consequence of introducing the concepts of *thinking* and *intention* is considerable in that this elaborated version of everyday psychology implicitly views action as resulting from active, constructive processes. Wellman characterizes the difference between the two versions of everyday psychology by saying that the basic version views the mind as a simple repository of beliefs, whereas the elaborated version views it as an information processor and planning device. But even this expanded version of everyday psychology needs to go further if it is to approximate the average adult's version.

So far, the emphasis has been upon identifying those constructs which enable the everyday psychologist to understand the mental causes of *specific* actions. But often we want to go beyond specific actions, and seek to understand recurrent patterns in a person's action – that is, we identify *personality traits*. So, in viewing someone's action, we might not be interested simply in the 'here and now' of their desires and beliefs; we might also want to know whether their actions reflect their general personality. 'Is he talking about himself so much because he believes I'm interested, or is he just vain?' Having identified a trait – here, vanity – we may then speculate that specific desires and beliefs may flow from it: the person in question might be seen as desiring attentive 'victims', and as believing that he is blessed with many attractive qualities. Thus, according to Wellman, once in possession of the trait construct, the everyday psychologist has a basis for predicting all sorts of desires and beliefs that a person might have. Moreover, particular actions can now be understood within a broader psychological context than is afforded by desires and beliefs alone. We may view them as part of an overall, coherent picture rather than as disconnected and discrete elements.

Wellman's analysis may seem obvious. He has charted out territory that is navigated so readily by the everyday psychologist that it is easy to be unimpressed. However, this would be to underestimate the difficulty of standing back from one's taken-for-granted knowledge, unwrapping it, and showing how the different pieces fit together. We should not be unimpressed – but neither should we assume that Wellman provides a complete chart as far as the everyday psychologist's navigational skills are concerned.

As Wellman himself indicates, his efforts are directed at describing everyday *mentalistic* psychology. That is, he is interested in those constructs which are taken to be internal, or psychological, determinants of action. This, however, is to neglect what Dahrendorf (1967) has referred to as 'the vexatious fact of society' – that we are often obliged to act in ways required of us by social rules and roles, sometimes quite against what we might personally want. For the ordinary person on the street, as for the sociologist Durkheim, 'society confronts us . . . . It is *there*, something that cannot be denied and must be reckoned with' (in Berger, 1963, p. 108). And this brings us to the matter of everyday *social* psychology.

1.3.3 Everyday social psychology

As adults, we have many expectations concerning what types of behaviour 'go with' what types of situation (Price and Bouffard, 1974). Wearing a swimsuit on the beach is fine, but wearing one at a funeral would at best be viewed as tactless. Smoking on the street may go unnoticed, but lighting up a cigarette whilst one is getting married would, at the very least, be seen as idiosyncratic. Such examples abound – one need only think of particular actions and then transplant them into various situations. Some types of behaviour – for example, talking about the weather – will 'fit' many situations; others, like making love, will be appropriate to far fewer. This thought-game can often be quite amusing, but for our purposes it is important in that it brings to mind the extent to which action is constrained by forces beyond the individual.

'The common expectation of regularities in conduct is the fundamental feature of *social norms*' (Hollander, 1967, p. 228). Plainly, we recognize that much that we observe in everyday action is a reflection of norms, or social rules. We need not stop and ask: 'Why did she do that?' every time we see someone braking at a red light. We know that there is a rule, or *convention*, that specifies that we must stop when traffic lights are at red. Rules pervade our lives and are reflected in much that we do.

The sense of familiarity aroused by the preceding examples supports Wegner and Vallacher's (1977) assertion that ordinary people are 'implicit situation theorists' who subscribe to 'a set of expectations concerning the rules of behaviour in various settings' (p. 48). But these are not the only sorts of expectations held. Not only do we understand much of what we see in terms of common-to-all *rules*, we interpret some aspects of action with reference to particular *roles*. Roles refer to 'those particular expectancies regarding appropriate behaviour for a person occupying a position in a given situation' (Hollander, 1967, p. 240). For example, although doctor and patient are both subject to some general *rules* (to be fairly formal, to be deferential, etc.), each has clearly defined roles. The doctor's role permits the asking of personal questions; the patient's role the disclosing of personal information. The doctor may ask the patient to undress, and in the role of patient it is quite acceptable to undress before this virtual stranger. But try turning all this around: 'How have you been feeling lately, doctor? I'd like to examine you. Would you mind undressing and lying down over here for me?' Though we might not *explicitly* formulate the concept of role in our everyday social psychology, examples like this indicate the extent to which it is *implicitly* formulated.

Social life is often understood in terms of quite particular and isolated roles and rules. For example, in response to the question 'Why did you give him that money?', we might reply: 'I owed it to him' (i.e. a rule is implied); and in response to the question 'Why did you follow her orders?', we might answer: 'She's my boss' (i.e. a role-relationship is implied). Frequently, however, much that we observe is understood in terms of *event episodes*. To illustrate this, consider the example of a visit to a restaurant. In a restaurant we are aware of a considerable range and sequence of expectations about how we must conduct ourselves in relation to people in other roles (waiters, waitresses, our companions, etc.): in the role of diner we know that upon entering the restaurant we request a table (if it hasn't already been booked) and are then shown to the table and given menus; some time afterwards, we order our food (in a particular order, note – main course *before* dessert); we are brought the food, eat it, and finally pay for it and leave. In this particular case, all sorts of rules and roles are implicated.

An event episode, then, is characterized by a 'predetermined stereotyped sequence of actions' (Schank and Abelson, 1977, p. 41). You can probably identify many such events in your own day-to-day life – foremost amongst them, perhaps, the lecture: stated simply, you take a seat, the lecturer arrives and talks for around fifty minutes, invites questions, answers them, then all disperse. In terms of our everyday understanding, the important point to note about 'scripted' episodes is that they involve highly stereotyped sequences of action. As soon as it is apparent that we are dealing with such an episode, all sorts of things can be taken for granted simply *because* of their stereotypy. Schank and Abelson have suggested that such events give rise to schematic knowledge structures which they refer to as *scripts*. (See Judith Hudson's chapter [6] below for further discussion.)

The striking thing about our everyday social psychology is that we have a relatively impoverished vocabulary for talking about some of its major constructs – rules, roles, events, and the like. Seldom do people talk explicitly about the way in which their action reflects, for example, norms, roles, social conventions, etc. In this sense it seems very different from everyday mentalistic psychology, which, as we have seen, is brimming with all sorts of terms marking quite subtle distinctions (e.g. between believing and knowing). Why should this be? Why should one aspect of everyday psychology be so *explicit* when another is so *implicit*? The most likely explanation runs as follows. When action conforms to a particular convention, we understand it *without* having to explain it: it 'fits' with a background of taken-for-granted knowledge. 'Asking "why" of a scripted action is an odd thing reserved for children, foreigners and social scientists. Behaving in script-appropriate ways seems explanation enough' (Lalljee and Abelson, 1983, pp. 71–3). In short, there is no need to juggle with the complexities of explanation if action conforms to what is expected.

But clearly, not all our everyday understandings of action *do* derive from scripts and so on. Many actions are unscripted, and it may then become necessary to resort to our everyday mentalistic psychology (e.g. 'Why did you order champagne?' 'I wanted to surprise you'). Often, too, we will seek explanations when actions run *counter* to a convention ('Why didn't you leave a tip?' 'I thought service was included').

In summary, it must be said that adults clearly rely to a great extent on an implicit everyday social psychology. The foregoing discussion has not attempted to provide an exhaustive account of the tools of the naive social psychologist, but has sought to highlight some of the major ones. The important point to note, however, is that we hold a great many expectations about action – expectations which, more often than not, are fulfilled. Quite often, then, we have no need for the sorts of constructs discussed by Wellman (desires, beliefs, etc.) and see particular actions as reflections of general rules or roles. But when there are no obvious expectations, or when what we see is *un*expected, we typically appeal to our everyday mentalistic psychology. (For further discussion of this point, see Lalljee and Abelson, 1983.)

Having looked in some detail at adults' everyday explanatory constructs, the question that inevitably comes to mind is: 'What do *children* understand of all this?' It is this very question, of course, that is tackled in the remainder of this book. Before moving on to the answers provided, however, it may be useful, finally, to consider how everyday psychologists differ from academic psychologists.

1.3.4 Psychologist and everyday psychologist compared

As we have seen, the everyday psychologist draws upon a substantial set of constructs in making sense of everyday action. Although people may differ in the importance they attach to the various constructs, the constructs we have outlined can be seen to constitute the 'core' of our everyday theories of action. But how far can the everyday psychologist be likened to an academic psychologist or scientist? In particular, we need to ask whether everyday knowledge about action can be viewed as a 'theory'. We also need to ask how far everyday theorists' approach to 'theory-use' corresponds to that of psychologists.

What is a theory?

This apparently simple question has given rise to much debate in the philosophy of science, and there is no universally accepted definition of the term 'theory'. For present purposes, however, it will be helpful to answer the question by saying that a theory is 'a way of structuring observations of reality, of placing them in a rational system that specifies their interrelations' (Wegner and Vallacher, 1977, p. 15) which enables us to explain events and make predictions. On this definition, everyday psychology might reasonably be viewed as a theory: concepts such as desire, belief, personality, social rule, and so on enable us to structure our observations of action, and place them into a rational explanatory system which specifies interrelations and makes predictions.

Wellman (1990) has suggested that there are three essential features of a theory: that it should be *coherent*, that it should make *ontological distinctions*, and that it should provide a *causal explanatory framework*. Let us look at each in turn, and consider whether everyday psychology measures up.

By coherence Wellman means the *interconnectedness* of the theory's concepts. He suggests that within a theory:

> it becomes impossible to consider a single concept in isolation because its meaning and significance are determined by its role in an interrelated web of other constructs and terms. The notion of a planet, for example, is a concept entrenched in a larger understanding of the solar system, comets and asteroids and how bodies revolve around others because of differing mass and gravitational forces. (1990, p. 6)

Wellman makes the case that everyday psychology is clearly coherent in this sense, since its concepts are strongly interconnected: when we try to define dreams, we refer to thoughts and mental images; when we define personality, we invoke desire and belief; and when we define a script, we may appeal to rules, roles, desires and beliefs. Everyday psychology, then, satisfies Wellman's coherence criterion.

The second key feature of a theory is that it makes ontological distinctions. In simple terms, this means that it will 'carve phenomena into different kinds of entities and processes' (p. 7). That is, it makes fundamental distinctions between different classes of thing. Everyday psychology quite clearly provides us with a basic ontological distinction – between mental phenomena (thoughts, desires, dreams, etc.) and external phenomena (observable actions [like touching], situational pressures, the physical environment, etc.).

Finally, a theory should offer a causal-explanatory framework. This means that it should provide a basis for *explaining*, or identifying the *causes* of, the phenomena it deals with. In everyday psychology, the terms used – particularly desire, belief and intention – carry with them an obvious capacity to explain actions (and one another – e.g. I *want* to see that dentist because I *believe* she's the best).

So, in terms of the three criteria discussed by Wellman, everyday psychology *can* reasonably be viewed as a theory. (For recent alternatives to this position, however, see Chapter 2 below by Sue Leekam.) Thinking of everyday psychology as theory is useful in that it helps us to frame the matter of *conceptual change* – that children's conceptualizations of human action are likely to undergo substantial change during childhood. Just as scientists' views evolve and are refined, so too children's views about action may develop in important ways. But is this to say that psychologist and everyday psychologist are essentially the same in terms of their *use* of theory? I tackle this question in the next section.

Before turning to the question of theory-use, however, it is important to point out that although there are senses in which everyday psychology can be viewed as theory (or theories), the scope of everyday psychology is nothing like as broad as that of academic psychology. Quite simply, much in our daily lives happens so naturally that we may see little need for explanation. We hardly notice, for example, the processes of perception and attention. Such processes are taken for granted by the everyday psychologist, yet a little reflection shows them to be extremely complex and problematic phenomena in need of explanation. Thus, although the academic psychologist is interested in the sorts of things which absorb the everyday psychologist (notably the causes and consequences of actions and emotions), his or her preoccupations are much more extensive, as will be clear from even the briefest perusal of a general psychology text.

Theory-use

Although, as we have seen, there are obvious parallels between layperson and scientist, Berger and Luckmann (1966) have suggested that the purpose of lay theories is significantly different from that of scientists' theories. In particular, they maintain that 'everyday life is guided by the pragmatic motive' (p. 56). By this they mean that the person in the street is primarily concerned with 'recipe knowledge' – knowledge that gets results. As Yates (1990) has put it: 'usefulness, not truth, is the relevant criterion for intuitive theories . . . ' (p. 95). Thus, in everyday life the main need is to 'get by'. For example:

> I know what I must do to apply for a passport. All I am interested in is getting the passport at the end of a certain waiting period. I do not care, and do not know, how my application is processed in government offices, by whom and after what steps approval is given, who puts which stamp in the document. I am not making a study of government bureaucracy – I just want to go on a vacation abroad. (Berger and Luckmann, 1966, p. 57)

The scientist, by contrast, wants to go beyond recipe knowledge and construct as full an account as possible of the structures, processes and contents associated with a particular phenomenon. Although the 'scientific motive' *will* sometimes get results, results are not primary, as they are with the pragmatic motive.

The academic psychologist's or scientist's approach will typically involve a close look at the presuppositions and implications of a theory – what does the theory *assume*, and what follows from it? It will also involve an examination both of the theory's logic and of how far it goes in accounting for observations of behaviour. In other words, there is a set of rules governing theory-use by scientists – the scientific method. Perhaps the most notable rule here concerns the *falsification* of theories: rather than attempting to verify a theory, it is usual in science to attempt to refute it, since no number of supportive observations can finally *prove* a theory, yet relatively few negative observations can show it to be flawed (Popper, 1959). In everyday life, however, people are inclined to look for evidence which verifies rather than falsifies their position (e.g. Snyder and Gangestad, 1981).

This point about scientists' regulative rules of inquiry leads us to a further difference. The 'scientific motive' is self-evidently deliberate and self-conscious: scientists use theory *as* theory. Theory is constructed, tested and modified *as such*. In this sense, what academic psychologists do is quite at odds with what everyday psychologists do. For the everyday psychologist there is little – if any – *awareness* of using a 'theory'. Rather, he or she draws on it in an unselfconscious way. The theory is lived, and what is specified by it is taken as reality. To state it differently: academic psychologists' theories are *explicit*, whereas everyday psychologists' theories are largely *implicit*.

This distinction between theories *as lived* versus theories *as theories* leads us to a final and quite basic point made by Schutz (1962). He argued that a key difference between social scientists and laypersons is that social scientists must develop 'constructs of the second degree, namely, constructs of constructs made by the actors on the social scene' (1962, p. 6). And this point brings us back more or less to where this chapter began: Schutz, like Heider, was committed to the view that social scientists' constructs need to refer to the constructs of ordinary people. For both Heider and Schutz, the social scientist is obliged to develop theories which incorporate the theorizing of laypersons, since, as Schutz (1964) put it, he or she 'confronts a reality whose structure originates in subjective common-sense constructs' (p. 2).

In summary, then, the academic psychologist's theory-use differs from that of the everyday psychologist in a number of important ways. Most notably we have seen that academic and lay psychologists differ with respect to whether or not there is self-consciousness about holding a theory, and the related presence or absence of a methodology. Arguably, the key to these points of departure is provided by Berger and Luckmann: the psychologist and the person in the street have different orientations. One is driven by the 'pragmatic motive'; the other by the desire to explicate formally the nature, function and consequences of the pragmatic motive.

1.3.5 Summary

We have seen that everyday psychology (or naive or folk psychology) is populated with a variety of concepts which provide different types of insights into behaviour. Attention was given to a range of psychological and social concepts. The case was made that these concepts can be viewed as constituting a theory about human behaviour. However, it was suggested that the way in which lay psychologists use 'theory' is substantially different from the way in which scientists do so. (For recent discussion of the nature of everyday psychology, see Greenwood, 1991.)

1.4 Closing remarks

In *The Child's Conception of the World*, Piaget (1929) asserted that the child 'knows nothing of the nature of thought' (p. 37). It is a measure of how far we have come that we can now say confidently that this is quite simply wrong. As will be evident from the chapters that follow, children's competence as everyday psychologists is considerable. This book provides what I hope is a useful and interesting review of contemporary research on children's social cognition. It is not meant to be an exhaustive account of research, but reflects instead some of the major areas in which developmental social cognition work has been conducted.

It would be particularly gratifying to learn that these chapters might have played a small role in generating new ideas and research – the interested student should be encouraged by the fact that despite all we now know, much remains to be done. First, as will become evident, there are various disagreements between researchers, and such disagreements clearly provide a basis for future research. Furthermore, answers frequently give rise to new questions, and all the contributors to this volume indicate the sorts of directions that future investigation might take. Finally, whole areas of uncharted territory in the domain of social cognition remain – for example, very little is known about children's understanding of social *processes*, such as conformity and social influence. Furthermore, relatively little is known about how and when children deploy their conceptual knowledge in everyday contexts of action. In looking to the future, it seems probable that joint enterprises between developmental and social psychologists will be especially fruitful, as Paul Light indicates in the closing chapter. In short, though we now know a good deal, the future of this research area promises to be at least as interesting as its past.

Acknowledgements

I would like to express my gratitude to Eithne Buchanan-Barrow, Linda
Galpert, Sue Leekam and Nicola Yuill for giving me useful comments on an
earlier version of this chapter.

References

Ackerman, B.P., Jackson, M. and Sherrill, L. (1991) 'Inference modification by
children and adults'. *Journal of Experimental Child Psychology*, 52, 166–96.
Asch, S.E. (1952) *Social Psychology*. Englewood Cliffs, NJ: Prentice Hall.
Bargh, J.A. (1982) 'Attention and automaticity in the processing of self-relevant
information'. *Journal of Personality and Social Psychology*, 43, 425–36.
Bar-Tal, D., Raviv, A. and Sharabany, R. (1977) *Cognitive basis of the development of
altruistic behaviour*. Paper presented at the biennial conference of the International
Society for the Study of Behavioral Development, Pavia, Italy.
Berger, P. (1963) *Invitation to Sociology*. Harmondsworth: Penguin.
Berger, P. and Luckmann, T. (1966) *The Social Construction of Reality*. Harmonds-
worth: Penguin.
Berti, A.E. and Bombi, A.S. (1988) *The Child's Construction of Economics*. Cambridge:
Cambridge University Press.
Brainerd, C.J. (1978) 'The stage question in cognitive-developmental theory'.
Behavioural and Brain Sciences, 2, 173–213.
Cantor, N. and Mischel, W. (1979) 'Prototypes in person perception'. In L. Berkowitz
(ed.) *Advances in Experimental Social Psychology*, vol. 12. New York: Academic Press.
Carey, S. (1985) *Conceptual Change in Childhood*. Cambridge, MA: MIT Press.
Case, R. (1985) *Intellectual Development: Birth to adulthood*. New York: Academic Press.
Chi, M.T.H., Glaser, R. and Rees, E. (1982) 'Expertise in problem solving'. In R.J.
Sternberg (ed.) *Advances in the Psychology of Human Intelligence*, vol. 1. Hillsdale, NJ:
Erlbaum.
Dahrendorf, R. (1967) *Pfade as Utopia*. Munich: Piper.
Davidson, D. (1980) *Essays on Actions and Events*. London: Oxford University Press.
DeVries, R. (1969) 'Constancy of generic identity in the years three to six'. *Monography
of the Society for Research in Child Development*, 34 (3).
DiVitto, B. and McArthur, L.Z. (1978) 'Developmental differences in the use
of distinctiveness, consistency and consensus information for making causal
attributions'. *Developmental Psychology*, 14, 474–82.
Doise, W. and Mugny, G. (1979) 'Individual and collective conflicts of centrations in
cognitive development'. *European Journal of Social Psychology*, 9, 105–9.
Doise, W., Mugny, G. and Perret-Clermont, A. (1975) 'Social interaction and the
development of logical operations'. *European Journal of Social Psychology*, 5, 367–83.
Doise, W., Mugny, G. and Perret-Clermont, A. (1976) 'Social interaction and
cognitive development: Further evidence'. *European Journal of Social Psychology*, 6,
245–7.
Donaldson, M. (1979) *Children's Minds*. London: Fontana.

Duveen, G. and Lloyd, B. (eds) (1990) *Social Repesentations and the Development of Knowledge*. Cambridge: Cambridge University Press.

Emerich, W., Goldman, K., Kirsch, B. and Sharabany, R. (1977) 'Evidence for a transitional phase in the development of gender constancy'. *Child Development*, 48, 930–6.

Feffer, M. (1970) 'Developmental analysis of interpersonal behaviour'. *Psychological Review*, 77, 197–214.

Feffer, M. and Gourevitch, V. (1960) 'Cognitive aspects of role-taking in children'. *Journal of Personality*, 28, 383–96.

Fincham, F.D. and Jaspars, J. (1979) 'Attribution and responsibility to the self and others in children and adults'. *Journal of Personality and Social Psychology*, 37, 1589–1602.

Fiske, S. and Linville, P. (1980) 'What does the schema concept buy us?'. *Personality and Social Psychology Bulletin*, 6, 543–57.

Fiske, S. and Taylor, S. (1991) *Social Cognition*. New York: McGraw-Hill.

Flavell, J.H. (1985) *Cognitive Development*. Englewood Cliffs, NJ: Prentice Hall.

Forguson, L. and Gopnik, A. (1988) 'The ontogeny of common sense'. In J.W. Astington, P.L. Harris and D.R. Olson (eds) *Developing Theories of Mind*. Cambridge: Cambridge University Press.

Furth, H. (1978) 'Children's societal understanding and the process of equilibration'. In W. Damon (ed.) *New Directions for Child Development, vol. 1: Social Cognition*. San Francisco, CA: Jossey-Bass.

Greenwood, J.D. (ed.) (1991) *The Future of Folk Psychology*. Cambridge: Cambridge University Press.

Hanson, N.R. (1958) *Patterns of Discovery*. Cambridge: Cambridge University Press.

Harris, B. (1977) 'Developmental differences in the attribution of responsibility'. *Developmental Psychology*, 13, 257–65.

Hastie, R. (1988) 'A computer simulation model of person memory'. *Journal of Experimental Social Psychology*, 24, 423–47.

Heelas, P. and Lock, A. (eds) (1981) *Indigenous Psychologies*. London: Academic Press.

Heider, F. (1958) *The Psychology of Interpersonal relations*. New York: Wiley.

Heider, F. (1976) 'A conversation with Fritz Heider'. In J. Harvey, W.J. Ickes and R.F. Kidd (eds) *New Directions in Attribution Research*, vol. 1. Hillsdale, NJ: Erlbaum.

Hewstone, M. (1989) *Causal Attribution*. Oxford: Blackwell.

Hollander, E.P. (1967) *Principles and Methods of Social Psychology*. New York: Oxford University Press.

Jones, E.E. and Davis, K.E. (1965) 'From acts to dispositions: The attribution process in person perception'. In L. Berkowitz (ed.) *Advances in Experimental Social Psychology*, vol. 2. New York: Academic Press.

Karniol, R. and Ross, M. (1976) 'The development of causal attributions in social perception'. *Journal of Personality and Social Psychology*, 34, 455–64.

Karniol, R. and Ross, M. (1979) 'Children's use of a causal attribution schema and the inference of manipulative intentions'. *Child Development*, 50, 463–8.

Kassin, S.M. (1981) 'From laychild to "layman": Developmental causal attribution'. In S.S. Brehm, S.M. Kassin and F.X. Gibbons (eds) *Developmental Social Psychology*. New York: Oxford University Press.

Kassin, S.M. and Gibbons, F.X. (1981) 'Children's use of the discounting principle in their perceptions of exertion'. *Child Development*, 52, 741–4.

Kelley, H.H. (1967) 'Attribution theory in social psychology'. In D. Levine (ed.) *Nebraska Symposium on Motivation*, vol. 15. Lincoln, NB: University of Nebraska Press.

Kelley, H.H. (1972) 'Causal schemata and the attribution process'. In E.E. Jones, D.E. Kanouse, H.H. Kelley, R.E. Nisbett, S. Valins and B. Weiner (eds) *Attribution: Perceiving the causes of behaviour*. Morristown, NJ: General Learning Press.

Kelly, G.A. (1955) *The Psychology of Personal Constructs*. New York: Norton.

Kohlberg, L. (1963) 'The development of children's orientations toward a moral order: 1. Sequence in the development of moral thought'. *Vita Humana*, 6, 11–33.

Kohlberg, L. (1966) 'A cognitive-developmental analysis of children's sex-role concepts and attitudes'. In E. Maccoby (ed.) *The Development of Sex Differences*. Standford, CA: Stanford University Press.

Kruglanski, A.W. (1975) 'The endogenous–exogenous partition in attribution theory'. *Psychological Review*, 82, 387–406.

Kruglanski, A.W. (1989) *Lay Epistemics and Human Knowledge*. New York: Plenum.

Lalljee, M. and Abelson, R. (1983) 'The organisation of explanations'. In M. Hewstone (ed.) *Attribution Theory: Social and functional extensions*. Oxford: Blackwell.

Lawrence, V.W. (1991) 'Effects of socially ambiguous information on white and black children's behavioral and trait perceptions'. *Merrill-Palmer Quarterly*, 37, 619–30.

McArthur, L. (1981) 'What grabs you? The role of attention in impression formation and causal attribution'. In E.T. Higgins, C.P. Herman and M.P. Zanna (eds) *Social Cognition: The Ontario Symposium*. Hillsdale, NJ: Erlbaum.

McNiell, D. (1970) *The Acquisition of Language*. New York: Harper & Row.

McShane, J. (1991) *Cognitive Development: An information processing approach*. Oxford: Blackwell.

Markus, H. and Zajonc, R.B. (1985) 'The cognitive perspective in social psychology'. In G. Lindzey and E. Aronson (eds) *The Handbook of Social Psychology*. New York: Random.

Martin, C. and Halverson, C. (1981) 'A schematic processing model of sex-typing and stereotyping in children'. *Child Development*, 52, 1119–34.

Miller, P.H. (1985) 'Children's reasoning about the causes of human behaviour'. *Journal of Experimental Child Psychology*, 39, 343–62.

Montemayor, N. and Eisen, M. (1977) 'The development of self-conceptions from childhood to adolescence'. *Development Psychology*, 13, 314–19.

Nelson, K. (ed.) (1985) *Event Knowledge: Structure and function in development*. Hillsdale, NJ: Erlbaum.

Nisbett, R. and Ross, L. (1980) *Human Inference: Strategies and shortcomings of social judgement*. Englewood Cliffs, NJ: Prentice Hall.

Ostrom, T.M. (1984) 'The sovereignty of social cognition'. In R.S. Wyer and T.K. Srull (eds) *Handbook of Social Cognition*, vol. 1. Hillsdale, NJ: Erlbaum.

Papineau, D. (1977) *For Science in the Social Sciences*. London: Macmillan.

Pepitone, A. (1981) 'Lessons from the history of social psychology'. *American Psychologist*, 36, 972–85.

Piaget, J. (1929) *The Child's Conception of the World*. Hillsdale, NJ: Littlefield, Adams (1960).

Piaget, J. (1932) *The Moral Judgement of the Child*. Glencoe, IL: Free Press (1948).

Pleban, R. and Richardson, D.C. (1979) 'Research and publication trends in social psychology: 1973–7. *Personality and Social Psychology Bulletin*, 5, 138–41.

Popper, K. (1959) *The Logic of Scientific Discovery*. New York: Basic Books.

Potter, J. and Wetherell, M. (1987) *Discourse and Social Psychology*. London: Sage.

Price, R.H. and Bouffard, D.L. (1974) 'Behavioural appropriateness and situational constraint as dimensions of social behaviour'. *Journal of Personality and Social Psychology*, 30, 579–86.

Ross, L. (1977) 'The intuitive psychologist and his shortcomings: Distortions in the attribution process'. In L. Berkowitz (ed.) *Advances in Experimental Social Psychology*, vol. 10. New York: Academic Press.

Ross, L. (1981) 'The "intuitive scientist" formulation and its developmental implications'. In J.H. Flavell and L. Ross (eds) *Social Cognitive Development*. Cambridge: Cambridge University Press.

Scarlett, H.H., Press, A.N. and Crockett, W.H. (1971) 'Children's descriptions of peers: A Wernerian analysis'. *Child Development*, 42, 439–53.

Schank, R. and Abelson, R. (1977) *Scripts, Plans, Goals and Understanding*. Hillsdale, NJ: Erlbaum.

Schutz, A. (1962) *Collected Papers*, vol. 1. The Hague: Nijhoff (first published 1932).

Schutz, A. (1964) *Collected Papers*, vol. 2. The Hague: Nijhoff (first published 1932).

Scott, M.B. and Lyman, S. (1968) 'Accounts'. *American Sociological Review*, 33, 46–62.

Secord, P. and Backman, C. (1974) *Social Psychology*. London: McGraw-Hill.

Sedlak, A. (1979) 'Developmental differences in understanding plans and evaluating actors'. *Child Development*, 50, 536–60.

Shultz, T.R. and Butkowsky, I. (1977) 'Young children's use of the scheme for multiple sufficient causes in the attribution of real and hypothetical behaviour'. *Child Development*, 48, 464–9.

Shultz, T.R., Butkowsky, I., Pearce, I. and Shanfield, H. (1975) 'Development of schemes for the attribution of multiple psychological causes'. *Developmental Psychology*, 11, 502–10.

Snyder, M. and Gangestad, S. (1981) 'Hypothesis-testing processes'. In J.H. Harvey, W. Ickes and R.F. Kidd (eds) *New Directions in Attribution Research*, vol. 3. Hillsdale, NJ: Erlbaum.

Taylor, S. and Crocker, J. (1981) 'Schematic bases of social information processing'. In E.T. Higgins, C.P. Herman and M.P. Zanna (eds) *Social Cognition: The Ontario Symposium*. Hillsdale, NJ: Erlbaum.

Tomlinson-Keasey, C., Eisert, D.C., Kahle, L.R., Hardy-Brown, K. and Keasey, B. (1979) 'The structure of concrete operational thought'. *Child Development*, 50, 1153–63.

Tversky, A. and Kahneman, D. (1974) 'Judgements under uncertainty: Heuristics and biases'. *Science*, 185, 1124–31.

Valenti, S.S. and Good, J.M.M. (1991) 'Social affordances and interaction'. *Ecological Psychology*, 3, 77–98.

Valsiner, J. (1991) 'Construction of the mental'. *Theory and Psychology*, 1, 477–94.

Wegner, D.M. and Vallacher, R. (1977) *Implicit Psychology: The study of social cognition*. New York: Oxford University Press.

Wellman, H.M. (1990) *The Child's Theory of Mind*. Cambridge, MA: MIT Press.

Werner, H. (1957) *Comparative Psychology of Mental Development*. New York: International Universities Press.

Yates, J. (1990) 'What is a theory?' *Cognition*, 36, 91–6.

Zebrowitz, L.A. (1990) *Social Perception*. Milton Keynes: Open University Press.

Chapter 2

Children's understanding of mind

Sue Leekam

I

2.1 Understanding what?

What does it mean to 'understand mind'? What is mind, and in what sense can it be 'known' or 'understood'? Philosophers have been debating such questions for centuries. My purpose in raising them is to examine what developmental psychologists actually *mean* when they use terms like 'understanding mind' and 'theory of mind' to refer to children's development. My first task in this chapter, then, is to clarify what people are talking about when they refer to the child's understanding of mind. This done, we can then look at what children understand about the mind at different ages, and the relevance or significance of such understanding for children's lives.

The chapter starts with a tour through the terminology of this area. I think it is important to start here because there are many terminological confusions and disagreements in this subject area so it helps to clarify what is being referred to. Also, putting these terms under the microscope helps to remind us that innocuous-sounding phrases like 'understanding mind' and 'theory of mind' are actually minefields of philosophical and theoretical debate. Having looked at some of the theoretical and terminological issues at the beginning of the chapter, I then move on in the second section to a review of the empirical literature. In the third section I look at the social significance of understanding mind – its importance for moral, social and communicative development. In the final section I look at what we still need to know about children's understanding of the mind, and why some of the major, challenging questions remain unresolved.

I have divided this chapter into two parts. Part I deals with some of the main theoretical ideas; and part II deals with the implications of these ideas. To some extent the content of each part could stand separately, but I think it is important to include both aspects side by side. Overall, what I want to get across in this chapter is the scope of this subject area, its theoretical flexibility for explaining cognitive and social development, normal and abnormal development, and its importance in developmental psychology as a whole. First, though, on with the terminological tour and the question of what we mean by 'children's understanding of mind'.

2.1.1 Mind

Let us start with *'mind'*. What is mind – this thing that children are meant to acquire an understanding of? It is difficult to find a one-line answer to this question. Whiten and Perner (1991), however, supply a good 'quick-and-ready' answer when they talk about what one person might 'read' into the mind of another: 'the mind consists of mental states for which we have expressions in our language, like knowing, thinking, feeling, wanting and so on' (p. 8). This quick-and-ready definition, whilst not intending to capture all that belongs to a definition of 'mind', reminds us that what is usually referred to in the phrase 'understanding of mind' is the child's understanding of *mental states* like belief, desire and intention – their understanding that people have states of knowing, thinking, doubting, remembering, wanting, hoping, feeling, perceiving, imagining, etc.

What is the nature of these mental states? What do they consist of, and what is it that children have to learn about them in order to have an 'understanding of mind'? These essentially philosophical questions about the nature and existence of mental states are answered differently by different theoretical camps in philosophy (see Churchland, 1984; Greenwood, 1991). There is a division, for example, between dualist theories which subscribe to the view that mental states are unobservable and non-physical in nature, and non-dualist, materialist theories which claim that mental states are products of the physical brain. Within each of these different philosophical camps there are further theoretical divergences over the question of what mental states consist of.

In philosophy, then, a number of theories of mind are possible. Which of these theories of mind do children have? The starting point for research on children's understanding of mind has not tended to address the question of *which* philosophical theory of mind children acquire (though see Perner, 1991a, ch. 11; Wimmer and Hartl, 1991 for discussion on this). Instead, research tends to start with the question of whether children have a theory of mind at all, and how they acquire it. The origin of this discussion comes from the accepted view that in everyday life people constantly talk about mental states in order to explain and predict other people's behaviour. We talk about what people 'want' to do, what people 'think', what people 'know' and 'perceive'. The question is how the child comes to develop concepts of mental states from this language of everyday life. The widely held view is that such concepts come from a network of common-sense generalizations known as 'folk psychology' (see also Bennett, this volume, Chapter 1), and much developmental research is devoted to characterizing the origins and development of this folk (or common-sense) psychology (see Olson, 1988).

The term 'folk psychology' can be loosely described as common folklore for explaining how human beings work. Common-sense principles or 'platitudes' (Stich, 1983) populate this everyday folklore – for example, generalizations like: 'A person who has lost something will be sad', 'A person who has not eaten will be hungry', 'A person who believes X will act in accordance with X'. Such generalizations connect mental states to external events in the world. The term 'folk psychology' (also 'mentalistic', 'everyday' or 'common-sense psychology'), then, refers to these common-sense generalizations, and to the framework of understanding that underlies them. Many writers have made a strong case for the importance of this common-sense psychology in our everyday life. Forguson and Gopnik (1988), for example, stress:

> It is difficult to overestimate the extent to which our commitment to CS (common-sense) psychology is implicated in our everyday lives as adults. Our ability to make cooperative plans, our deeply ingrained practice of blaming, excusing and justifying behaviour; our ability to predict what others will do under various conditions; our ability to influence others' behaviour (e.g. to cajole, entreat, persuade, bribe, motivate etc.) all depend on attributing beliefs, expectations, knowledge, wants, fears, wishes, motives, strategies and the like to others and using these attributions in 'practical reasoning'. (p. 227)

2.1.2 A theory of mind?

How should this common-sense understanding be characterized? What kind of understanding do children acquire when they acquire folk psychology? Many developmentalists argue that what is acquired is a 'theory of mind'. What makes them think that children have a *theory* of mind? As the term 'theory of mind' has become such a popular catch phrase, it might be helpful to look at where it came from and how useful it is as a description of the child's understanding.

The 'theory view' in philosophy of mind proposes that the mental terms we use in everyday life – e.g. 'want', 'think', 'know', etc. – are not just arbitrary, unconnected common-sense terms. They are *theoretical concepts* which form part of a larger framework of understanding, or theory (see Churchland, 1984). The idea is that the meaning of terms like think, believe, etc., is fixed by a set of laws in the same way that the meanings of other theoretical terms become determined in any theory of the physical world. These laws originate from the many generalizations or principles we use in everyday life. Consider statements like 'A person who wants X and gets X will be happy', or 'A person who wants X and believes X is in P will look in P.' These statements have certain characteristics. They connect mental states with other mental states, and they connect mental states with events in the world and with human action. It is argued that a collection of such laws forms a theory. The theory, therefore, prescribes a set of mental states and causal relations between these mental states and the world.

The 'theory view' in developmental psychology grew out of this philosophical background following a question originally asked by Premack and Woodruff as to whether chimpanzees have a 'theory of mind'. By 'theory of mind', Premack and Woodruff were referring to the ability to impute mental states to others. This ability, they argued, can be seen as a 'theory' because it involves a 'system of inferences' which can be used to make predictions about others' behaviour – inferences concerning states that are unobservable. Following Premack and Woodruff's (1978) study, developmental psychologists started to investigate whether children have a theory of mind. The use of the term 'theory of mind' has changed along the way and it is now used in a number of different ways. At its loosest, the term 'theory of mind' is simply used as a label for a research area in developmental psychology – the *study* of children's understanding of the mind. Second, the term 'theory of mind' is used by some to refer to 'theory' in the widest sense: as Astington and Gopnik put it, 'a kind of *catch-all term for any organized body of knowledge*' (1991, p. 16; emphasis added). Third, the term has been used by developmentalists in the sense intended by Premack and Woodstuff (1978): as the *ability to impute mental states to self and other* (Bretherton, 1991; Bretherton, McNew and Beeghly-Smith, 1981). And finally, a number of developmentalists have taken a more formal and specific definition of the term 'theory of mind' – the 'theory theory' of children's understanding (see Astington and Gopnik, 1991). The view here is that children's everyday common-sense knowledge, their folk psychology, is *essentially theoretical* in nature. It has the status of a theory in the same way that scientific theories do.

But why should common-sense be treated as science – or, more specifically, as scientific theory? The rationale for this view which links everyday knowledge to scientific theory has been most strongly advocated by Wellman (1990), who combines ideas from philosophy of mind, philosophy of science, and cognitive developmental research on children's theory formation in support of his view.

Wellman's central argument is that children have a theory of mind. This proposal rests on the claim that adults have one. But how do we know that adults have a theory of mind? The claim that adults have a theory of mind rests on two other claims. One claim, from philosophy of mind, is the view I mentioned above: that folk-psychological generalizations can be seen as a collection of laws that together form a naive theory. The claim is that people hold a naive theory, which is not a developed or scientific theory, but is nevertheless a theory. Wellman's second claim, based on ideas from philosophy of science, is a stronger one: that adults' reasoning about the mind demonstrates three important features that can be found in scientific theories. First, a person's body of knowledge about mental states demonstrates *coherence* – an interconnectedness of concepts. Second, their reasoning demonstrates *ontological distinctions* between mental and physical phenomena – the specification or 'carving up' of phenomena into classes and kinds. And finally, the adult's understanding of mind provides a *causal explanatory scheme* – a framework for explaining and predicting changes and relationships between phenomena, in this case explaining human action in terms of mental states (see also Bennett, this volume, Chapter 1). Such features, Wellman claims, are evidence for a 'theory of mind', and through a detailed process of experimentation he has shown that the same three features found in adults' understanding are also apparent in even 3-year-olds' understanding. According to Wellman, the child, like the adult, has a 'theory of mind' which is made up of mentalistic common-sense laws or principles and works in a way that is analogous to a scientific theory.

Many developmentalists agree with Wellman that the child's understanding of mind is 'theory-like'. This general position is consistent with the view that cognitive development can be seen in terms of theory formation. The claim is that cognitive development progresses through the development of theories of physics, psychology and biology which become increasingly specialized as they unfold (Carey, 1985). Such theories rely on the grasp of specific explanatory mechanisms to provide the key to how things work. This theoretical knowledge contrasts with other types of 'knowledge' like scripts, rules or associations. Although these other types of knowledge may provide a cumulative store of working strategies for dealing with the world, they do not offer a core explanatory mechanism which can account for how or why aspects of the world work as they do. Theoretical knowledge, in contrast, is flexible and economical. Central 'foundational' concepts and key ideas generate explanations across multiple different situations. The view that having a theory is not only the best way to proceed but also the way that children actually do acquire knowledge has been persuasively argued by both Karmiloff-Smith (1988) and Carey (1985).

Whilst many agree that the child's understanding of the mind can be seen as theoretical, not everyone agrees with Wellman's formulation. As Perner (1991a, 1991b) and Samet (in press) point out, the analogy between scientific theories and children's theories of mind rests rather precariously on the definition of what a theory is. Perner (1991a, ch. 11) in particular takes issue with Wellman's contention that the 2- and 3-year-old child has a 'theory of mind'. Nevertheless, Perner (1991a, 1991b) argues that the 'theory view' as an explanation for children's understanding of mind is justified. For one thing, he argues, it gives us important insights into children's conceptual development. In particular, the child's acquisition of particular 'foundational' concepts can have a major role in creating new theories and major theory changes. These 'foundational' concepts provide a deeper level of explanation that can be applied to a wide range of phenomena and create a 'theoretical revolution' in the child's development. Perner argues that the concept of 'representation' plays this role and has a major effect on the child's theory formation. Once the child understands the explanatory mechanism of representation, he or she has a 'theory of mind' (see below, pp. 39–41, for a fuller discussion of this point).

Although Perner and Wellman disagree in their analysis of the child's theory of mind, they both subscribe to the 'theory' view of children's understanding of the mental world. This position is strongly supported by a number of other developmentalists such as Leslie, Gopnik and Flavell, all of whom take the child's developing understanding of representation as central to their explanation, but present a different formulation from either Perner or Wellman (see Astington, Harris and Olson, 1988; Butterworth, Harris, Leslie and Wellman, 1991, for further detail of these explanations).

2.1.3 Not a theory of mind?

The research I have discussed so far makes the claim that children have a theory of mind. What would children's knowledge of mind look like if it was not theoretical? One problem with trying to answer this question is that the term 'theory' has such a wide application. Samet (in press) points out five different uses or connotations of this term. For example, 'theory' can be used in the sense of 'engaging in a process of deliberate theorizing' (psychogenetic sense) or in the sense of 'forming explanations by correlating events' (functional sense). Since the term 'theory of mind' can easily be applied to children's understanding in at least five different ways, it is important to take account of all these different applications when we are trying to decide when a child does *not* have a theory of mind.

Several developmental theorists, however, do take the view that young children's understanding of mind is not a theory at all. Hobson (1991), for example, proposes that the child's understanding of mind is not theoretical. Although he agrees that there are ways in which children's concepts of mind are 'theory-like', he claims that theorizing is not the primary source of their knowledge. Instead he argues that our knowledge of other people (including their minds) is founded upon 'directly experienced' attitudes towards others. We acquire knowledge of mental states through a process that begins with perceiving attitudes in the expressions of others. We read certain mental states directly from other people's behaviour, acquiring knowledge of these states through the invariant information provided in perception. Such information specifies social meaning for us. Butterworth (1991) also proposes the idea of direct perception in his claim that visual attention provides signals for sharing information with others without any need for 'mind-reading'.

Another position in the non-theory-of-mind camp is the 'simulation' view, a view which also employs the idea of direct perception and experience. Johnson (1988) originally proposed the view that children do not need a theory because their own subjective experiences provide all the information about the mind they need. Children can read off their own subjective experiences of thoughts, desires, and so on, to get information about other peoples inner states. Harris (1989, 1991, in press, and Chapter 3 below) has extended Johnson's idea by proposing a 'simulation' account of children's understanding. Children, he argues, experience their own beliefs, desires and perceptions directly. These experiences are personal, first-hand mental states, not theoretical constructs. In order to understand what someone else would think or feel, you have to imagine being in the same situation and read off or *simulate* the desire, belief or emotion you would feel. This view is quite different from the 'theory' view I discussed above, in which children use their conceptual knowledge to make *inferences* about both their own and another person's mental state in order to explain external observable events.

As Harris (1991) and Perner (1991a) point out, this simulation view is reminiscent of the idea put forward in the 1960s and 1970s for social role-taking (e.g. Flavell, Botkin, Fry, Wright and Jarvis, 1968) and children's problems with egocentrism (Piaget and Inhelder, 1948/1956). The idea is that you put yourself in 'another person's shoes' in order to take their role or perspective. The 'putting-yourself-in-another-person's-shoes' view associated with the social role-taking literature, and the more recent simulation view, has also been linked by Wimmer and Hartl (1991) to the philosophical position originally taken by Descartes. Descartes (1639/1970) argued that we have direct access to our mental states by internally observing our own minds. Our own mind, in other words, is transparent to itself. Its contents are available and accessible to us, while the contents of other people's minds are not.

Some philosophers and psychologists argue against the 'simulation' view. Churchland (1991), for example, proposes that in order to possess even an understanding of oneself, one would need a conceptual framework that is already a theory. Perner (1991a) also argues that simulation is not the prime mechanism by which minds are understood, since theoretical understanding is already in place before simulation appears. Perner's view is supported with evidence provided by Wimmer and Hartl (1991) and Wimmer, Hogrefe and Perner (1988) showing that children do not find it easier to attribute mental states to themselves than to others, which is what you would expect if you had direct access to your own but not to others mental states. However, Harris (in press) argues that all this evidence concerns the attribution of *past* mental states, which simulation theory would predict to be no easier to attribute to oneself than to others. In contrast, when children report what they are *currently* pretending, wanting and thinking, the evidence does seem to support the simulation view that children have privileged access to their own mental state.

In weighing up the 'theory theory' versus 'simulation theory' debate, Harris (in press) states that 'we cannot adjudicate between theory theory and simulation theory by attempting to show that either one of them is an implausible account of how we predict and explain other people's action and speech . . . it is pretty clear that we deploy both tacit theories and simulation'. The important thing seems to be to establish under what conditions we may simulate and under what conditions we use theoretical understanding. The simulation account may better explain how children become more accurate in their ability to predict mental states, and may offer a better explanation for the developmental transitions of the first two years of life. Freeman (1992) also makes the point that when we evaluate 'simulation' versus 'theory theory' explanations, we need to be careful about the basis for our comparisons. We need to look at what each theory is directed towards (for example, the child's understanding of 'representation' or 'personhood') and evaluate the theory in terms of what it is attempting to explain.

Other developmentalists in the 'non-theory' camp have turned their attention to the *source* of children's later theoretical knowledge. They argue that knowledge of the mind does not appear in a vacuum – it arises *out of* something. In particular, it arises out of perceptual experiences (Butterworth, 1991; Hobson, 1991) and affective experiences (Hobson, 1991; Reddy, 1991) with others. Interactions are set in a social world (Dunn, 1991), in a narrative context, within a stream of temporal events (Carrithers, 1991; Forrester, 1992) and take a dynamic form with an interactive partner who is continually acting back (Forrester, 1992). Accounts such as these, which stress the experiential basis of understanding, must be set against the 'theory theory' position, which stresses only the inferential basis of understanding.

2.1.4 Summary

The study of children's understanding of the mind has emerged from the view that mentalistic reasoning is central for our everyday understanding as adults. We talk about mental states, impute intentions and beliefs to others, and reason about human actions by referring to mental states. We can think of the term 'understanding mind' as referring to knowledge of mental states which is organized and develops in a particular way. The view of how it is organized depends on the theorist. Most in the field argue that it takes the form of a theory, and give central importance to the development of this theoretical knowledge and to the child's understanding of representations. Some, however, have argued against the view that the child has a 'theory' of mind.

2.2 *What understanding?*

Having defined children's understanding of mind in its widest sense as their understanding of mental states like desire, belief and intention, the next question is: What understanding do children actually have? When do they start getting ideas about others' minds, and how do these ideas develop? Research within the 'theory view' makes the proposal that some notion of other minds can be found even in infants, but not until much later do children acquire a theory of mind that resembles the understanding that adults are said to possess. Moreover, there are specific age points at which sudden transformations in knowledge occur. It is these changes that have interested theorists, because of the underlying cognitive abilities that appear to be emerging at this time.

In this section I examine these proposals for children's developing knowledge of mind by describing some of the main research findings on their understanding of imagination, pretence, perception, intention, desire, knowledge and belief. In line with the focus of research in this area, I concentrate particularly on the changes that occur between the age of 2 and the age of 5 (see also Astington and Gopnik, 1991; Perner, 1991a; Wellman, 1990 for excellent reviews of this literature).

2.2.1 Pre-schoolers' understanding of mind

Perception　Children's understanding of perception emerges quite early on. At 18 months to 2 years of age they begin to show objects to others, bringing objects in front of another person's eyes into their line of sight (Lempers, Flavell and Flavell, 1977). By the age of 3, children also understand that this line of sight must remain unobstructed for a person to see an object that they themselves cannot see (Flavell, Everett, Croft and Flavell, 1981). By the time they are 3 years old, then, children understand the physical relationship between line of sight and behaviour – that something in front of another person's eyes is 'seen' or registered by that person. The same goes for perception in other modalities: smell, touch and hearing (Yaniv and Shatz, 1988). Not until the age of 4 or 5, however, do children understand that if other people view an object from different aspects, orientations or viewpoints, this will lead them to have quite different interpretations according to their viewpoint (Masangkay, McCluskey, McIntyre, Sims-Knight, Vaughn and Flavell, 1974). From the same age the child also begins to understand that an ambiguous picture could be interpreted differently by different people (Ruffman *et al.*, 1991; Taylor, 1988). So by the age of 2 or 3 children understand that two people can see two quite different things, but not until the age of 4 or 5 do they understand the idea that two people can see exactly the same thing, but form two quite different interpretations of it.

Imagination and pretence　The ability to pretend indicates that children are aware of the distinction between the real world and the mental world. Pretend play emerges in the second year of life. From the second year onwards, children engage in pretence in several different ways: pretending that one object is another, creating imaginary objects, and endowing real objects with imaginary attributes (Leslie, 1987). Even at 18 months they engage not only in pretend play by themselves but also in shared pretence, and they recognize pretence in others (Dales, Dunn and Dale, cited in Leslie, 1987). Although pretend play first emerges at the age of 12 to 24 months, this ability continues to develop in the next four years, becoming increasingly sophisticated throughout this period. At the age of 2, children still often confuse pretence and reality (DeLoache and Plaetzer, 1985; DiLalla and Watson, 1988; Slade, 1986; cited in Harris, 1989), but by the age of 3 they can clearly distinguish between the real world and the world of imagination. Three-year-olds know, for example, that imaginary objects cannot be touched or seen (Wellman and Estes, 1986) but can be mentally transformed (Estes, Wellman and Woolley, 1989). If children are asked to imagine a cup, they know that they cannot really see the cup or touch it, but they also know that by just thinking about it they can make it turn upside down. By the age of 4, children can deal with make-believe ideas in quite an advanced way. They competently attribute pretend mental states, such as beliefs, to dolls (Wolf, Rygh and Altshuler, 1984) and can logically reason from within a hypothetical, make-believe world (Dias and Harris, 1988; Harris, 1991). In sum, pretence is an early emerging ability. By 28 months, children display an impressive range of make-believe skills (Harris and Kavanaugh, in press), and these continue to develop throughout the pre-school years.

Desires and intentions By the age of 2, young children have a clear understanding of goal-directed action. They can switch between different means to achieve goals (Frye, 1991), are conscious of when goals fail to be achieved (Kagan, 1981) and understand other people as intentional agents whose actions are directed at achieving goals. From the age of 2 or 3 children also recognize that a person's action depends on what that person wants (Wellman and Woolley, 1990). From the age of 3 they can distinguish intended actions from accidents (Shultz, Wells and Sarda, 1980). They also understand how the relationship between what you want (desire) and what you get (outcome) affects emotional consequences – i.e. whether you are happy or sad (Hadwin and Perner, 1991; Yuill, 1984). By the age of 4 to 5, children become able to understand intentions independently of actions. That is, they recognize that someone's *intention* to – for example – paint a picture or go on a swing is quite different from the act of painting the picture or swinging itself. So by the time they are 4 to 5 years old children can conceptualize prior intention and understand the causal link between intentions and actions (Astington, 1991). To summarize: from the age of 2 or 3 the child already has an understanding of goals and desires, and by the age of 4 or 5 they have developed an advanced understanding of the causal relationship between intentions and actions.

Knowledge   Two-year-olds and even 3-year-olds are not very good at playing hide-and-seek (Perner, 1991a). Although they like to engage in hide-and-seek games, they do not appreciate that the purpose of the game is to conceal an object to prevent another person from knowing where it is. Three-year-olds, however, do understand that there is some connection between perceptual activities like seeing and hearing and some resulting state of 'knowing'. For example, if a 3-year-old is asked to choose which of two people knows what is in a box, they will choose the person who looked into the box rather than the person who did not look into it (Hogrefe, Wimmer and Perner, 1986; Pillow, 1989; Pratt and Bryant, 1990). At the same time, however, children of this age cannot justify their own or another person's knowledge. That is, they cannot say *how* a person came to know something – i.e. because the person looked, or was told, etc. (Gopnik and Graf, 1988; Perner and Ogden, 1988; Wimmer, Hogrefe and Sodian, 1988). They are also unable to appreciate that knowledge of different aspects of an object is acquired from different perceptual modalities. For example, looking at an object will give information about its colour, while feeling it will give information about its texture or weight (O'Neill, Astington and Flavell, 1992). Not until about the age of 5 do children understand the 'aspectuality' of knowledge in this way, and not until they are 4 do they consistently justify their knowledge correctly when asked how or why they know something. At about the same age, children become able to distinguish between 'know' and 'guess' (Moore, Bryant and Furrow, 1989; Perner, 1991a). These later abilities suggest that by the time they are 5, children understand not only that informational access (i.e. seeing or being told something) is linked with 'knowing', but that this informational access actually *causes* knowledge.

Thinking and belief   Children start to talk about 'thinking' from an early age, using the term 'think' in their spontaneous speech at 24 months or earlier (Bretherton *et al.*, 1981). Yet not until much later, at around the age of 4, do they really understand the concept of belief. Understanding the concept of belief is an important step in the child's understanding of the mind. Beliefs are representational – that is, when someone holds a belief, they represent the world in a particular way. Children's *understanding* of belief, therefore, tells us something about their understanding of the mind as representational.

An enormous amount of research has concentrated on children's understanding of this representational type of understanding and, in particular, the child's understanding of *false belief*. Children's understanding of false belief gives us the acid test for investigating their understanding of mental representations. When people hold a false belief, they act not according to how the world actually is but according to their mental representation of the world. In the now-classic false-belief task (Wimmer and Perner, 1983) the child has to make a prediction about someone's action in the following situation. A person (Maxi) puts an object in a particular place (location A) and leaves the room. In Maxi's absence, the object is moved to another location (B). The child then has to predict where Maxi will look for the object when he returns. In this case Maxi will act not according to how the world really is – by looking in the new location – but according to his representation – by looking in the wrong place. The evidence shows that the ability to attribute false beliefs develops between the ages of 3½ and 5. This shift in ability between younger and older pre-school children is remarkably robust. Astington and Gopnik (1991) report that the results have been replicated in twenty different studies, with variations in tasks, materials and questions asked. The results of these studies show a distinct shift in ability between younger and older pre-school children which has been attributed to a clear change in conceptual understanding.

2.2.2 Theoretical explanations for pre-schoolers' understanding of mind

Even this brief review of the literature on children's understanding of these mental states, I hope, demonstrates that there are some quite distinct changes in children's understanding between the ages of 2 and 5.

The 2-year-old At the age of 2 children understand the physical relation between a person's line of sight and their behaviour, engage in pretend play and start to understand the hypothetical world of make-believe. They also understand the link between means and ends – the idea of goal-directed action.

The 3-year-old At the age of 3 children understand that other people see the world differently from themselves – for example, see things that they themselves do not see. They also understand that imaginary objects are altogether different from real objects, that people's actions can be determined by their desires, intentions and thoughts. In addition, 3-year-olds understand that perceptual activity (seeing, being told) is in some way connected to a concept of 'knowing'.

The 4- and 5-year-old At the age of 4 to 5, other abilities emerge. Children recognize that different perceptual viewpoints can lead people to have different interpretations of an object or event. They can also reason within a counterfactual world and understand intentions independently of actions. They understand how access to information by seeing or hearing is causally related to knowledge (someone knows about something because they have seen it) and how knowledge and belief can be causally related to actions in the world (beliefs cause people to act in certain ways). In particular, the 4- to 5-year-old understands that someone who misrepresents a situation will act wrongly because of their false belief about this situation.

What is going on in children's cognitive development between the ages of 2 and 5 to create such changes in their understanding of others' minds? Whilst I cannot do justice to the range of theoretical positions that explain the evidence I have presented, I will outline two major theoretical interpretations of these data: the positions of Wellman (1990) and Perner (1988, 1991a) (see Astington and Gopnik, 1991; Astington, Harris and Olson, 1988, for a fuller account of different theoretical positions by Leslie, Flavell, Gopnik and others).

Wellman: from desire psychology to belief–desire psychology
Wellman (1990) argues that what is developing is a theoretical understanding which reveals two distinct theory 'shifts' between the ages of 2 and 5. Wellman claims that by the age of 2 children have already developed a very simplified theory, a 'desire psychology'. The 2-year-old's theory consists of the simple notion that human action is driven by internal dispositions, or desires, or drives. The 2-year-old understands the mental world by conceptualizing internal states as simply being *directed* at objects or states of affairs in the world. At this stage, however, they do not yet understand mental states as representations. The 3-year-old, in contrast, can conceptualize internal states as *representing* truths in the world. The 3-year-old, then, understands not only desires but also beliefs.

The first theory change in Wellman's scheme thus occurs at about the age of 3, when the child changes from simple desire psychology to belief–desire psychology. The 3-year-old becomes able to understand mental states not only as internal dispositions directed at states in the world but also as representations of the world. Three-year-olds, however, have a peculiar kind of representational understanding. Wellman suggests that they understand representations such as beliefs only as direct *copies* of reality, faithfully depicting what is truthfully the state of affairs in the real world. Although this early notion of belief is representational in Wellman's account, it is not interpretative. Beliefs are seen as truthful copies of the world rather than as interpretations of the world which may be *either* true *or* false. A second theory change then takes place between the ages of 4 and 6, when children move from a copy-container notion of mind to an interpreter view of mind. That is, they come to understand 'representational' mental states like belief as interpretative devices rather than simply as copies of reality. At this age they then become able to appreciate false as well as true beliefs.

In terms of the findings I have reported above on children's understanding of mental states, Wellman's account suggests three distinct developmental stages: age 2 (desire psychology), age 3 (belief–desire psychology) and age 4–6 (interpreter view of mind). Wellman suggests that the ability at each stage is somehow 'pulled out of' or constructed from the earlier one. Understanding desires provides the bedrock for understanding beliefs. The developmental mechanism by which these theory changes take place is not specified; however, Wellman makes it clear that understanding of desire does not cease at this point of the belief–desire transition. Instead, once children understand belief, their theory of mind is transformed to encompass understanding of both kinds of mental state, desires and beliefs.

Perner: from situational theory to representational theory
Perner's (1988, 1991a) account is both similar to and different from Wellman's: similar in the sense that it is an account of changes in theoretical knowledge; different in its analysis of what is *representational*. Perner (1991a) asserts that the term 'representation' has a very specific meaning. Following Frege (1892/1960), he points out that a representation, like belief, represents something (e.g. a state of affairs in the world) as being a certain way (Perner, 1991a, p. 40). In the false-belief task, for example, Maxi represents the chocolate, which is really in location B, as being a certain way – i.e. in location A. The ability to understand that Maxi is *representing* something rests on understanding the distinction between *what* is represented (chocolate in location B) and what it is represented *as* (i.e. chocolate in location A). Only once this distinction is grasped can the child be said to understand the mind as representational. Wellman's idea that children first have a 'representational' understanding, in which they view beliefs as copies of the world, would not, therefore, count as representational understanding according to Perner's theory.

Apart from the question of representation, another major departure from Wellman's position is Perner's analysis of the *conditions* under which people treat mental states as representational. Whilst it is true that understanding belief as a representation does involve recognizing that someone represents the world in a particular way, Perner argues that in everyday life we just do not do this most of the time. Instead, we usually refer to 'beliefs' or 'thoughts' without considering representations at all. Remember the last time you referred to someone thinking something? The chances are that you didn't consider that the person was actually representing a particular state of affairs in a particular way – as a particular interpretation of an event. Take as an example 'Mary thinks the cat is in the garden'. Perner suggests that we do not need to consider in what way her thought *represents* a particular situation. All we need do is connect her with a situation – in this case, a garden with a cat in it. Thinking can be viewed simply as an activity which relates people to particular thought-of *situations* – real or imaginary. It does not have to be conceived of as a *representational* activity, except in certain circumstances (see Perner, 1991, p. 173, for further discussion).

There are occasions, however, when thoughts – or, more correctly, 'beliefs' – do need to be construed as representations. This becomes necessary in order to understand how someone could misrepresent reality. It is important in these situations to understand that a person represents a state of affairs in a particular way. In the case of false belief, for example, a person misrepresents a state of affairs as true when it is really false. Confronted with another person's misrepresentation or false belief, therefore, you need to consider another person's belief *as* a representation, not simply as an objective situation or a state of affairs that can be linked with what that person is thinking about. Perner argues that children do not understand misrepresentations until about the age of 4. At this point they see the mind as a representational device, and this understanding allows them to understand false belief. It also allows them more generally to conceive of mental states as interpretations, to understand the causal relationship between information and knowledge, and the causal relationship between mental states and behaviour. Before the age of 4, according to Perner, children do not have a representational understanding of mind. Instead, they understand beliefs and mental states as links between a person and situations or states of affairs. Perner describes the younger child as having a 'situation theory' of behaviour, whilst the older child of 4 upwards has a 'representational theory of mind'. Once a representational view of the mind is acquired, however, it does not supplant or encompass the early situation theory. Instead, the two exist side by side. Even adults are 'situation theorists at heart' (Perner, 1991a, p. 251). Once the representational view of mind has appeared, however, it can be drawn on when it is needed.

In terms of the findings I reported above on children's understanding of mental states, Perner suggests two distinct developmental stages. At around the age of 4, children come to understand that knowledge, beliefs, intentions and perceptions are causally related to the real world, and that these mental states can represent the world in a particular way. One example is the case of understanding false belief in which a state in the world is (falsely) represented as being a different way. Before this time, however, 2- and 3-year-olds simply understand knowledge, thinking, perception and pretence as situations in the world (either real or hypothetical) that are linked to a person, but they do not need to understand these mental states as representations.

To summarize, compare Perner's account with Wellman's three-stage scheme (see Table 2.1). Wellman argues that once children have some notion of 'thinking' at the age of 3, this can be counted as representational understanding to some degree. It is not representational understanding in its fullest sense, however, because 3-year-olds can conceptualize beliefs only as copies of reality. Then, at 4, this understanding changes: children become capable of understanding representations as interpretations of the world rather than as copies. This is reflected in their representational understanding of belief, but also in their understanding of other mental states such as perception and intention, and in their view of the mind as an active processor of information. Stages 1 and 2 of Wellman's account can therefore be incorporated into Perner's Stage 1. In Perner's account, thinking (belief) has

Table 2.1 Summary of Perner's and Wellman's Developmental Stages

Wellman	Perner
1. Desire psychology (age 2)	1. Situational theory of behaviour (age 18 mths +)
2. Belief–desire psychology (age 3)	
3. Beliefs as both interpretations and representations (ages 4–6)	2. Representational theory of mind (ages 4–5)

to be understood as representational only in special circumstances; for the most part it can be seen as situational rather than representational.

In this account I have deliberately focused on the changes in the pre-school years, as most of the research has been directed at this age group. But why the fuss over 2- to 4-year-olds? Why is this important? It is important because it relates back to the point mentioned above about understanding mind as a representational device. The child's discovery of representation as an explanatory mechanism facilitates his or her theory development. As Perner (1991a) puts it: 'one can think of representation as playing a catalytic role in children's reconceptualization of what the mind is, similar to the catalytic role that important scientific concepts play in the development of new scientific theories' (p. 11). The emergence of representational understanding, then, is important for cognitive-developmental accounts of the child as a theorist. Representation is seen as a central concept – not only in cognitive-developmental theory, but also in cognitive psychology and cognitive science more generally.

Apart from these important concerns with representation, let us look again at the question of *development*. I have talked about the pre-school period, but what do we know about understanding of the mind in the infant under 2, and again later in the school-aged child or adolescent? The answer is: a lot less than we know about the 2- to 5-year-old. Most research has been focused on the pre-school years, but we now need to look at how mental concepts might first emerge in infancy, and how they come to be elaborated as the child develops into the school years.

2.2.3 Infancy

So far I have skimmed over the issue of when understanding of mind first emerges. This is clearly an important issue. In a sense there are two questions here. First, where does 'theory of mind' come from? Is it, as Leslie (1987, 1988) suggests, an innate cognitive 'module' which is either functioning from the start of life or set to unfold along a maturational time-course? Or is it acquired through cultural practices and social interaction: a social product of family discourse and the emotional experiences associated with conflict and cooperation (see Dunn, 1991)? Second, when (and in what form) does understanding of the mind first appear? Is there evidence for understanding of the mind before the second year of life? In this section I deal with this later question, saving the 'origin' issue for later in the chapter.

Both Perner and Wellman argue that young infants do not have a theory of mind. Both claim that it is not until well into their second year that infants understand other people's inner states as mental. Perner argues that evidence on early social awareness (Trevarthen, 1979), emotional awareness, and joint attention (e.g. pointing) in 9–12-month-olds can be explained in ways other than the existence of an explicit (or implicit) theory of mind. The infant does not need to appreciate the mental state of emotion or attention underlying their care-giver's emotional expression or pointing behaviour. Instead their ability may be explained in terms of other factors: innate recognition of meaning in emotional expressions, learned contingencies between facial expressions and consequences, and mastery over another's eyes or behaviour to produce particular effect. Only from the second year (around 18 months) is there evidence for an understanding of inner states as mental. At this time the child shows empathic reactions to another person's distress, the ability to engage in hypothetical thinking by imagining oneself in the other person's situation.

Even if there is no evidence that infants understand mental states as *theoretical constructs*, however, the abilities of the infant are important in their own right. Naturalistic observations of infants' playfulness and teasing (Reddy, 1989, 1991) and their pre-verbal communicative behaviour (Bretherton, McNew and Beeghly-Smith, 1981) show that even 9–12-month-olds are able to manipulate other people's beliefs and intentions in teasing exchanges, and can make their messages understood. Even if these abilities cannot yet be called 'mental-state knowledge', it can be argued that a rich store of interpersonal knowledge develops in the first year. The problem for the 'theory-of-mind' position has been how to integrate accounts of early ability into an explanation which is essentially based on *theoretical* knowledge. Reddy (1989) points out that in this view development ends up being seen as *discontinuous*, so at an early point the child is seen to be engaging in behaviour using knowledge of behaviour, and from a later point using a developing knowledge of mental states. One way of trying to get round this is to view the early abilities as *precursors* to the later-developing mental-state knowledge (Wellman, 1990; Baron-Cohen, 1991a). Some researchers have turned their attention to the way in which infants develop an understanding of intentionality *out of* their own intentional actions (Bretherton, 1991; Frye, 1991; Premack, 1991), but more work is needed on the functional continuity between infancy and later childhood.

2.2.4 The school years

What kind of developments would you expect to see in the school years? If children's understanding of mental states is in place by the end of the pre-school years, what more can one say about their developing understanding of mind? Because there is little research on understanding of mind in older children and adults, it is difficult to know what it means to achieve competence and *what* exactly might be developing in later childhood or adolescence. Nevertheless, a few suggestions have been proposed.

Perner (1988) suggests that what develops is a higher level of representational skill. Between the ages of 6 and 9 the child becomes able to attribute second-order mental states (i.e. can attribute beliefs about beliefs, intentions about beliefs, etc.). This is made possible by the ability to apply mental states *recursively*. So the child becomes able to understand embedded mental states like: 'John knows (Mary doesn't know (the teacher is arriving)). Work by Perner and Wimmer (1985) suggests that this recursive understanding may be a fairly advanced ability, not emerging fully until the age of 6–9.

Wellman (1990) also suggests that various advances in conceptual structures appear in the school years. These advances form extensions and developments to the child's theory of mind. In the years beyond the age of 6, children are able to form *specific* theories within their general *framework* theory of mind. These specific theories include theories of self, intelligence and memory. Perner (1988) also argues that the ability to attribute higher-order mental states allows children to deepen their knowledge in other areas, particularly understanding of social concepts such as trust, commitment and intention to deceive.

Other developments may also be occurring in the school years (see Chandler, 1988, for further discussion). In addition to the increases in conceptual understanding that may be taking place, children will probably become more proficient at spontaneously identifying when to use or call up their conceptual competencies without cues or support from others (Bennett and Galpert, 1992). More research is needed to investigate the circumstances under which children spontaneously draw on their representational understanding of mind. We also need to know more about how adults reason about mental phenomena.

2.2.5 Summary

Research within the 'theory' view of children's understanding of mind has shown that specific changes take place across the pre-school years in children's understanding of mental states (perception, pretence, desire, intention, knowledge, thinking, belief). Wellman has attributed these changes to specific theory shifts (desire to belief–desire psychology, copy to interpreter view of mind), whilst Perner has attributed them to the development of understanding mind as representational. While both theorists agree that what changes is the child's theoretical knowledge, they differ in their analysis of (a) what a 'representational' understanding of mind is, and (b) the conditions under which people treat mental states as representational.[1] The focus of study on changes within the pre-school period has meant that a developmental picture across childhood has not emerged, and developments in infancy and the school years have tended to be overlooked. Research on infancy shows that the richness of the pre-verbal child's understanding is important in its own right, and stands as an important source of later knowledge. Research on the school years suggests that firmer links must be drawn between earlier and later development, and that we should clarify what we mean by an 'adult' theory of mind.

II

2.3 So what?

Why is it important for children to develop an understanding of mind? How important is such understanding for children's lives? One of the major contributions of the 'theory-of-mind' perspective is its value as a flexible explanatory framework which can account for a number of aspects of human functioning. It has relevance for cognitive, social and language development, and has provided important insights on abnormal development in the case of autism. Also, beyond child development, the 'theory-of-mind' orientation has had an impact in the analysis of animal deception and work on computer simulation (see Whiten, 1991). The point of the second part of this chapter is to look at the significance of children's understanding of mind for their developing moral, social and communication skills. First, however, I want to think about understanding of mind as a *cognitive* achievement. Research on children's understanding of mind comes from within a cognitive-developmental research tradition, and the findings are important in informing us about how thinking develops with age. I have already mentioned the developing understanding of hypothetical situations, understanding representations and causal understanding. Evidence in other aspects of cognitive development that do not involve understanding of mind suggests that similar abilities emerge at the same time. For example, at the same time that children develop an understanding that people can form interpretations of the world in terms of mental states, they also understand the distinction between appearance and reality in objects (Flavell, Flavell and Green, 1983). In addition, recent research shows that 3-year-old children not only fail tests of their understanding of *mental* representations but also have similar difficulties with representations that are not mental – e.g. photographic representations

(Leekam and Perner, 1991; Zaitchik, 1990). Understanding of mind, then, may tell us a great deal about the child's cognitive development.

2.3.1 Social development

Having a theory of mind may also be important for understanding certain kinds of social, moral and emotional situations. A range of social (and antisocial) acts may depend on having some understanding of another's mind – for example, deception, mistakes, lies, misunderstandings, jokes, irony, trust, commitment, politeness and appropriateness. Much communication seems to involve taking account of anothers intentions and beliefs. Having a proper understanding of emotion also seems to require some understanding of desires, expectations and beliefs being thwarted or fulfilled. What exactly is the relationship between these social abilities and the developing understanding of mind? Throughout this section I try to look at two things: first, what evidence there is for linking theory of mind and social abilities; second, the nature of this relationship.

Understanding emotions
Various researchers have suggested that children's initial attempts to understand emotions are based on emotion 'scripts'. Donaldson and Westerman (1986), for example, propose that young children assume that 'feelings are wedded to events' (p. 655), so that birthday parties are associated with happiness and the loss of toys, pets, etc. will be associated with sadness. It seems probable, however, that children's conception of the mental world may facilitate understanding of emotions: once they begin to understand emotions in terms of mental states, they will also realize that the same situation can evoke different emotions in different people, depending on their prior expectations and desires. For example, it will be understood that if someone doesn't want to be at a birthday party yet has to go, they will probably be unhappy.

A number of studies now show that the child's developmental achievement in grasping certain mental states is closely matched or followed by an understanding of the emotions relevant to those mental states. In the case of desire, for example, Yuill (1984) asked children to make judgements about how pleased a person would be in a particular situation. She found that even 3-year-olds took account of the person's desire – so, someone wanting a particular object would be happier when they received it than someone who had not really wanted that object. In a different study, Wellman and Woolley (1990) showed that even 2-year-olds understand the link between desires, outcomes and emotions. So it seems that by the age of 3, children do understand something about the emotional consequences of desires.

Understanding of belief can also be linked to understanding emotion, and several studies have now investigated the understanding of 'belief-based' emotions (e.g. surprise, which results from a mismatch between what is expected and what actually occurs). A study by Harris, Johnson, Hutton, Andrews and Cooke (1989) suggests that although children can match happy and sad according to what someone wants and gets (desire-based judgement), they have more difficulty when it comes to beliefs. Even 4-year-olds could not understand that a potentially happy event will be interpreted as sad by a story character who has a false belief (e.g. s/he believes there are no chocolates left, when in fact there are).

To summarize: it seems that once children can reason about mental states, especially their own (Beckwith, 1991), they may come to apply this to their understanding of emotion. However, as will be clear from the next chapter in this volume, by Meerum Terwogt and Harris, an understanding of emotion does not *depend* upon an understanding of mental states such as desire and belief.

Deception and lying

The important role of intention and belief in acts of deception and lying has been noted by both moral philosophers (Chisholm and Feehan, 1977) and cognitive developmentalists (Piaget, 1932/1965) across the years. Research on children's understanding of mind has attempted to explicate the actual mental states involved in different acts of falsity. For instance, (a) a mistaken speaker *intends* to be truthful, and *believes* he is speaking the truth, whilst a lying speaker does not; (b) the deceived person who is misled may end up holding a *false belief*; (c) a deceitful liar *intends* the listener to *believe*, whilst the joking or ironic speaker does not.

How does children's understanding about deception and lying relate to their understanding of mental states? Research in this area works from the assumption that as children acquire an understanding of mind, they should become better able to deceive and to understand lying and deception in others (for discussion see Leekam, 1992; Ruffman, Olson, Ash and Keenan, in press). The evidence seems to support this picture. First, as far as understanding deception is concerned, Wimmer, Gruber and Perner (1984) showed that by the age of 4, when children understand false belief, they are also able to distinguish mistakes from lies on the basis of the speaker's *intention* to tell the truth. At 5 years old children could also distinguish jokes from lies on the basis of the speaker's second-order intention (i.e. John *doesn't want* his mother to *believe* versus John *wants* his mother to *believe*) (Leekam, 1991), and 5–7-year-olds can distinguish white lies from irony on the same basis (Winner and Leekam, 1991).

Evidence on children's own *ability* to lie and deceive also shows that once they can attribute false beliefs, they also become very successful at misinforming someone in order to deceive them (Russell, Mauthner, Sharpe and Tidswell, 1991; Sodian, 1991). In fact, in interviews with parents and teachers, Stouthamer–Loeber (1986; cited in Perner, 1991a) found that only

30 per cent reported an incident of lying when their children were 3–3½ years old, compared with over 75 per cent when their children were 4 years old, the age at which they also acquire understanding of false belief. This is not to say, however, that children are incapable of engaging in deceptive behaviour before the age of 4. Children may start off with simple strategies to manipulate others' behaviour, and research suggests that even 2- and 3-year-olds are capable of this (Lewis, Stanger and Sullivan, 1989; Chandler, Fritz and Hala, 1989). Indeed, early signs of deceptive and teasing behaviour are apparent even in infancy (Reddy, 1991). Yet it seems that not until the age of 4 do children understand that deception is a means of creating a false belief in another person (Ruffman, Olson, Ash and Keenan, in press). A range of studies (Russell *et al.*, 1991; Sodian, 1991; Sodian, Taylor, Harris and Perner, 1991) with one exception (Hala, Chandler and Fritz, 1991) – point to this conclusion: that 4-year-olds, but not 3-year-olds, appreciate that deception can create a state of false belief in another.

The development of deception and lying suggests a close 'fit' between theory of mind and moral development. However, further research needs to establish what the correlations between deception and false belief understanding actually mean. How relevant is false belief really to deception? So much deception involves simply wanting to mislead another person by creating a particular outcome (e.g. saying 'I didn't do it' in order to avoid punishment). In most cases there is no specific need to represent another person's representational activity by plotting that they should represent a particular situation in a particular way. Even if understanding false belief is not directly implicated in many acts of deception, of course, understanding representation may still provide a kind of conceptual 'key' in which the child suddenly grasps the point of deception. The emergence of this deeper understanding allows the child to engage in deception and other kinds of social manipulation more readily and flexibly. Even if this is so, it is possible that both abilities may have emerged owing to the development of an independent factor. Russell and colleagues (Hughes and Russell, in press; Russell *et al.*, 1991), for example, have proposed that both the false-belief test and the test of deceptive pointing require 'executive control'. In both cases children have to disengage their own knowledge and inhibit themselves from pointing to where an object really is. In both cases, if children focus or perseverate on what *they* know is in a box, they will point to the wrong box.

Communication
Speech act theorists (Austin, 1962; Grice, 1975; Searle, 1969) make it clear that communication relies on both speaker and hearer taking account of each other's intentions and knowledge. Whether asserting, requesting, promising or declaring, the speaker's intentions and beliefs are a central part of what is communicated, independent of the precise linguistic meaning of the utterance. Sperber and Wilson (1986) claim that communication proceeds

according to a principle of relevance. Relevance is established by the speaker communicating what he or she believes is relevant, and by the hearer working to recover the speaker-intended meaning. Bretherton (1991) also points out that what an utterance conveys and how it is conveyed depend on a framework of 'intersubjectivity', a framework of mutual interest and shared understanding. The emergence of communicative intent and use of speech acts in infancy has been of great interest to language acquisition theorists over the years (Bates, Benigni, Bretherton, Camaioni and Volterra, 1979; Bruner, 1975; Lock, 1980), and recently researchers have linked this subject directly to the phenonenon of 'theory of mind'.

A number of studies have investigated the relationship between children's understanding of mind and their use or understanding of communication. Observational studies of children's use of mental verbs have shown that by 28 months virtually all children are talking about perceptions, sensations and physiological states, and most talk about basic emotions (Bretherton, McNew & Beeghly-Smith, 1981). At the end of the third year, children also start to use mental-state terms to express degrees of certainty – i.e. think versus know (Bloom, Rispoli, Gartner and Hafitz, 1989; Shatz, Wellman and Silber, 1983), and at 4 years old they recognize the relative certainty implied in these terms when they are used by others (Moore, Bryant and Furrow, 1989), appreciating that 'knowing' implies more certainty than 'guessing' or 'thinking'. Between the ages of 3 and 4, children also show sensitivity to their listener's mental state by adjusting their communication to what their listener already knows or does not know (Perner and Leekam, 1986). From the age of 5, they understand ambiguous statements by distinguishing the *speaker's* meaning from the *message* meaning (Beal and Flavell, 1984; Mitchell and Russell, 1991; Robinson, Goelman and Olson, 1983), and can distinguish non-literal ironic statements from white lies by basing their judgements on the speaker's second-order intention (whether the speaker intended the listener to believe them) (Winner and Leekam, 1991).

So far I have talked only about the link between understanding of mind and communication once children develop language. But what about communication in the pre-verbal period? Any discussion of infant communication brings us back to the discussion earlier in the chapter on what *counts* as understanding of mind. Shatz *et al.* (1983) argue that even the earliest *verbal* references to mental states might not count as evidence for understanding of mental states, because mental-state references can so often be used in conversation without taking account of actual mental states (e.g. 'know what?' or 'you know'). If even verbal communication cannot always reveal explicit understanding of mind, what conclusions can be drawn from pre-verbal communication?

Bretherton (1991) reviews the communicative achievements of the infant in the run-up to language acquisition. These pre-verbal achievements, she argues, demonstrate 'intersubjectivity'. The communicative gestures of the 9–12-month-old, including pointing, gaze direction, timing of signals and repair of failed messages, are attempts to gain the hearer's attention and direct it to a subject of mutual interest. In being able to specify messages for the addressee, the infant at the end of the first year shows not only a rudimentary ability to impute mental states but also a recognition that minds can be 'interfaced' through the sharing of conventional or mutually comprehensible signals.

Leslie (1987) and Leslie and Happé (1989) also link 'theory of mind' to pre-verbal communication in their analysis of 'ostensive communication'. Ostensive acts are communicative acts that are intended to claim and direct the hearer's attention (Sperber and Wilson, 1986). Such acts draw attention to themselves, and thereby to what the actor *means*. Some acts of pointing and showing, for example, are acts in which one person deliberately claims someone else's attention and directs it to something. The ability to understand ostensive communication, they suggest, may require the representation of another's mental state (i.e. the child represents what the perceived agent intends or means by doing what he did).

Both Leslie and Happé (1989) and Perner (1991a) point out that even if infants do have an implicit notion of attention or intention, one would have to establish that they understand this state as something specifically *mental*. As yet there does not seem to be the evidence to establish this. The claim is that when infants use communicative gestures or are on the receiving end of ostensive communication, they are representing the *attention, interest* and *meaning* of their partner. It is not clear, however, that they do have a concept of these inner states and actually understand them as *mental* states. Perner's (1991a) alternative interpretation is that when infants first point in order to show something to another person, they may be manipulating attention not in order to produce a shared experience, but 'to check the effect of their pointing act on their mother's eyes because they enjoy mastery over her eyes' (Perner, 1991a, p. 131). Another possibility, I think, is that the infant *is* motivated by a strong goal to share experiences, as others suggest (Bates *et al.*, 1979; Bretherton, 1991; Hobson, 1991). This goal is achieved by 'conventional or mutually comprehensible signals' (Bretherton, 1991, p. 57). However, the infant's arrival at these mutually agreed signals may not require any recognition of another's inner state as *mental*. Instead, conventionalized communicative behaviour may emerge through routines and interactions with familiar partners (Lock, 1980), and such behaviour is used as a means to achieve the goal of shared experience.

2.3.2 Autism

The case of the autistic child gives a compelling demonstration of what life might be like without a theory of mind. Some of the most important studies in the theory-of-mind field have been done in autism, and the value of this research has been enormous. The work on the autistic child's theory of mind really constitutes a book on its own, and I cannot do justice to it here (see Baron-Cohen, Tager-Flusberg and Cohen, in press; Frith, 1989). My aim here is briefly to summarize the main proposals in order to support the argument of why a theory of mind may be important in our everyday life.

Autism is a developmental disorder characterized by a 'triad' of specific impairments: social, communicative and imaginative (Wing and Gould, 1979). Autistic children are unable to form normal social relationships; they have marked difficulty with verbal and non-verbal communication and no inner world of pretence and imagination. A recent theoretical claim is that all these symptoms can be explained by the hypothesis that the autistic child has an impaired theory of mind (Baron-Cohen, Leslie and Frith, 1985). There is now growing evidence in support of this claim (for reviews see Baron-Cohen, in press; Frith, 1989). A number of studies (e.g. Baron-Cohen, Leslie and Frith, 1985; Perner, Frith, Leslie and Leekam, 1989) show that autistic children have difficulty understanding false belief. They also have difficulty understanding knowledge and ignorance (Leslie and Frith, 1988; Perner *et al.*, 1989), pretence (Baron-Cohen, 1991b), belief-based emotions (Baron-Cohen, 1991c) and second-order beliefs (Baron-Cohen, 1989). In addition, autistic children tend not to use mental-state terms in their spontaneous speech (Tager-Flusberg, 1992), have difficulty distinguishing mental from physical entities, and do not recognize the mental function of the brain (Baron-Cohen, 1989).

The research on autism makes important connections between a range of different behavioural problems and a single underlying cognitive deficit. Leslie (1987, 1988) and Leslie and Frith (1990) propose that this deficit is a failure to form 'metarepresentations'. A *metarepresentation* in Leslie's sense of the term is a 'representation of a representation', e.g. a thought about a thought, a belief about a belief. The ability to form such representations is necessary for the emergence of pretend play, and for understanding mental states. In normal children, evidence of this ability is apparent by 18 months of age. In the case of the autistic child, however, the cognitive mechanism responsible for the formation of these metarepresentational structures is claimed to be faulty or developmentally delayed. Hence autistic children are impaired in imaginative activity and in understanding of mind.

Although the exact nature of this underlying cognitive mechanism has been the subject of debate (Leekam and Perner, 1991; Leslie and Thaiss, 1992), the central finding that autistic children have an impaired theory of mind has been well documented. One question that is relevant here is how autistic children's theory of mind impairment is related to their behavioural symptoms, particularly their social and communicative impairment.

As far as early social and communication abilities are concerned, some of the earliest behavioural symptoms that autistic children manifest are deficits in joint attention, communicative gestures, pointing and showing objects to others. These should develop from the first year of life in normal children. Baron-Cohen (1991a) argues that these early social abilities may be 'precursors' to a normal theory of mind for children, as they require an understanding of another's *attention*. As far as later social and communicative abilities are concerned, it is interesting to look at the small proportion of autistic children who do pass 'theory-of-mind tests' to see what their social and communication skills are like. The evidence so far suggests that autistic children who pass theory-of-mind tests have a higher verbal mental age (Prior, Dahlstrom and Squires, 1990) and may be more proficient in some aspects of pragmatic language (Eisenmajer and Prior, 1991) and some measures of social functioning (Siddons, Happé, Whyte and Frith, 1990). Yet even those subjects who pass theory-of-mind tests are not free of many of the basic social and communicative impairments of autism (Happé, 1991; Ozonoff, Rogers and Pennington, 1991).

More research is needed in order to examine the relationship between verbal deficits, social and communicative impairments, and theory-of-mind impairments. In particular we need to look at the direction of the relationship and determine what causes what. Does the theory-of-mind impairment cause the social and communication problems associated with autism? In what way could the relationship work in the other direction, with social and communicative ability influencing the formation and development of theory of mind? Alternatively, could social and communicative ability and mental-state knowledge develop independently and in parallel, or could verbal ability be a separate factor which could control both developments and therefore link them? A number of alternative possibilities must be considered.

Summary
In this section I have explored some of the implications of understanding mind in everyday life, in particular its possible importance for moral and emotional understanding and communication. It seems that the development of a theory of mind may make a number of things possible. Normal children may develop a deeper understanding of a range of social and emotional events in their lives by applying their new-found theoretical knowledge of the mind. However, I think we should be wary of making the assumption that understanding of deception, emotion, communication, and so on, *depends* on understanding of mind. There may be many aspects of social life which do not involve making complicated inferences about mental states (see, for example, Chapter 6 below, by Hudson, on children's use of scripts). The *development* of social understanding may not necessarily emerge from the developing understanding of mind. We need to look more closely at the relationship between understanding of mind and social and communicative development.

2.4 Conclusions

2.4.1 What we know and what we don't know

Despite all the research, there is still a great deal we don't know about what children understand about the mind, and some major issues remain to be sorted out. An important issue, for example, concerns the *nature* of children's knowledge of the mind. Is it theoretical or not? In the first part of this chapter I looked at whether children can be said to have a *theory* of mind. Ultimately, I think the only way this question can be answered is by examining the assumptions that are held – assumptions, for example, like the view that the mental terms we use in everyday life are *theoretical* concepts (i.e. the 'theory view' in philosophy of mind) and the view that children's development takes place through the formation of theories in different domains such as physics, biology, psychology (i.e. the 'theory view' in cognitive development). These assumptions must be explicitly set against competing views if we want to answer the question of whether or not the child has a theory of mind. In addition, we need greater consensus on what we mean by the concept of 'theory', and more information about the kind of knowledge adults have. To date only philosophy, rather than psychology, has informed our views about what an adult's understanding of mind looks like.

A second major issue concerns the *origin* of the child's understanding of mind – where it comes from, and whether it is innate or acquired. In the second part of this chapter (pp. 41–2) I reviewed evidence that indicates an early appreciation of others' minds well before the pre-school years, and even in the first year of life. People argue that these signs of understanding of mind in infancy do not constitute evidence for a 'theory of mind', but if theoretical knowledge does not appear until the pre-school years, when and how does it start? One explanation is that it begins in the early interactions between infants and care-givers: early joint attention and communicative abilities can be seen as 'precursors' to later-developing mental-state knowledge. Pre-verbal communicative gestures, eye gaze and joint attention facilitate an awareness of what others are attending to and an early understanding of their state of 'attention' or 'interest'.

One way of viewing the idea of 'precursors' is within a nativist view of the child's understanding of mind. Leslie (1987, 1988) proposes an innate 'theory-of-mind module'. He argues that child's understanding of mind is innate but is pre-set to unfold along a maturational time-course. However, the development of theory of mind may not simply be the case of a maturational timetable unfolding. Astington and Gopnik (1991) suggest that precursors to theory of mind may be based on early social abilities which allow children to learn from their first experiences with others. These abilities allow children to develop and revise a concept of mind within the maturational constraints that are set for their later understanding. If, as Astington and Gopnik suggest, one's eventual theory of mind is influenced by these early precursors, then people with autism, who do not start with the infant apparatus, might never converge on the prescribed adult view.

However, perhaps these early and later abilities could also be seen as quite separate developments. Could the non-theoretical abilities (i.e. precursors) that first appear in social interaction exchanges in infancy also continue to thrive and develop separately as non-theoretical social and communicative skills in later life? We need to know more about how these earlier abilities are functionally related to theory of mind, whether they provide the basis for later theoretical knowledge – i.e. prerequisites as well as precursors – and the mechanism for the transition from infant to pre-school understanding. Overall, we need to know more about the mechanism for development, what part social and cultural factors play (Dunn, 1991; Perner, Ruffman and Leekam, 1992) and how perceptual and emotional experiences affect development.

The third major issue concerns the *relationship* between understanding of mind and other domains of development (social, moral understanding, language) and also the relationship between reasoning or hypothetical understanding on the one hand and behaviour in everyday life on the other. I have addressed this issue in the second part of this chapter (pp. 45–51). An important aspect of the research on children's understanding of mind is its theoretical flexibility – it uses a single explanatory framework to account for a range of cognitive, social, moral and language developments. This has been particularly helpful in the research on autism, in which a range of different behaviours could be accounted for by a single underlying impairment. Nevertheless, as I suggest in that section, research on understanding of mind may tell us a lot more about cognitive development than it will ever tell us about social development. The view proposed by Forguson and Gopnik (1988) that our ability to influence and understand other people *depends* on our attributing mental states to them suggests that everything rests on this ability. Other chapters in this book – by Smetana, Hudson, Emler and Dickinson – make it clear that children gain social understanding in a number of different ways, and we need to know more about the necessity of mentalistic reasoning for many aspects of social life. Furthermore, many aspects of social interaction tap not reasoning ability and hypothetical understanding but on-line skills and behaviours. There may, however, be *some* social developments that are better explained by the child's developing understanding of mind than in any other way. My suggestion is that we look more closely at the relationship between understanding of mind and social and communicative development by comparing different developmental accounts of social understanding.

So what do we know about children's understanding of mind? First, we now know a great deal about young children's ability to reason about a range of mental states, such as belief, knowledge, desire, intention, seeing, pretence and second-order beliefs. We know about the normal course of these developments, and we know that normal development can go wrong, as the case of the autistic child shows us. In addition, we have some insight into how children might apply this understanding to their understanding of emotion, deception and communication. Second, researchers have proposed important ways to *characterize* this understanding. Although there are continuing debates over what is the *best* way, the theoretical claims are coherent and well articulated.

So we have clear ways in which we can characterize the child's understanding – as the development of a theory (Wellman, 1990), the development of representational understanding (Perner, 1991a) or the development of the ability to simulate (Harris, 1991, in press).

Against the rich store of empirical data and strength of the theoretical arguments, there are also problems in the research field. These include an overemphasis on one view of folk psychology (the 'theory theory'), assumptions about 'stages' of development, an artificial methodology (see Freeman, Lewis and Doherty, 1991; Lewis and Osborne, 1990, for comment on how the traditional methodology may underestimate ability), and lack of attempt to falsify. To some extent this research field has become 'paradigm bound' (Kuhn, 1962) – caught in the grip of its own philosophical and methodological assumptions. We need to remain aware of these assumptions, and perhaps to loosen the 'grip' of theory of mind on developmental psychology.

Notes

1. Perner (personal communication) suggests a third difference between his and Wellman's theories: that Wellman's stages are descriptions of what children actually can do, while Perner's are theoretical frameworks which specify the potential of the child's ability which still needs to be worked out. At 18 months, for example, the child has a situational theory framework within which an understanding of desire is possible, but that understanding may not be worked out until later, at around 3 years of age. See Perner (1991a) for further discussion.

Acknowledgements

I am especially grateful to Mark Bennett for nursing this chapter to life and health. I also thank Josef Perner, Jim Russell, Mike Forrester and Peter Hobson for their helpful comments on an earlier draft.

References

Astington, J.W. (1991) 'Intention in the child's theory of mind'. In D. Frye and C. Moore (eds) *Children Theories of Mind: Mental states and social understanding.* Hillsdale, NJ.: Erlbaum.

Astington, J.W. and Gopnik, A. (1991) 'Theoretical explanations of children's understanding of the mind'. *British Journal of Developmental Psychology*, 9, 7–31.

Astington, J.W., Harris, P.L. and Olson, D.R. (eds) (1988) *Developing Theories of Mind*. New York: Cambridge University Press.

Austin, J. (1962) *How To Do Things with Words*. Oxford: Blackwell.

Baron-Cohen, S. (1989) 'The autistic child's theory of mind: A case of specific developmental delay'. *Journal of Child Psychology and Psychiatry*, 30, 285–98.

Baron-Cohen, S. (1991a) 'Precursors to a theory of mind: Understanding attention in others'. In A. Whiten (ed.) *Natural Theories of Mind*. Oxford: Blackwell.

Baron-Cohen, S. (1991b) 'The theory of mind deficit in autism: Deviance and delay?' *Psychiatric Clinics of North America*, 14, 33–51.

Baron-Cohen, S. (1991c) 'Do people with autism understand what causes emotion?' *Child Development*, 62, 385–95.

Baron-Cohen, S. (in press) 'From attention-goal psychology to belief–desire psychology: The development of theory of mind and its dysfunction'. In S. Baron-Cohen, H. Tager-Flusberg and D. Cohen (eds) *Understanding Other Minds: Perspectives from autism*. Oxford: Oxford University Press.

Baron-Cohen, S., Leslie, A.M. and Frith, U. (1985) 'Does the autistic child have a theory of mind?' *Cognition*, 21, 37–46.

Baron-Cohen, S., Tager-Flusberg, H. and Cohen, D. (eds) (in press) *Understanding Other Minds: Perspectives from autism*. Oxford: Oxford University Press.

Bates, E., Benigni I., Bretherton, I., Camaioni, L. and Volterra, V. (1979) *The Emergence of Symbols*. New York: Academic Press.

Beal, C.R. and Flavell, J.H. (1984) 'Development of the ability to distinguish communicative intention and literal message meaning'. *Child Development*, 55, 920–8.

Beckwith, R.T. (1991) 'The language of emotion, the emotions and nominalist bootstrapping'. In D. Frye and C. Moore (eds) *Children's Theories of Mind: Mental states and social understanding* (pp. 47–96). Hillsdale, NJ: Erlbaum.

Bennett, M. and Galpert, L. (1992) 'Complex belief–desire reasoning in children'. *Social Development*, 1, 201–10.

Bloom, L., Rispoli, M., Gartner, B. and Hafitz, J. (1989) 'Acquisition of complementation'. *Journal of Child Language*, 16, 101–20.

Bretherton, I. (1991) 'Intentional communication and the development of an understanding of mind'. In D. Frye and C. Moore (eds) *Children's Theories of Mind: Mental states and social understanding*. Hillsdale, NJ: Erlbaum.

Bretherton I., McNew, S. and Beeghly-Smith, M. (1981) 'Early person knowledge as expressed in gestural and verbal communication: When do infants acquire a "theory of mind"?'. In M.E. Lamb and L.R. Sherrod (eds) *Infant Social Cognition* (pp. 333–73). Hillsdale, NJ: Erlbaum.

Bruner, J. (1975) 'The ontogenesis of speech acts'. *Journal of Child Language*, 2, 1–19.

Butterworth, G. (1991) *Towards an ecology of mind*. Paper presented at the BPS Developmental Section Conference, Cambridge University, September.

Butterworth, G., Harris, P.L., Leslie, A.M. and Wellman, H.M. (eds) (1991) *Perspectives on the Child's Theory of Mind*, Oxford: BPS and Oxford University Press.

Carey, S. (1985) *Conceptual Change in Childhood*. Cambridge, MA: MIT Press.

Carrithers, M. (1991) 'Narrativity: Mindreading and making societies'. In A. Whiter (ed.) *Natural Theories of Mind*. Oxford: Blackwell.

Chandler, M. (1988) 'Doubt and developing theories of mind'. In J. Astington, P.L. Harris and D.R. Olson (eds) *Developing Theories of Mind*. New York: Cambridge University Press.

Chandler, M., Fritz, A.S. and Hala, S. (1989) 'Small-scale deceit: Deception as a marker of two-, three-, and four-year-olds' early theories of mind'. *Child Development*, **60**, 1263–77.

Chisholm, R.M. and Feehan, T.D. (1977) 'The intent to deceive'. *Journal of Philosophy*, **74**, 143–59.

Churchland, P.M. (1984) *Matter and Consciousness*. Cambridge, MA: MIT Press/ Bradford Books.

Churchland, P.M. (1991) 'Folk psychology and the explanation of human behaviour'. In J.D. Greenwood (ed) *The Future of Folk Psychology*, Cambridge: Cambridge University Press.

Descartes, R. (1639/1970) *Philosophical Letters*, ed. & transl. A. Kenny. Oxford: Clarendon Press.

Dias, M. and Harris, P.L. (1988) 'The influence of the imagination on deductive reasoning'. *British Journal of Developmental Psychology*, **6**, 207–21.

DiLalla, L.F. and Watson, M.W. (1988) 'Differentiation of fantasy and reality: Preschoolers' reactions to interruptions in their play'. *Developmental Psychology*, **24**, 286–91.

Donaldson, S.K. and Westerman, M.A. (1986) 'Development of children's understanding of ambivalence and causal theories of emotion'. *Developmental Psychology*, **22**, 655–62.

Dunn, J. (1991) 'Understanding others: Evidence from the naturalistic studies of children'. In A. Whiten (ed.) *Natural Theories of Mind*. Oxford: Blackwell.

Eisenmajer, R. and Prior, M. (1991) 'Cognitive linguistic correlates of "theory of mind" ability in autistic children'. *British Journal of Developmental Psychology*, **9**, 351–64.

Estes, D., Wellman, H.M. and Woolley, J.D. (1989) 'Children's understanding of mental phenomena'. In H. Reese (ed) *Advances in child development and behaviour*, **22**, 41–87, New York: Academic Press.

Flavell, J.H., Botkin, P., Fry, C., Wright, J. and Jarvis, D. (1968) *The Development of Role-Taking and Communicative Skills in Children*. New York: Wiley.

Flavell, J.H., Everett, B.A., Croft, K. and Flavell, E.R. (1981) 'Young children's knowledge about visual perception: Further evidence for the Level 1–Level 2 distinction'. *Developmental Psychology*, **17**, 99–103.

Flavell, J.H., Flavell, E.R. and Green, F.L. (1983) 'Development of the appearance–reality distinction'. *Cognitive Psychology*, **15**, 95–120.

Forguson, L. and Gopnik, A. (1988) 'The ontogeny of common sense'. In J.W. Astington, P.L. Harris and D.R. Olson (eds) *Developing Theories of Mind*. New York: Cambridge University Press.

Forrester, M. (1992) *'The Development of Young Children's Social-Cognitive Skills*. Hove: Lawrence Earlbaum Associates.

Freeman, N.H. (1992) *Theories of mind in collision: A functional approach*. Paper presented at workshop on normal and autistic children's theory of mind, University College, Swansea, March.

Freeman, N.H., Lewis, C. and Doherty, M.J. (1991) 'Preschoolers' grasp of a desire for knowledge in false belief prediction: Practical intelligence and verbal report.' *British Journal of Developmental Psychology*, **9**, 139–57.

Frege, G. (1892/1960) 'On sense and reference'. In P. Geach and M. Black (eds) *Philosophical Works of Gottlob Frege* (pp. 56–78). Oxford: Blackwell.

Frith, U. (1989) *Autism: Explaining the Enigma*. Oxford: Blackwell.

Frye, D. (1991) 'The origins of intention in infancy'. In D. Frye and C. Moore (eds) *Children's Theories of Mind: Mental states and social understanding*. Hillsdale, NJ: Erlbaum.

Gopnik, A. and Graf, P. (1988) 'Knowing how you know: Young children's ability to remember the source of their beliefs'. *Child Development*, 59, 1366–71.

Greenwood, J.D. (ed.) (1991) *The Future of Folk Psychology*. Cambridge: Cambridge University Press.

Grice, H.P. (1975) 'Logic and conversation'. In P. Cole and J.L. Morgan (eds) *Speech Acts*. New York: Academic Press.

Hadwin, J. and Perner, J. (1991) 'Pleased and surprised: Children's cognitive theory of emotion'. *British Journal of Developmental Psychology*, 9, 215–34.

Hala, S.M., Chandler, M.J. and Fritz, A.S. (1991) 'Fledgling theories of mind: Deception as a marker of three-year-olds understanding of false belief'. *Child Development*, 57, 567–82.

Happé, F.G.E. (1991) 'The autobiographical writings of three Asperger syndrome adults: Problems of interpretation and implications for the theory'. In U. Frith (ed.) *Autism and Asperger Syndrome*. Cambridge: Cambridge University Press.

Harris, P.L. (1989) *Children and Emotion: The development of psychological understanding*. Oxford: Blackwell.

Harris, P.L. (1991) 'The work of the imagination'. In A. Whiten (ed.) *Natural Theories of Mind*. Oxford: Blackwell.

Harris, P.L. (in press) 'From simulation to folk psychology: The case for development'. *Mind & Language*.

Harris, P.L., Johnson, C.N., Hutton, D., Andrews, G. and Cooke, T. (1989) 'Young children's theory of mind and emotions'. *Cognition and Emotion*, 3, 379–400.

Harris, P.L. and Kavanaugh, R.D. (in press) 'Young children's comprehension of pretence'. *Society for Research in Child Development Monographs*.

Hobson, R.P. (1991) 'Against the theory of "Theory of Mind" '. *British Journal of Developmental Psychology*, 9, 33–51.

Hogrefe, G-J., Wimmer, H. and Perner, J. (1986) 'Ignorance and false belief: A developmental lag in attribution of epistemic states'. *Child Development*, 57, 567–82.

Hughes, C.H. and Russell, J. (in press) 'Autistic children's difficulty with mental disengagement from an object: Its implications for theories of autism'. *Developmental Psychology*.

Johnson, C.N. (1988) 'Theory of mind and the structure of conscious experience'. In J.W. Astington, P.L. Harris and D.R. Olson (eds) *Developing Theories of Mind*. New York: Cambridge University Press.

Kagan, J. (1981) *The Second Year*. Cambridge, MA: Harvard University Press.

Karmiloff-Smith, A. (1988) 'The child is a theoretician not an inductivist'. *Mind and Language*, 3, 183–97.

Kuhn, T.S. (1962) *The Structure of Scientific Revolutions*. Chicago, IL: Chicago University Press.

Leekam, S.R. (1991) 'Jokes and lies: Children's understanding of intentional falsehood'. In A. Whiten (ed.) *Natural Theories of Mind*. Oxford: Blackwell.

Leekam, S.R. (1992) 'Believing and deceiving: Steps to becoming a good liar'. In S.J. Ceci, M. DeSimone and M. Putnick (eds) *Social and Cognitive Factors in Early Deception*. Hillsdale, NJ: Erlbaum.

Leekam, S.R. and Perner, J. (1991) 'Does the autistic child have a metarepresentational deficit?' *Cognition*, 40, 203–18.

Lempers, J.D., Flavell, E.R. and Flavell, J.H. (1977) 'The development in very young children of tacit knowledge concerning visual perception'. *Genetic Psychology Monographs*, 99, 3–53.

Leslie, A.M. (1987) 'Pretence and representation: The origins of "theory of mind" '. *Psychological Review*, 94, 412–26.

Leslie, A.M. (1988) 'Some implications of pretence for mechanisms underlying the child's theory of mind'. In J.W. Astington, P.L. Harris and D.R. Olson (eds) *Developing Theories of Mind* (pp. 47–63). New York: Cambridge University Press.

Leslie, A.M. and Frith, U. (1988) 'Autistic children's understanding of seeing, knowing and believing'. *British Journal of Developmental Psychology*, 6, 315–24.

Leslie, A.M. and Frith, U. (1990) 'Prospects for a cognitive neuropsychology'. *Psychological Review*, 97, 122–31.

Leslie, A.M. and Happé, F. (1989) 'Autism and ostensive communication: The relevance of metarepresentation'. *Development and Psychopathology*, 1, 205–12.

Leslie, A.M. and Thaiss, L. (1992) 'Domain specificity in conceptual development: Neuropsychological evidence from autism'. *Cognition*, 143, 225–31.

Lewis, C. and Osborne, A. (1990) 'Three-year-olds' problems with false belief: Conceptual deficit or linguistic artifact?' *Child Development*, 61, 1514–19.

Lewis, M., Stanger, C. and Sullivan, M.W. (1989) 'Deception in 3-year-olds'. *Developmental Psychology*, 25, 439–43.

Lock, A. (1980) *The Guided Reinvention of Language*. London: Academic Press.

Masangkay, Z.S., McCluskey, K.A McIntyre, C.W., Sims-Knight, J., Vaughn, B.E. and Flavell, J.H. (1974) 'The early development of inferences about the visual percepts of others'. *Child Development*, 45, 357–66.

Mitchell, P. and Russell, J. (1991) 'Children's judgements of whether slightly and grossly discrepant objects were intended by the speaker'. *British Journal of Developmental Psychology*, 9, 331–49.

Moore, C., Bryant, D. and Furrow, D. (1989) 'Mental terms and the development of certainty'. *Child Development*, 49, 1107–13.

Olson, D.R. (1988) 'On the origins of beliefs and other intentional states in children'. In J.W. Astington, P.L. Harris and D.R. Olson (eds) *Developing Theories of Mind*. New York: Cambridge University Press.

O'Neill, D.K., Astington, J.W. and Flavell, J.H. (1992) 'Young children's understanding of the role that sensory experiences play in knowledge acquisition'. *Child Development*, 63, 474–90

Ozonoff, S., Rogers, S.J. and Pennington, B.F. (1991) 'Asperger's syndrome: Evidence of an empirical distinction from high-functioning autism'. *Journal of Child Psychology and Psychiatry*, 32, 1107–22.

Perner, J. (1988) 'Higher-order beliefs and intentions in children's understanding of social interaction'. In J.W. Astington., P.L. Harris and D.R. Olson (eds) *Developing Theories of Mind*. New York: Cambridge University Press.

Perner, J. (1991a) *Understanding the Representational Mind*. Cambridge, MA: MIT Press.

Perner, J. (1991b) *Grasping the concept of representation: Its impact on four-year-olds' theory of mind and beyond*. Paper presented at the BPS Developmental Section Conference, Cambridge, September.

Perner, J., Frith, U., Leslie, A.M. and Leekam, S.R. (1989) 'Exploration of the autistic child's theory of mind: Knowledge, belief and communication'. *Child Development*, 60, 689–700.

Perner, J. and Leekam, S.R. (1986) 'Belief and quantity: Three year olds' adaptation to listener's knowledge'. *Journal of Child Language*, 13, 304–15.

Perner, J. and Ogden, J. (1988) 'Knowledge for hunger: Children's problem of representation in imputing mental states'. *Cognition*, 29, 47–61.

Perner, J., Ruffman, T. and Leekam, S.R. (1992) 'Theory of mind is contagious: You catch it from your sibs. Experimental Psychology'. University of Sussex. Under review.

Perner, J. and Wimmer, H. (1985) ' "John thinks that Mary thinks that . . .": Attribution of second-order beliefs by 5 to 10-year-old children'. *Journal of Experimental Child Psychology*, 39, 347–471.

Piaget, J. (1932/1965) *The Moral Judgement of the Child*. New York: Free Press.

Piaget, J. and Inhelder, B. (1948/1956) *The Child's Construction of Space*. London: Routledge & Kegan Paul.

Pillow, B.H. (1989) 'Early understanding of perception as a source of knowledge'. *Journal of Experimental Child Psychology*, 47, 116–29.

Pratt, C. and Bryant, P.E. (1990) 'Young children understand that looking leads to knowing (so long as they are looking into a single barrel)'. *Child Development*, 61, 973–82.

Premack, D. (1991) 'The infant's theory of self-propelled objects'. In D. Frye and C. Moore (eds) *Children's Theories of Mind: Mental states and social understanding*. Hillsdale, NJ: Erlbaum.

Premack, D. and Woodruff, G. (1978) 'Does the chimpanzee have a theory of mind?' *Behavioural and Brain Sciences*, 1, 515–26.

Prior, M.R., Dahlstrom, B. and Squires, T.L. (1990) 'Autistic children's knowledge of thinking and feeling states in other people'. *Journal of Child Psychology and Psychiatry*, 31, 587–601.

Reddy, V. (1989) *Teasing in infancy: Doing what they 'shouldn't' be doing?* Paper presented at the BPS Developmental Psychology Section Conference, University of Surrey, September.

Reddy, V. (1991) 'Playing with others' expectation: Teasing and mucking about in the first year'. In A. Whiten (ed.) *Natural Theories of Mind*. Oxford: Blackwell.

Robinson, E., Goelman, H. and Olson, D.R. (1983) 'Children's understanding of the relation between expressions (what was said) and intentions (what was meant)'. *British Journal of Developmental Psychology*, 1, 75–86.

Ruffman, T., Olson, D.R. and Astington, J.W. (1991) 'Children's understanding of visual ambiguity'. *British Journal of Developmental Psychology*, 9, 89–102.

Ruffman, T.K., Olson, D.R., Ash, T. and Keenan, T. (in press) 'The ABC's of Deception: Do young children understand deception in the same way as adults?' *Developmental Psychology*.

Russell, J., Mauthner, N., Sharpe, S. and Tidswell, T. (1991) 'The "windows task" as a measure of strategic deception in preschoolers and autistic subjects'. *British Journal of Developmental Psychology*, 9, 331–49.

Samet, J. (in press) 'The theory of mind deficit in autism: Philosophical perspectives'. In S. Baron-Cohen, H. Tager-Flusberg and D. Cohen (eds) *Understanding Other Minds: Perspectives from autism*. Oxford: Oxford University Press.

Searle, J. (1969) *Speech Acts*. Cambridge: Cambridge University Press.

Shatz, M., Wellman, H.M. and Silber, S. (1983) 'The acquisition of mental verbs: A systematic investigation of the first reference to mental state'. *Cognition*, 14, 301–21.

Shultz, T.R., Wells, D. and Sarda, M. (1980) 'The development of the ability to distinguish intended actions from mistakes, reflexes and passive movements'. *British Journal of Social and Clinical Psychology*, 19, 301–10.

Siddons, F., Happé, F., Whyte, R. and Frith, U. (1990). *Theory of mind in everyday life: An interview-based study with autistic, retarded and disturbed children*. Paper presented at the European Conference of Developmental Psychology, Stirling University, August.

Sodian, B. (1991) 'The development of deception in young children'. *British Journal of Developmental Psychology*, 9, 173–88.

Sodian, B., Taylor, C., Harris, P., and Perner, J. (1991) 'Early deception and the child's theory of mind: False trails and genuine markers'. *Child Development*, 62, 468–83.

Sperber, D. and Wilson, D. (1986) *Relevance: Communication and cognition*. Oxford: Blackwell.

Stich, S. (1983) *From Folk Psychology to Cognitive Science*. Cambridge, MA: MIT Press/ Bradford Books.

Tager-Flusberg, H. (1992) 'Autistic children's talk about psychological states: Deficits in the early acquisition of a theory of mind'. *Child Development*, 63, 161–72.

Taylor, M. (1988) 'The development of children's ability to distinguish what they know from what they see'. *Child Development*, 59, 703–18.

Trevarthen, C. (1979) 'Communication and cooperation in early infancy: A description of primary intersubjectivity'. In M. Bullowa (ed.) *Before Speech: The beginning of interpersonal communication*. Cambridge: Cambridge University Press.

Wellman, H.M. (1990) *The Child's Theory of Mind*. Cambridge, MA: MIT Press/ Bradford Books.

Wellman, H.M. (1991) 'From desires to beliefs: Acquisition of a theory of mind'. In A. Whiten (ed.) *Natural Theories of Mind*. Oxford: Blackwell.

Wellman, H.M. and Estes, D. (1986) 'Early understanding of mental entities: A reexamination of childhood realism'. *Child Development*, 57, 910–23.

Wellman, H. and Woolley, J. (1990) 'From simple desires to ordinary beliefs: The development of everyday psychology'. *Cognition*, 35, 245–75.

Whiten, A. (ed.) *Natural Theories of Mind*. Oxford: Blackwell.

Whiten, A. and Perner, J. (1991) 'Fundamental issues in the multidisciplinary study of mindreading'. In A. Whiten (ed.) *Natural Theories of Mind*. Oxford: Blackwell.

Wimmer, H., Gruber, S. and Perner, J. (1984) 'Young children's conception of lying: Lexical realism – moral subjectivism'. *Journal of Experimental Child Psychology*, 37, 1–30.

Wimmer, H. and Hartl, M. (1991) 'The Cartesian view and the theory view of mind: Developmental evidence from understanding false belief in self and other'. *British Journal of Developmental Psychology*, 9, 125–38.

Wimmer, H., Hogrefe, G.-J. and Perner, J. (1988) 'Children's understanding of informational access as a source of knowledge'. *Child Development*, 59, 386–96.

Wimmer, H., Hogrefe, G-J. and Sodian, B. (1988) 'A second stage in children's conception of mental life: Understanding informational access as origins of knowledge and belief'. In J.W. Astington, P.L. Harris and D.R. Olson (eds) *Developing Theories of Mind*. New York: Cambridge University Press.

Wimmer, H. and Perner, J. (1983) 'Beliefs about beliefs: Representations and constraining function of wrong beliefs in young children's understanding of deception'. *Cognition*, 13, 103–28.

Wing, L. and Gould, J. (1979) 'Severe impairments of social interaction and associated abnormalities in children: Epidemiology and classification'. *Journal of Autism and Developmental Disorders*, 9, 11–29.

Winner, E. and Leekam, S. (1991) 'Distinguishing irony from deception: Understanding the speaker's second-order intention'. *British Journal of Developmental Psychology*, 9, 257–70.

Wolf, D.P., Rygh, J. and Altshuler, J. (1984) 'Agency and experience: Actions and states in play narratives'. In I. Bretherton (ed.) *Symbolic Play*. Orlando, FL: Academic Press.

Yaniv, I. and Shatz, M. (1988) 'Children's understanding of perceptibility'. In J.W. Astington, P.L. Harris and D.R. Olson (eds) *Developing Theories of Mind*. New York: Cambridge University Press.

Yuill, N. (1984) 'Young children's coordination of motive and outcome in judgements of satisfaction and morality'. *British Journal of Developmental Psychology*, 2, 73–81.

Zaitchik, D. (1990) 'When representations conflict with reality: The preschooler's problem with false beliefs and "false" photographs'. *Cognition*, 35, 41–68.

Chapter 3

Understanding of emotion
Mark Meerum Terwogt and
Paul L. Harris

Interviewer: Say you were missing your friends and family back home, and you wanted to cheer yourself up. Is there anything that you could do to cheer yourself up?
13-year-old: The worst thing to do is to ring home because the time comes when you have to say goodbye. I'd get into things, try and mix with society, try and make a lot of friends quickly and then they could comfort me. Hopefully, I could make myself forget – keep myself occupied the whole time. When you get homesick, you say goodbye and burst into tears. You wander round for a quarter of an hour and then you get picked up by some mates and feel great again.

This exchange took place between a 13-year-old boy who had just arrived at his new boarding school and an interviewer (Harris, 1989, ch. 7). It illustrates one of the themes that we shall discuss in this chapter: the control of emotion. The 13-year-old realizes that one's initial impulse – to phone home – may actually make matters worse. Instead, he emphasizes the longer-term strategy of making friends who can offer emotional comfort and help you to stop thinking about home so much. The boy clearly knows something about what causes particular emotions, such as happiness or homesickness, and he knows how to put that causal knowledge to use in order to redirect his emotional reactions. In this chapter we examine the origins and development of such knowledge. We begin by asking when children start to identify particular emotions and their causes.

3.1 The early years

Not long ago, any discussion of emotion in developmental psychology textbooks was almost completely limited to the infancy period (e.g. Fein,

62

1978). Since emotional reactions can be observed at a very early stage, a major part of this discussion dealt with the 'nature–nurture' issue. For instance, soon after birth we can elicit a spontaneous smile in babies by cuddling or various sounds, especially that of a human voice (Wolff, 1963). The origin and meaning of such early emotional expressions remain the object of much debate.

3.1.1 Recognition of emotional expressions in infancy

Particularly relevant to the child's understanding of emotions is Darwin's hypothesis that babies have an innate ability to recognize the meaning of some 'basic' emotional expressions (Darwin, 1872). In fact, this hypothesis pre-supposes another of Darwin's claims: that the facial expression of these emotions is constant across different human cultures. Otherwise, nature would have no way to equip the child with foreknowledge about the meaning of a smile versus a frown, for example.

Ekman and Friesen (1971) adopted Darwin's line of reasoning and tried to find evidence for cross-cultural invariance. They studied isolated groups that had had no contact with Westerners, presenting them with the simple task of picking out a photo depicting the emotional expression that would be provoked in a number of emotionally charged situations. For happiness, anger, disgust and sadness the results were straightforward: adults as well as children from these communities were able to select the appropriate photo-graphs, even though they depicted the emotional expressions of Western adults and children. The subjects in these experiments obviously took a given expression to have the same meaning as do Westerners. Fear and surprise were somewhat harder to discriminate, but in general Darwin's universalist claim was strongly supported by this study.

Developmental studies show that the ability to produce these universally recognizable facial expressions is also innate. Newborns produce discrim-inably different facial expressions highly similar to the expressions of adults in similar circumstances (Ganchrow, Steiner and Daher, 1983). Admittedly, it is sometimes argued that babies who are only a few days old can imitate facial expressions (Kaitz, Meschulach-Sarfaty, Auerbach and Eidelmann, 1988; Reissland, 1988). However, imitation could not easily teach babies how to produce these expressions in the appropriate circumstances. It seems much more plausible to suppose that particular stimuli automatically elicit an emotional reaction and the accompanying facial expression from the baby without the necessity for any learning or imitation.

Given that emotional expressions are universal, and produced via an innate ability, how do babies start to recognize emotional expressions in other people? Their capacity for recognition has been studied by using the selective-attention paradigm. This paradigm makes use of the fact that babies devote more attention to something new as compared with something they have seen before. Caron, Caron and Myers (1982) showed babies a number of pictures of different women with the same emotional expression. Gradually the babies lost interest, but their attention was reactivated when a different emotional expression was presented. Although this experiment shows that babies can see a difference between one expression and another, its main weakness is that it tells us virtually nothing about the meaning they attach to those expressions.

A more appropriate way to study babies' recognition is to observe their spontaneous reactions to an adult's facial expressions. Haviland and Lelwica (1987) studied 10-week-old babies' reactions to their mother. A happy, angry or sad face of the mother clearly had a different impact. The babies reacted with a happy face to a happy facial expression. In response to anger, they looked angry too, or remained still. In response to sadness, an increase in mouthing, chewing and sucking behaviour was observed. The nature of these reactions clearly shows that the babies were not simply copying the mother's expression. The increased immobility in response to anger and the search for comfort in response to sadness suggest that at this early stage babies react not only selectively but also appropriately to the emotion the mother expresses.

3.1.2 Social referencing

It is generally acknowledged that the emotional bond with the care-taker is very important for the child's development in the early years (Bretherton and Waters, 1985). We will see that the mother's emotional expressions are not only influential in direct interaction with the child, but they also guide the child's reactions to the surrounding world.

We have all probably witnessed the following scene. An infant meets with a little accident. The baby is not really hurt, but sits still for a moment, looks at the mother and then starts to cry. It almost looks as if the child consults the mother about whether to cry or not. Could this be true? In a way, it is. A careful observer might have noticed that the mother, who witnessed the accident, looked anxiously at the child. If she had reacted with a reassuring smile instead, the child would probably have gone on playing.

In line with attachment theory (Bowlby, 1973), it could be argued that this is a global effect. The developing child has to explore the world guided and protected by its care-taker. The adult's facial expression serves as a signal that activates or suppresses the entire exploratory system. In fact, recent evidence suggests that the adult's facial expression has a more selective effect. Children seem to appreciate what specific object their mother's emotion is directed at. Hornik, Risenhoover and Gunnar (1987) let 12-month-old children play in a room full of toys. They asked the mothers to express their delight or disgust when children focused on particular randomly chosen toys. Later on, when the mothers acted neutrally again, it was observed that children played less with the 'disgusting' toys. In 15-month-old children this effect persisted for more than half an hour (Bradshaw, Campos and Klinnert, 1986). So, children not only keep track of an adult's emotional expression, they also notice which object it is directed towards. Moreover, that knowledge influences their attitude towards that particular object for some time. The attitude of their care-takers is taken as a social reference point for their decision about whether to approach or avoid the object in question.

3.1.3 The onset of the manipulation of other people's emotions

By the end of the first year of life, a major step in the understanding of emotion has been taken. As we have seen, the infant to some extent understands the targeting or intentionality of other people's emotions and reacts appropriately to those targets. However, their reactions are not yet governed by the notion that they can effect the intensity or nature of other people's emotions. Deliberate attempts to change other people's emotional states begin to appear in the course of the second year. Dunn, Kendrick and MacNamee (1981) asked mothers to observe the interaction of their 2- to 4-year-old children with their younger siblings (8 or 14 months). The mothers reported that the older children tried deliberately to upset a younger brother or sister. On the other hand, almost all of them also tried to comfort a younger sibling in distress. The older children's efforts to comfort appeared to be successful because by 14 months, almost a third of the younger children actively sought the elder child's attention for comfort. Several of the younger children had also begun to reciprocate by comforting their older brothers and sisters when they were upset. Wolf (1982) even reported attempts at this age to comfort a sad or hurt parent. Comforting behaviour becomes increasingly frequent during the second year (Zahn-Waxler and Radke-Yarrow, 1982), but the same can be said about teasing. If we look closely at the way that 2- or 3-year-old children annoy their brother or sister, we see that hitting, poking and pinching are often part of a deliberate strategy, a planned technique (Dunn and Munn, 1985). It is clear that children at this age appreciate and exploit their power to change other people's emotions – for better or worse.

The frequency of these interventions varies considerably from child to child (Dunn and Kendrick, 1982). Some children show sympathy more often, whereas others show aggression more often. Although it is clear that children know by the age of 3 that comforting is 'right' and hurting is 'wrong' (Smetana, 1981; see also Chapter 5 below), the internalization of such moral rules is probably not equally strong among all children.

Cognitive factors also influence the variation among children. Stewart and Marvin (1984) found that children who made no attempt to comfort a distressed younger brother or sister during their mother's temporary absence were poor at so-called perspective-taking: they were poor at imagining the emotion or visual experience of another child. If children do not ask – or cannot answer – the question 'How would I feel if something like this happened to me?', they will not respond to the needs of others. In the next two sections, we elaborate on other cognitive and social factors that influence children's understanding of emotion.

3.2 The development of an early theory of emotion: cognitive elements

3.2.1 Sources of knowledge

Harris and Olthof (1982) mentioned three different sources of information that might teach children about emotion: observation of their own mental states; observation of other people's emotional reactions; and instruction, particularly verbal instruction, by the verbal community. It is plausible to assume that these three sources are not equally powerful throughout development. For example, children might be responsive to the emotional expressions of other people, even in the first year, but have little awareness of their own mental states. In the first year of life, and perhaps beyond, children do not possess the introspective attitude that is necessary to scan the 'inner environment' (Meerum Terwogt and Olthof, 1989). Therefore, mental states will not be part of their earliest conception of emotion; they will start out by focusing on the overt expression of emotion (Harris, Olthof and Meerum Terwogt, 1981).

Even when they appreciate that an emotional state is composed of both a subjective mental experience and an emotional expression, children may fail to grasp that these two aspects of emotion are not perfectly correlated. Thus, not until 4 years old or older do children realize that emotional expressions can be used strategically to conceal what one actually feels (Harris, Donnelly, Guz and Pitt-Watson, 1986; Saarni, 1979).

3.2.2 The acquisition of emotion concepts

Children start to use emotion terms quite early – around the beginning of their second year (Bretherton and Beeghly, 1982; Smiley and Huttenlocher, 1989). There is some evidence that words for emotional expressions ('laugh' and 'cry') are understood earlier than emotion words ('happy' and 'sad') (Honkavaara, 1961). By 2½ to 3 years old they realize that there can be a variety of personal reasons for an emotional reaction, and they start asking spontaneously for these reasons (Bretherton and Beeghly, 1982; Cairns and Hsu, 1977). Connections between emotional states and emotional determinants are sought. Around 4 years of age there is quite a good consensus among children about the kinds of situation that will provoke emotions like happiness, sadness and anger (Barden, Zelko, Duncan and Masters, 1980). Other emotions will follow in a fairly stable order, mainly determined by the complexity of the emotions involved (Harris, Olthof, Meerum Terwogt and Hardman, 1987). For example, the understanding of 'social emotions' like shame, guilt or pride requires an appreciation of social standards or rules, an ability to recognize violations of those standards or rules, and an ability to anticipate other people's reactions to such violations. The early understanding of 'basic emotions', like happiness, is probably also related to the fact that these emotions are characterized by a unique facial expression that makes them easy to identify (Reichenbach and Masters, 1983).

3.2.3 Imaginative projection

Although an understanding of the common causal links between particular situations (e.g. receiving a present) and particular emotions (e.g. happiness) is very important, it is not sufficient. For a full understanding of emotion, children must have the ability to detach their thinking from the objective characteristics of a situation. The emotional impact of a situation is determined by a person's subjective appraisal of it – an appraisal (de)formed by personal beliefs, expectations and desires (Harris, 1989). Even a gift, for example, will not elicit happiness if the recipient dislikes it or suspects the motive of the donor.

If we want to understand somebody else's emotions, we can often take ourselves as a frame of reference: 'What would I feel in these circumstances?' But in many cases that is not enough to make an accurate prediction. No two people are identical. We have to take into account as much information as we know about that particular person. We have to put ourselves in the position of 'a shy person', in the position of 'somebody who is afraid of dogs', or in the position of 'somebody who is very fond of his parents', and make adjustments in the light of that knowledge.

One of the most powerful indications that even very young children can manage this complex task is pretend play (Leslie, 1987; Piaget, 1952). For most children, the first signs of pretend play emerge somewhere in their second year of life. A young girl acts as if her doll is a genuine person (Wolf, Rygh and Altshuler, 1984). At first, the young 'mother' treats her 'child' as a passive recipient of her own actions, but later the doll is made to talk and act independently and eventually credited with desires, sensations and emotions. When the child is around 3½ to 4 years old we can hear her using a different voice if she talks for the doll. In the act of playing 'hide-and-seek' the child puts her doll in the closet, and shouts directly afterwards 'Where are you?' Or at feeding time, despite hating spinach herself, she spoons pretend spinach into the doll's mouth, claiming that this is the doll's favourite food.

These examples show that the child acknowledges that her make-believe companion is not simply an extension of herself. The 'other person' has distinct qualities, can do things that the child pretends not to know about, and has different preferences. Despite occasional confusion between the rules of play and the rules of reality (DiLalla and Watson, 1988; Harris, Brown, Marriott, Whittall and Harmer, 1991), even 3-year-olds can make a systematic distinction between the real world and the world of the imagination (Wellman and Estes, 1986).

This capacity for imaginative projection helps the child to take another person's perspective. In particular, it allows children to make allowances for other people's particular desires and beliefs. This is demonstrated in an experiment by Harris, Johnson, Hutton, Andrews and Cooke (1989). They told children about an elephant who went out for a walk. Meantime, the can of Coke that she would drink when she came home thirsty was emptied and refilled with milk by a mischievous monkey who wanted to play a trick on the poor elephant. The children were asked to predict the elephant's feelings before and after discovering the switch. Even 4-year-olds were able to take the elephant's desires into account. They realized, for example, that the elephant would be sad on discovering the trick if she preferred Coke to milk, or pleased if she preferred milk to Coke. On the other hand, the 4-year-olds were quite poor at working out that at first the elephant's feelings would be based on her mistaken belief about the contents of the can. Six-year-olds and some 5-year-olds were much better at this. They realized that at first, before sipping from the can, the elephant would be happy if she liked Coke, or sad if she liked milk, because she would not yet have discovered the trick. This experiment shows how young children start to realize that it is not the objective situation that triggers emotion, but someone's appraisal of that situation. The 4-year-olds had a partial understanding of this. They understood that the elephant's emotion would depend on whether she liked Coke or milk. The older children also realized that the elephant's appraisal would include her mistaken belief.

3.3 The development of an early theory of emotion: social elements

3.3.1 Social regulation of emotional behaviour

When the other person's facial expression and the situational clues are in conflict, young children tend to rely on the emotional expression (Gnepp, 1983; Greenspan, Barenboim and Chandler, 1976; Reichenbach and Masters, 1983). They fail to appreciate that facial expressions do not always give reliable information, and that people sometimes try to hide their true feelings. They are still unaware of the social rules that regulate such behaviour (Saarni, 1979). When facial expressions are not visible these children infer an emotion from the situation, although they sometimes overlook obvious social category factors such as age (Gnepp, 1989) that might moderate the impact of the situation. Later on (roughly between 5 and 8 years of age) children increasingly rely on situational cues, and the emotional impact of the situation for the person in question, in making their judgements. Moreover, they expand their repertoire of situations whose emotional significance they comprehend (Harris *et al.*, 1987).

In the preceding section, we discussed the way appraisal processes will moderate someone's emotional reaction to a situation. In particular, we considered the role of an individual's beliefs and desires. Situations are also appraised in the light of interpersonal standards, and to appreciate the full impact of many emotionally charged situations, children must take these standards into account. For instance, a young boy will have difficulty in understanding why his sister starts crying when she discovers that her new dress will not be finished in time for the school ball, if he does not acknowledge that 'girls have to look pretty' at such occasions.

An appreciation of the role of interpersonal standards is especially critical for understanding complex emotions like guilt, shame or pride. In fact, these emotions can be regarded as part of the moral system that maintains such standards. Hence they are often called 'social emotions'. Before we take a closer look at children's understanding of these emotions, we need to step back and consider two different conceptions of emotion: the biological and the social constructivist.

3.3.2 Emotional culture

Following Darwin's claim that human beings express certain basic emotions such as happiness, anger, disgust, and so forth, with the same facial expressions irrespective of culture, psychologists have pursued the idea that there is a universal set of biologically determined emotions (Ekman and Friesen, 1971; Izard, 1977). Social anthropologists, by contrast, emphasize the possibility that different cultures cultivate particular emotions in different ways (e.g. Levy, 1984). For example, cultures – and, indeed, different epochs within the same culture – vary in the extent to which they cultivate emotions such as humility, vengeance or romantic love. Indeed, some authors have argued that biology exerts very little influence on our emotional repertoire; rather, there is a potentially infinite number of different emotions, contingent only upon the possible permutations of social variables and cultural inter-pretations (Harré, 1986).

There is no reason, however, why the two approaches should not be integrated (Gordon, 1989; Kemper, 1987). The study of child development helps us to think about how this integration can be achieved. Children's emotional behaviour and knowledge might be initially constrained by an innate repertoire of basic emotions, but internal developmental processes and an expansion of the child's social environment might engender new, more complex emotions. Gordon (1990) remarks that exposure to the 'emotional culture' of our society – that is, exposure to a set of beliefs, vocabulary, regulative norms, and other ideational resources to emotion – is essential to the development of these emotions and the child's competence to handle them. Exposure will include both deliberate instruction and also the un-intended consequences of interaction (Lewis and Saarni, 1985). Children, for their part, will be actively engaged in hypothesis-testing, especially when they have discovered that they can benefit in terms of interpersonal advantage or self-esteem by monitoring emotional signals in others.

3.3.3 Pride, shame and guilt

When we present children of different cultures with a wide variety of emotion terms and ask them to tell us about a situation that would elicit each emotion, they can not offer appropriate and recognizable situations for emotions like jealousy, worry, pride, shame or guilt before the age of 7. The situations mentioned by the children clearly reflect the circumstances and concerns of their lives. Whereas European children are typically worried about things like school exams, children living in a small agricultural community in Nepal are worried about the crops and the animals for which they are partially responsible. None the less, the timing and sequence in which the emotions are understood is roughly the same (Harris *et al.*, 1987).

If we take a closer look at emotions like pride, shame and guilt, it seems that there are two elements that are essential for understanding them: the concept of personal responsibility and the role of social standards. Pride, for example, involves an achievement brought about by the self that meets a social criterion. It can be demonstrated that 5-year-olds have some insight into these two elements. They clearly distinguish between success that is obtained by internal factors (effort; ability) as compared with external factors (an easy task; help from somebody else). They do not, however, incorporate that distinction into their conception of pride: they claim that someone will be proud whether the achievement is due to internal or external factors (Graham, 1988; Graham and Weiner, 1986). The same phenomenon can be observed with respect to the normative aspects of a situation. Five-year-olds appreciate the difference between good and bad (e.g. reaching one's goal in an honest way or by stealing), but they do not include this moral standard in their judgements about whether or not someone will feel guilty (Nunner-Winkler and Sodian, 1988). Instead, their judgements are guided by the outcome of the action (Graham and Weiner, 1986). If one succeeds, one is proud (or happy); if one fails, one feels sad (or guilty). The fact that it takes another few years for children to incorporate all the relevant elements into their conception of pride, shame or guilt, shows that the problem is a cognitive one. Although young children understand the elements that are relevant, they do not immediately combine them into one integrated perspective.

Children's care-takers are probably important in encouraging that integration. They link the separate elements together, by telling the child: 'Mummy feels proud of you, because . . .'. Indeed, 6- and 7-year-olds often link the emotions of pride and shame to their parents rather than to themselves (Harter and Whitesell, 1989). Later, when the internalization of values is completed, they no longer need an external judgement, and they talk about feeling proud or ashamed of themselves.

When it takes children at least eight years to grasp the finer nuances of pride and the like, how is it that we can sometimes observe reactions in very young children that closely resemble pride, guilt or shame? One explanation is that younger children do not genuinely experience guilt, although we adults are tempted to attribute it to them. Social emotions are not accompanied by a unique facial expression. So if a 3-year-old child looks guilty after we have scolded him for not finishing his meal, his expression may be indistinguishable from an ordinary sad expression, but we automatically read into his facial expression a more complex emotion that is based on our own evaluation of the circumstances.

However, there may be more to children's social emotions than adult projection. Sometimes, we can observe the child displaying additional reactions that fit in with our more complex interpretation. For example, the 'embarrassed' child stops protesting or makes him- or herself small. Semin and Papadopoulou (1990) present an interesting explanation for such phenomena. They point out that when children misbehave – for example, by making a mess of their food in a public restaurant – their mothers are likely to exhibit embarrassment themselves. Semin calls this their 'extended identity'. They display the feeling that the child is not yet expected to feel. So when young children show such behaviour in an appropriate situation, it is possible that they are just copying their care-takers. Recall the phenomenon of social referencing: even in the first year of life, children can 'echo' a care-taker's reaction to a given situation. Eventually, having established in the child the appropriate feeling of embarrassment, the mother will assert her own perspective and express the more common, corrective attitude: anger, which is intended to induce authentic and not just mimetic feelings of guilt, shame or embarrassment in the child.

Hoffman (1982) predicts that the nature of these disciplinary reactions will be important for the child's later proneness to feel guilt (which implies a recognition of moral wrongdoing) versus shame (which need not include a moral component). Stegge, Ferguson and Meerum Terwogt (1991) obtained support for this prediction. Withdrawal of love and affection or simple rejection produces children who are inclined to explain this parental reaction in terms of their own global inadequacy. They are more likely to react with shame and, if possible, withdraw from the scene. If, on the other hand, the parent criticizes the child's behaviour, presents the reasons for his or her anger or tells the child how to avoid such circumstances in the future, the child is prone to feel guilty and tries to correct his or her faults.

3.4 Strategic control of emotions

During middle childhood there is a rapid accumulation of knowledge about
the antecedents and consequences of emotion. The child learns how people's
emotions influence their behaviour, and begins to take advantage of that
influence – for example, by asking for a special treat when the parent is in a
good mood rather than a bad mood. Children also learn that emotions affect
their own mental processes and activities. For example, they realize that
sadness will limit their creativity or concentration (Harris, 1989, ch. 7; Harris
et al., 1981). We may ask ourselves what purpose this knowledge serves. How
does it shape children's emotional behaviour? Does it stimulate spontaneous
self-control, and if so, how does it do so?

3.4.1 Automatic emotional response programs

It is often taken for granted that knowledge guides emotional behaviour. For
example, if we discover that someone deliberately lied to us, we become angry
with him. However, it is doubtful that we are always aware of the cognitive
determinants of our affect-related behaviour. Our 'reasons' often turn out to
be *post hoc* constructions that we use to justify our immediate emotional
reactions (Nisbett and Wilson, 1977). Take, for instance, the well-known
phenomenon of someone being attacked in a crowded street while other
people stand by without intervening. Latané and Darley (1970) noticed that
the 'unresponsive bystanders' offered all kinds of reasons for their behaviour,
but they all ignored the empirical fact that people are less likely to help when
there is a large number of other people in the immediate environment. Even
when they were asked directly, bystanders persistently denied that the number
of people in the immediate vicinity had any influence. Clearly, our emotional
reactions are guided by conscious reasoning less often than we like to think
(Zajonc, 1980).

Many of our emotion patterns can be regarded as modular, organized
behavioural programs that are executed in response to specific situations. We
run away from frightening situations, we attack when something or someone
arouses our anger, and we approach joyful events. Such 'response programs'
(Plutchik, 1980) or 'adaptive specializations' (Rozin, 1975) are executed
automatically. None the less, as in the case for every automatism, we can
disrupt the program by making it the object of our attention. For instance, if
we ask someone at the balancing bar how he manages to keep his equilibrium,
he is likely to fall off. Similarly, if an experienced driver is not seated in his car
and we ask him to describe the position of his gears, he often makes mistakes
even though he reaches out and changes gear quite smoothly when he is
actually driving. Both examples demonstrate that automatic processes are not
guided – and may even be disrupted – by conscious thought. Of course, the

disruption of successful programs such as these is not very useful. Within the context of our present society, the same cannot always be said about primary emotional programs. They are not always socially acceptable. When we feel the impulse to hit an exasperating teacher or boss on the nose, we should block that program and think again.

So: learning to monitor our feelings is not simply a question of acquiring knowledge about our emotional system. Self-monitoring may also call for an inhibitory system that allows us to block our primary action tendencies. It is here that the acquired emotional knowledge and cognitive abilities of children become effective. They are needed to recognize the situation as one in which the primary action impulse is inadequate and has to be halted, and they are needed to find a more acceptable outlet for the emotional impulse that remains.

3.4.2 When to control?

Young (1961) once defined emotion as an 'acute disturbance of the individual as a whole'. Indeed, emotions, sometimes suddenly and unexpectedly, break into our cognitive activities and take over. We feel overpowered. Adults and children alike, therefore, sometimes describe emotion as an involuntary, autonomous process that takes you by surprise (Frijda, 1986; Harris *et al.*, 1981). It is not difficult to see that this special characteristic of at least some of our emotions is sometimes very useful. Take fear as an example. If we find ourselves on the point of crossing a busy street completely involved in our own important thoughts and not paying attention to anything else, it is of life-saving importance that our fear, aroused by some 'unconscious' danger signal, immediately takes over, and saves us from the approaching cars by provoking a quick retreat.

A crucial element in such an incident is 'not paying attention'. We probably would not have experienced fear at all if we had paid attention to our surroundings, since we are accustomed to the danger of traffic and how to avoid it. Fear is especially likely to occur if we experience a sudden and unexpected 'lack of control' (Abramson, Seligman and Teasdale, 1978).

Sometimes, all we need in order to get rid of our initial fear is further experience. Think of the young child who touches a hot stove by accident. After this experience, the stove will certainly remain a feared object for some time. But gradually the child will discover that when you keep your distance, the stove can do you no harm; on the contrary, it spreads an ageeable warmth. This simple knowledge changes the child's attitude completely. The potential danger is still acknowledged, but the child trusts her ability to control this danger. Respect has taken the place of fear.

These examples suggest that when we are surprised by our emotions it is often because we do not expect or do not pay attention to the stimuli that arouse them. Children have to learn the value and importance of these stimuli in order to anticipate their effects. Once an emotional state is elicited and surpasses a certain intensity, it will be hard to avoid the immediate acting out of the stereotypic impulse (Frijda, 1986). In this connection, it is interesting to note that emotionally disturbed children, as compared to normal children of the same age, are more likely to describe emotions as autonomous and unalterable processes. Moreover, they are more likely to say that they do not pay attention to emotional signals in themselves and the environment (Meerum Terwogt, Schene and Koops, 1990).

In summary, in order to be aware of when an emotion will occur and of whether control is needed, we must use various kinds of knowledge: knowledge about the antecedents of emotion, knowledge about the cues for identifying an emotion in ourselves at an early stage, knowledge about our uncontrolled action patterns following an emotion, and knowledge about the consequences of acting out these patterns for ourselves and our environment (Meerum Terwogt and Olthof, 1989).

3.4.3 How to control?

We mentioned above that simply by making our emotions the object of our attention we can sometimes activate an inhibitory mechanism that prevents an automatic execution of the emotional program. This observation stresses the importance of self-monitoring (Snyder, 1979), since this gives us the time and opportunity to cope with our emotions.

Coping mechanisms can be used to modify either the expression of an emotion or the emotion itself by means of a cognitive 'reappraisal' of the situation (Lazarus, Averill and Opton, 1970). For example, if a child takes the social constraints of the occasion into account, he may quickly realize that it is not acceptable to hit the person he is angry with (e.g. a parent), but in order to give expression to the impulse he mutters a sarcastic comment instead. In other cases, he finds that in anger he has badly hurt his baby sister, and his anger turns into shame or anxiety. So in dealing with the situation not only is the information rearranged, but also new aspects are taken into account. Moreover, children can search their memory system for similar experiences or use generalized knowledge about their emotional functioning. As in any other type of problem-solving, therefore, coping benefits from the availability of relevant information and appropriate stategies – a body of knowledge that gradually accumulates with age.

None the less, it is probable that emotional coping has some distinctive aspects that distinguish it from other kinds of problem-solving. Coping deals with so-called 'hot cognitions' (Abelson, 1963; Zajonc, 1980). Pressed by the need to find a quick solution – in order to express the emotional impulse that has been aroused – we are often ready to follow shaky or unrealistic appraisals that serve only our short-term interests. Recall, for example, the interview quoted at the beginning of this chapter. The boy mentions the strategy of ringing home if you feel homesick, but points out that it helps only very briefly. If anything, you feel more homesick when the telephone conversation comes to an end.

Such short-term strategies are understandable if we bear in mind that the memories used in the process are likely to have an emotional connotation. For example, the homesick child may recollect memories of conversations with the family at home and these memories will have a comforting glow, strengthening the impulse to renew contact. The enterprise of finding a suitable response can therefore be described as a constant interplay between cognitive appraisals, emotion, subsequent information processing, reappraisals, and so on (Lazarus, Coyne and Folkman, 1982).

3.4.4 Hiding emotions

People may, for various reasons, attempt to conceal their emotions. How far can they do so successfully? Ekman and Friesen (1974) asked a group of student nurses who had just watched a training film that included pictures of amputations, severe burns, and so on to pretend afterwards that they had seen a pleasant film. Another group of nurses really did watch a pleasant film. Judges who were asked to decide which film each nurse had watched had difficulty in discriminating between the 'dishonest' and 'honest' nurses. When they were successful, they claimed that it was often bodily movements that gave the nurses' real emotion away. This was corroborated by the fact that although the nurses themselves mentioned efforts to control their facial expressions, they either did not realize the importance of posture or limb movements or thought that they could not control those expressive clues in any case. It also turned out that it was much harder to deceive a judge if he or she had had some previous acquaintance with the nurse. Nevertheless, the main finding of Ekman and Friesen's study is that emotion can often be concealed quite successfully, especially through misleading facial signals.

What do children think about the possibility of hiding emotions from others? We asked 6-, 11- and 15-year-old children this question directly (Harris, Olthof and Meerum Terwogt, 1981). About a third of the 6-year-olds claimed not to know, but the remaining 6-year-olds as well as all the 11-year-olds claimed that it is possible to hide one's feelings. By the age of 15, some subjects expressed their doubts. Their answers revealed that these older subjects had in mind situations involving a very familiar person, such as their mother or a close friend. This probably explains why they thought that their attempts at concealment would fail. These children had not started to doubt the possibility of trying to hide one's emotions, but they were more alert to the fact that it is hard to deceive a careful observer who knows a lot about you.

We can observe partially successful attempts to conceal emotions at a very early stage. Saarni (1984) gave 6- to 10-year-old children a gift that turned out to be very disappointing when it was unwrapped. None the less, she observed that most children managed a slight smile or mumbled their thanks. Cole (1986) used the same situation with even younger children – 3- to 4-year-old girls – and compared their behaviour in two situations: when they unwrapped the gift alone, or when they were watched by the adult who had given them the gift. In the first situation the girls expressed their disappointment in an uninhibited fashion, but in the second, they often masked their disappointment with a half-smile.

Do children as young as this conceal their emotions consciously and deliberately, or do they do it automatically 'without thinking'? Cole asked her subjects whether the adult would know how they felt when they opened their present. None of the children realized that the adult could be misled by their facial expression. So 3- to 4-year-old children can produce a misleading expression without being aware of its correspondingly misleading impact on an observer. At the age of 6, however, children clearly distinguish between the actual emotion and misleading facial expressions. For example, they now know that Diana, who 'tries to hide her feelings after winning a game because otherwise her friend won't play any more', probably feels happy, but will try to put on a neutral face. Even though they have to work out both the real and the apparent emotional state for themselves from this description, 6-year-olds appropriately attribute the real emotion ('She feels happy 'cos she won') and a deceptive intention ('She doesn't want her friend to know how she feels, 'cos then she won't play any more'). They also correctly answer the question 'How does the other girl think that Diana feels?' (Harris and Gross, 1988). This shows that they are able to work out two simultaneous but different views of what is going on: a view of the actual state of affairs, and also a view of the state of affairs apparent to the onlooker. This discovery is an important element in children's understanding of the potential privacy of their mental world (Harris, 1989). Other people will probably try to read your emotions, but you can try to mislead them or withhold the essential cues. If you have attended to the relevant information at the right moment, you yourself are the only one who has unhampered access to the information necessary for a full understanding of what you feel and why you feel it.

Display rules serve two functions. The boy who hides his fear because he wants to make sure that his friends will not laugh at him is clearly protecting himself. The boy who does not laugh at the amusing mishap that befalls his friend is protecting the feelings of his friend. Admittedly, the distinction between serving one's own interests and serving those of others may be hard to make. Sometimes, the fact that one does not try to spare another's feelings will not stay unpunished in the long run. Yet granted that the distinction can often be made, not all children understand both functions equally well. Emotionally disturbed children acknowledge just as readily as normal children that one can hide negative emotions, but they seem to be somewhat delayed in the simulation of positive emotions (Meerum Terwogt *et al.*, 1990). A plausible explanation is that it is seldom necessary to simulate a positive emotion except in order to spare somebody else's feelings. By contrast, the hiding of negative emotion can protect one's own feelings as well as those of another person. Thus, emotionally disturbed children may use simulation only to protect themselves. There is no clear evidence about their actual behaviour, but their own statements corroborate this conclusion. The majority of a group of 10-year-old emotionally disturbed boys, who were told about the 'disappointing gift situation', claimed that they would both feel and express their disappointment (Taylor and Harris, 1984).

3.4.5 Changing the emotional state

The situations we examined in the previous section leave us with a problem: the successful hiding of an emotion implies that we do not *express* the emotion, but we continue to *feel* it. A 13-year-old boy (interviewed in the study of boarding-school children mentioned above) put it like this: 'You can hide your feelings easily by day, if they are not too bad, when everyone's watching you, by joining in and by smiling and getting on with other people. But at night when no one is watching you, you can go back to normal. If you're upset, you're just upset' (Harris, 1989; Harris and Guz, 1986). How is it possible not just to hide the overt expression of emotion but to blunt or transform the experience itself? Do young children understand how this can be done?

One of Freud's important contributions to the study of emotion was the whole list of possibilities he mentioned: repression, denial, displacement, rationalization, and so on (Freud, S., 1936). The Freudian account also deals with the unconscious tendency to use these so-called 'defence mechanisms' selectively, and states that each person has a characteristic pattern of defence. According to Freud's daughter Anna, this is already true of young children (Freud, A., 1946).

In the present discussion we do not want to concern ourselves with individual differences. On the contrary, we want to illustrate that in everyday life the choice of a coping pattern is often 'rational' and strongly related to the restrictions of the situation. Let us consider three broad categories: delay or suppression of the emotional response, response modification, and modification of the state itself.

Even 6-year-old children understand the time-course of emotion. They know that although an emotion can be revived at certain moments, it will typically wane over time (Harris, 1983). In other words, they appreciate that provided one is able to wait long enough, the impulse to express the emotion – for example, by bursting into tears – will eventually disappear. Even after a short delay, the impulse to cry or to be aggressive will be weaker, thereby making it easier to find an appropriate alternative (e.g. confiding one's loss to a friend; teasing rather than hitting a sibling). Delay can also be used to find the right place (the privacy of one's own room) or the right opponent (the other team on the football field). In all cases, our behaviour will be strongly linked to our individual (and, of course, age-related) judgements about what is and is not acceptable.

Six-year-olds also realize that one need not simply wait. They suggest changing the external situation or environment: 'If I go to play outside, then I'll feel better' (Harris *et al.*, 1981). At this age, however, children have difficulty in explaining exactly why such strategies are effective. They do not mention, for example, the possibility that the new situation helps you to stop thinking about what upset you. By 10 years of age and upwards, children acknowledge this effect more explicitly. Recall, once again, the 13-year-old boarder quoted at the beginning of this chapter. He emphasized changing the situation by making new friends, but he also referred to the impact of that change on one's thought patterns: you could keep busy and stop being reminded of home.

Interview studies can often underestimate children's competence. This is especially true for younger children who may not be able to describe their emotion–control strategies in words. For this reason, we also looked directly at the strategies that 6-year-olds can use (Meerum Terwogt, Schene and Harris, 1986). We asked 6-year-olds to listen to a sad story about a child who was moving to a new town and losing his or her best friend. All the children were asked to listen very carefully: 'so that you can tell the story again afterwards'. In addition, a third of the children were instructed to listen so that: 'you won't get sad yourself' (detachment-instruction) and a third so that: 'you make yourself feel sad' (involvement-instruction). The remaining children served as a control group and were simply instructed to listen carefully. Afterwards the three groups proved to be quite different in their 'level of sadness'. Apparently, they had successfully used appropriate techniques to regulate their emotional reactions. None the less, the three groups were just as accurate in retelling the story (showing that successful detachment could not be explained by stimulus avoidance).

Most children were unable to tell us exactly what they had done, but a few did, and their explanations showed a remarkable resemblance to the strategies described by adults in a comparable experiment (Koriat, Melkman, Averill and Lazarus, 1972). The most frequently mentioned strategies, among adults and children alike, were 'reminding oneself that it is not real' (detachment) and 'imagining that it is happening to oneself' (involvement).

Although this experiment shows that young children are able to make use of strategic control when prompted, that does not mean that they will do so spontaneously. Even if they possess a strategy for controlling their emotions, they do not always realize that they should or could exercise that control. A negative mood generally reduces performance. Often we can prevent that reduction by an extra effort. In an experiment in which we wanted to show the influence of mood on a simple memory task, 10-year-old children countered the potentially deleterious effect of mood. By contrast, 5-year-olds performed markedly less well when they were in a negative mood, but they produced an optimal performance if we alerted them in advance by asking: 'What do you think your mood will do to your performance?' (Meerum Terwogt, 1986).

We do not know of any studies showing that 6-year-olds can deliberately alter the quality as well as the intensity of their emotional state. If we ask them about their own expectations, some of them are quite pessimistic, but others think they can (Harris and Lipian, 1989; Harris *et al.*, 1981; Meerum Terwogt *et al.*, 1990). It is likely that changing the quality of an emotion is different from changing its intensity. Telling oneself: 'It's a very sad story, but it is just a story' may moderate the intensity of one's emotion, but it will not arouse a different emotion. Yet as adults, we sometimes deliberately try to replace one emotion with another by focusing on a different aspect of the situation – we look on 'the bright side'. Are young children capable of such deliberate cognitive shifts? As we saw above, they do realize that replacing one situation with another is helpful, but the realization that the same situation can be construed differently seems a lot more difficult. One important obstacle is that young children find it hard to imagine that you can feel two emotions at the same time, especially if they are of opposite character (Harris, 1983; Harter, 1983; Harter and Buddin, 1987; Meerum Terwogt, Koops, Oosterhoff and Olthof, 1986). That does not mean that their behaviour is always ruled by one emotion at a time. In fact, children often show a mixture of emotions (Harris, 1989; Meerum Terwogt, 1987). What it does mean is that given their difficulty in recognizing the possible existence of two concurrent emotions, children will focus on the first emotional viewpoint that comes to mind in a certain situation, and probably will not look spontaneously for another perspective on that same situation (Meerum Terwogt, 1984). Lacking the conviction that there are other ways of looking at the situation, they make no effort to change their feelings in this fashion.

3.5 Conclusions: accessibility and flexibility

We have sketched various aspects of children's understanding of emotional functioning – their own as well as other people's. We have also explained why some insights come relatively easily, while others take considerable time and effort to acquire. We want to reserve this last section for a more general discussion. What is emotional experience? How does it turn into generalized knowledge? And what is the purpose of this structured and formalized knowledge?

Let us begin by considering a very simple and primitive emotional reaction: a neonate is given a bitter substance to taste, and wrinkles its mouth in disgust. Although the baby is expressing a specific emotion, it seems unlikely that it can code the nature of its own emotional reaction: it is not aware of the disgust that is expressed so clearly on its face. More generally, it is unlikely that infants can code any of the fixed emotional programs that we see them display. They are happy, or afraid, or disgusted, but they do not know that they are.

To encode one's own emotional experience requires cognitive processing. A particular emotional reaction needs to be identified as a member of a category. For instance, a fearful situation elicits a subjective response, a distinct facial expression and an autonomic response. To encode that complex event as being an instance of fear, we need to compare it with situations in which a similar response complex has occurred. These connections do not necessarily have to be made on a conscious level. If we follow the psycho-analytic point of view, the coding of the response complex could remain at an unconscious level – 'denied' or 'repressed', perhaps. When eventually this kind of encoding takes place at a conscious level, however, it can serve as the basis for a simple rule: I am frightened when I undergo these various subjective, facial and physiological reactions. In time, these rules are refined. For example, the child might learn that the physiological component – the change in heart rate – can vary sharply in intensity – indeed, similar variation can sometimes occur in the absence of fear. The child will gradually identify which elements are a recurrent component of the emotion, although 'mistakes' may continue to occur.

One problem for young children is that they are not yet accustomed to monitor internal signals. According to Rozin (1975), an increase in the conscious accessibility of pre-existing internal information is an essential feature of the ontogenetic (as well as phylogenetic) development of intelligence. Another component is the development of what Piaget called 'decentration' – the ability to switch attention smoothly between one stimulus and another: in this case between the inner and the outer environment so as to integrate several sources of information, or to take different perspectives with respect to one and the same situation. Both aspects are necessary for the development and enrichment of an emotional experience, and consequently for the development of emotional knowledge.

As soon as children acknowledge the connection between the emotional state and some of the other elements in the emotional process, we observe that their behaviour becomes more flexible. Take the example of the infant who is afraid of heights and avoids any sharp drop; at a later age, the child may realize that his or her behaviour is regulated by fear. Watching other children climb up a slide, the child may follow suit. The emotional value of the situation is reevaluated and the response pattern is adapted accordingly.

Logically – and we have seen this on several occasions throughout this chapter – knowledge lags behind behaviour: one has to be able to accomplish something before one knows that one can do it (Meerum Terwogt and Olthof, 1989). This does not mean that we should regard the development of knowledge as an interesting but ineffective by-product of normal develop-ment. An explicit and well-structured knowledge base – emotional knowledge – is a powerful instrument that provides important information for the evaluation of new situations, and therefore for the development of a new behavioural repertoire.

Finally, we may consider an important omission – one that is especially relevant to future research. Throughout this chapter we have emphasized the pattern of development that is typical of most children. It is probable, however, that there are individual differences among children in their understanding of emotion. We have mentioned some exploratory studies conducted with emotionally disturbed children in which such individual differences were observed. In future research, it will be important to investigate these individual differences and their causes. Two factors seem especially likely to produce variation: the child's own emotional experience, and the emotional climate that confronts the child at home. Children vary sharply in their emotional experience. Some must learn to cope with repeated separations from one or both parents, whereas others do not have to. Some must live through a frightening disaster, whereas others have a narrow but lucky escape. At home, children can be confronted by a predominantly happy or angry atmosphere. Families also differ in more subtle ways. They vary in the way that particular emotions are expressed – anger can be suppressed and silent, or it can be overt and explosive. They vary in their favoured strategies for controlling emotion – some parents will ignore or reprimand a miserable child; others will try distraction; and still others will try to find out what is causing the distress. Indeed, families vary markedly in the extent to which they encourage explicit and open discussion of emotion. These variations in emotional experience and family life will probably impinge on children's understanding of emotion. In the longer term, a study of these variations will help us to explain how most children gain the access and flexibility that we have described.

References

Abelson, R.P. (1963) 'Computer simulation of "hot cognitions" '. In S. Tomkins and S. Mesick (eds) *Simulation of Personality*. New York: Wiley.

Abramson, L., Seligman, M. and Teasdale, J. (1978) 'Learned helplessness in humans: Critique and reformulation'. *Journal of Abnormal Psychology*, **87**, 49–74.

Barden, R., Zelko, F., Duncan, S. and Masters, J. (1980) 'Children's consensual knowledge about the experiential determinants of emotion'. *Journal of Personality and Social Psychology*, **39**, 968–76.

Bowlby, J. (1973) *Attachment and Loss, vol. 2: Separation, Anxiety and Anger*. London: Hogarth Press.

Bradshaw, D.L., Campos, J.J. and Klinnert, M.D. (1986) *Emotional expressions as determinants of infants' immediate and delayed responses to prohibition*. Paper presented at the Fifth International Conference on Infant Studies, Los Angeles.

Bretherton, I. and Beeghly, M. (1982) 'Talking about internal states of mind: the acquisition of an explicit theory of mind'. *Developmental Psychology*, **18**, 906–21.

Bretherton, I. and Waters, E. (eds) (1985) 'Growing points of attachment theory and research'. *Monographs of the Society for Reserch in Child Development*, **50**, Serial No. 209.

Cairns, H. and Hsu, J. (1977) 'Who, why, when, and how: A developmental study'. *Journal of Child Language*, **5**, 477–88.

Caron, R.F., Caron, A.J. and Myers, R.S. (1982) 'Abstraction of invariant face expressions in infancy'. *Child Development*, **53**, 1008–15.

Cole, P.M. (1986) 'Children's spontaneous control of facial expression'. *Child Development*, **57**, 1309–21.

Darwin, C. (1872) *The Expression of the Emotions in Man and Animals*. London: Murray.

DiLalla, L.F. and Watson, M.W. (1988) 'Differentiation of fantasy and reality: Preschoolers' reactions to interruptions in their play'. *Developmental Psychology*, **24**, 286–91.

Dunn, J. and Kendrick, C. (1982) *Siblings: Love, envy and understanding*. Cambridge, MA: Harvard University Press.

Dunn, J., Kendrick, C. and MacNamee, R. (1981) 'The reaction of firstborn children to the birth of a sibling: Mother's reports'. *Journal of Child Psychology and Psychiatry*, **22**, 1–18.

Dunn, J. and Munn, P. (1985) 'Becoming a family member: Family conflict and the development of social understanding in the first year'. *Child Development*, **50**, 306–18.

Ekman, P. and Friesen, W.V. (1971) 'Constants across culture in the face and emotion'. *Journal of Personality and Social Psychology*, **17**, 124–9.

Ekman, P. and Friesen, W.V. (1974) 'Detecting deception from body and face'. *Journal of Personality and Social Psychology*, **29**, 288–98.

Fein, G.G. (1978) *Child Development*. Englewood Cliffs, NJ: Prentice Hall.

Freud, A. (1946) *The Ego and Mechanisms of Defense*. New York: International Universities Press.

Freud, S. (1936) *The Problem of Anxiety*. New York: Norton.

Frijda, N.H. (1986) *The Emotions*. Cambridge: Cambridge University Press.

Ganchrow, J.R., Steiner, J.E. and Daher, M. (1983) 'Neonatal facial expressions in response to different qualities and intensities of gustatory stimuli'. *Infant Behaviour and Development*, **6**, 473–84.

Gnepp, J. (1983) 'Children's social sensitivity: Inferring emotions from conflicting cues'. *Developmental Psychology*, **19**, 805–14.

Gnepp, J. (1989) 'Children's use of personal information'. In C. Saarni and P.L. Harris (eds) *Children's Understanding of Emotion* (pp. 151–77). Cambridge: Cambridge University Press.

Gordon, S.L. (1989) 'The socialisation of children's emotions: Emotional culture, competence and exposure'. In C. Saarni and P.L. Harris (eds) *Children's Understanding of Emotion* (pp. 319–49). Cambridge: Cambridge University Press.

Gordon, S.L. (1990) 'Institutional and impulsive cultural orientations in the selective appropriation of emotions to self'. In D. Franks and E.D. McCarthy (eds) *The Sociology of Emotions: Original essays and research papers*, Greenwich, CT: JAI Press.

Graham, S. (1988) 'Children's developing understanding of the motivational role of affect: An attributional analysis'. *Cognitive Development*, **3**, 71–88.

Graham, S. and Weiner, B. (1986) 'From an attributional theory of emotion to developmental psychology: A roundtrip ticket?' *Social Cognition*, **4**, 152–79.

Greenspan, S., Barenboim, C. and Chandler, M.J. (1976) 'Empathy and pseudo-empathy: The affective judgements of first and third graders'. *Journal of Genetic Psychology*, **129**, 77–88.

Harré, R. (1986) *The Social Construction of Emotions*. Oxford: Blackwell.

Harris, P.L. (1983) 'Children's understanding of the link between situation and emotion'. *Journal of Experimental Child Psychology*, **33**, 1–20.

Harris, P.L. (1989) *Children and Emotion: The development of psychological understanding*. Oxford: Blackwell.

Harris, P.L., Brown, E., Marriott, C., Whittall, S. and Harmer, S. (1991) 'Monsters, ghosts and witches: Testing the limits of the fantasy–reality distinction in young children'. *British Journal of Developmental Psychology*, **9**, 105–23.

Harris, P.L., Donnelly, K., Guz, G.R. and Pitt-Watson, R. (1986) 'Children's understanding of the distinction between real and apparent emotion'. *Child Development*, **57**, 895–909.

Harris, P.L. and Gross, D. (1988) 'Children's understanding of real and apparent emotion'. In J.W. Astington, P.L. Harris and D.R. Olson (eds) *Developing Theories of Mind* (pp. 295–314). New York: Cambridge University Press.

Harris, P.L. and Guz, G.R. (1986) 'Models of emotion: How boys report their emotional reactions upon entering an English boarding school'. Unpublished paper, Department of Experimental Psychology, University of Oxford.

Harris, P.L., Johnson, C.N., Hutton, D., Andrews, G. and Cooke, T. (1989) 'Young children's theory of mind and emotion'. *Cognition and Emotion*, **3**, 379–400.

Harris, P.L. and Lipian, M.S. (1989) 'Understanding emotion and experiencing emotion'. In C. Saarni and P.L. Harris (eds) *Children's Understanding of Emotion* (pp. 241–58). New York: Cambridge University Press.

Harris, P.L. and Olthof, T. (1982) 'The child's concept of emotion'. In G. Butterworth and P. Light (eds) *Social Cognition: Studies of the development of understanding* (pp. 188–209). Sussex: Harvester.

Harris, P.L., Olthof, T. and Meerum Terwogt, M. (1981) 'Children's knowledge of emotion'. *Journal of Child Psychology and Psychiatry*, **22**, 247–61.

Harris, P.L., Olthof, T., Meerum Terwogt, M. and Hardman, C.E. (1987) 'Children's knowledge of situations that provoke emotion'. *International Journal of Behavioural Development*, **10**, 319–43.

Harter, S. (1983) 'Children's understanding of multiple emotions: A cognitive-developmental approach'. In W.F. Overton (ed.) *The Relationship between Social and Cognitive Development* (pp. 147–94). Hillsdale, NJ: Erlbaum.

Harter, S. and Buddin, B. (1987) 'Children's understanding of the simultaneity of two emotions: A five-stage acquisition sequence'. *Developmental Psychology*, **23**, 388–99.

Harter, S. and Whitesell, N. (1989) 'Developmental changes in children's emotion concepts'. In C. Saarni and P.L. Harris (eds) *Children's Understanding of Emotion* (pp. 81–116). New York: Cambridge University Press.

Haviland, J.M. and Lelwica, M. (1987) 'The induced affect response: 10-week-old infants' responses to three emotional expressions'. *Developmental Psychology*, **23**, 97–104.

Hoffman, M. (1982) 'Affect and moral development'. In D. Cicchetti and P. Hesse (eds) *Emotional Development* (pp. 83–103). San Francisco, CA: Jossey-Bass.

Honkavaara, S. (1961) 'The psychology of expression'. *British Journal of Psychology Monograph Supplements*, **32**.

Hornik, R., Risenhoover, N. and Gunnar, M. (1987) 'The effects of maternal positive, neutral, and negative affective communications on infants' responses to new toys'. *Child Development*, 58, 937–44.

Izard, C.E. (1977) *Human Emotions*. New York: Plenum.

Kaitz, M., Meschulach-Sarfaty, O., Auerbach, J. and Eidelmann, A. (1988) 'A reexamination of newborn's ability to imitate facial expressions'. *Developmental Psychology*, 24, 3–7.

Kemper, T.D. (1987) 'How many emotions are there? Wedding the social and the autonomic components'. *American Journal of Sociology*, 93, 263–89.

Koriat, A., Melkman, R., Averill, J.R. and Lazarus, R.S. (1972) 'The self-control of emotional reactions to a stressful film'. *Journal of Personality*, 40, 601–19.

Latané, B. and Darley, J.M. (1970) *The Unresponsive Bystander: Why doesn't he help?* New York: Appleton–Century–Crofts.

Lazarus, R.S., Averill, J.R. and Opton, E.M., Jr (1970) 'Towards a cognitive theory of emotions'. In M. Arnold (ed.) *Feelings and Emotions* (pp. 207–32). New York: Academic Press.

Lazarus, R.S., Coyne, J.C. and Folkman, S. (1982) 'Cognition, emotion and motivation: The doctoring of Humpty-Dumpty'. In R.W. Neufield (ed.) *Psychological Stress and Psychopathology* (pp. 218–39). New York: McGraw-Hill.

Leslie, A.M. (1987) 'Pretense and representation: The origins of "theory of mind" '. *Psychological Review*, 94, 412–26.

Levy, R.I. (1984) 'Emotions, knowing, and culture'. In R.A. Shweder and R.A. LeVine (eds) *Culture Theory: Essays on mind, self, and emotion* (pp. 214–37). Cambridge: Cambridge University Press.

Lewis, M. and Saarni, C. (1985) *The Socialisation of Emotions*. New York: Plenum.

Meerum Terwogt, M. (1984) 'Emotional development in middle childhood: A cognitive view'. Unpublished dissertation. Amsterdam: Free University.

Meerum Terwogt, M. (1986) 'Affective states and task performance in naive and prompted children'. *European Journal of Psychology of Education*, 1, 31–40.

Meerum Terwogt, M. (1987) 'Children's behavioral reactions in situations with a dual emotional impact'. *Psychological Reports*, 61, 100–2.

Meerum Terwogt, M. (1990) 'Disordered children's acknowledgement of multiple emotions'. *Journal of General Psychology*, 117, 59–69.

Meerum Terwogt, M., Koops, W., Oosterhoff, T. and Olthof, T. (1986) 'Development in processing of multiple emotional situations'. *Journal of General Psychology*, 113, 109–19.

Meerum Terwogt, M. and Olthof, T. (1989) 'Awareness and self-regulation of emotion in young children'. In C. Saarni and P.L. Harris (eds) *Children's Understanding of Emotion* (pp. 209–37). Cambridge: Cambridge University Press.

Meerum Terwogt, M., Schene, J. and Harris, P.L. (1986) 'Self-control of emotional reactions by young children'. *Journal of Child Psychology and Psychiatry*, 27, 357–66.

Meerum Terwogt, M., Schene, J. and Koops, W. (1990) 'Concepts of emotion in institutionalised children'. *Journal of Child Psychology and Psychiatry*, 31, 1131–43.

Nisbett, R.E. and Wilson, T.D. (1977) 'Telling more than we can know: Verbal reports on mental processes'. *Psychological Review*, 84, 231–59.

Nunner-Winkler, G. and Sodian, B. (1988) 'Children's understanding of moral emotions'. *Child Development*, 59, 1323–38.

Olthof, T., Meerum Terwogt, M., van Panthaleon van Eck, O. and Koops, W. (1987) 'Children's knowledge of the integration of successive emotions'. *Perceptual and Motor Skills*, **65**, 407–14.

Piaget, J. (1947) *La Psychologie de l'intelligence*. Paris: Librairie Armand Colin.

Piaget, J. (1952) *The Origins of Intelligence in the Child*. London: Routledge and Kegan Paul.

Plutchik, R. (1980) *Emotion: A psycho-evolutionary synthesis*. New York: Harper & Row.

Reichenbach, L. and Masters, J. (1983) 'Children's use of expressive and contextual cues in judgments of emotion'. *Child Development*, **54**, 993–1004.

Reissland, N. (1988) 'Neonatal imitation in the first hour of life: Observations in rural Nepal'. *Developmental Psychology*, **24**, 464–9.

Rozin, P. (1975) 'The evolution of intelligence and access to the cognitive unconscious'. In J. Sprague and A.N. Epstein (eds) *Progress in Psychobiology and Physiological Psychology* (vol. 6, pp. 245–80). New York: Academic Press.

Saarni, C. (1979) 'Children's understanding of display rules for expressive behaviour'. *Developmental Psychology*, **15**, 424–9.

Saarni, C. (1984) 'Observing children's use of display rules: Age and sex differences'. *Child Development*, **55**, 1504–13.

Semin, G.R. and Papadopoulou, K. (1990) 'The acquisition of reflexive social emotions: The transmission and reproduction of social control through joint action'. In G. Duveen and B.B. Lloyd (eds) *Social Representation and the Development of Knowledge* (pp. 107–25). Cambridge: Cambridge University Press.

Skinner, B.F. (1971) *Beyond Freedom and Dignity*. New York: Knopf.

Smetana, J.G. (1981) 'Preschool children's conception of moral and social rules'. *Child Development*, **52**, 1333–6.

Smiley, P. and Huttenlocher, J. (1989) 'Young children's acquisition of emotion concepts'. In C. Saarni and P.L. Harris (eds) *Children's Understanding of Emotion* (pp. 27–49). Cambridge: Cambridge University Press.

Snyder, M. (1979) 'Cognitive, behavioral, and interpersonal consequences of self-monitoring'. In P. Pliner, K.R. Blankstein and I.M. Spigel (eds) *Perception of Emotion in Self and Others* (pp. 181–201). New York: Plenum.

Stegge, H., Ferguson, T. and Meerum Terwogt, M. (1991) *Parental disciplinary reactions and children's proneness to guilt and shame*. Presentation to the Fifth Congress of the International Society of Research on Emotion, Saarbrücken, 9–12 July.

Stewart, R.B. and Marvin, R.S. (1984) 'Sibling relations: The role of conceptual perspective taking in the ontogeny of sibling caregiving'. *Child Development*, **55**, 1322–32.

Taylor, D.A. and Harris, P.L. (1984) 'Knowledge of strategies for the expression of emotion among normal and maladjusted boys: A research note'. *Journal of Child Psychology and Psychiatry*, **24**, 223–9.

Wellman, H.M. and Estes, D. (1986) 'Early understanding of mental entities: A reexamination of childhood realism'. *Child Development*, **57**, 910–23.

Wolf, D. (1982) 'Understanding others: A longitudinal case study of the concept of independent agency'. In G.E. Forman (ed.) *Action and Thought* (pp. 297–328). New York: Academic Press.

Wolf, D.P., Rygh, J. and Altshuler, J. (1984) 'Agency and experience: Action and states in play narratives'. In I. Bretherton (ed.) *Symbolic Play*. Orlando, FL: Academic Press.

Wolff, P.H. (1963) 'Observations on the early development of smiling'. In B.M. Foss
(ed.) *Determinants of Infant Behaviour* (vol. 2, pp. 113–34). London: Methuen.

Young, P.T. (1961) *Motivation and Emotion*. New York: Wiley.

Zahn-Waxler, C. and Radke-Yarrow, M. (1982) 'The development of altruism:
Alternative research strategies'. In N. Eisenberg-Berg (ed.) *The Development of
Prosocial Behavior* (pp. 109–37). New York: Academic Press.

Zajonc, R.B. (1980) 'Feeling and thinking: Preferences need no inferences'. *American
Psychologist*, **35**, 151–73.

Chapter 4

Understanding of personality and dispositions
Nicola Yuill

4.1 Introduction

She is very nice because she gives my friends and me toffee. She lives by the main road. She has fair hair and she wears glasses. She is 47 years old. She has an anniversary today. She has been married since she was 21 years old. She sometimes gives us flowers. She has a very nice garden and house. We only go in the weekend and have a talk with her. (girl, 7 years, 11 months)

He smells very much and is very nasty. He has no sense of humour and is very dull. He is always fighting and he is cruel. He does silly things and is very stupid. He has brown hair and cruel eyes. He is sulky and 11 years old and has lots of sisters. I think he is the most horrible boy in the class. He has a croaky voice and always chews his pencil and picks his teeth and I think he is disgusting. (boy, 9 years, 11 months)

This girl is not in my form she is just in the same division as me. She is very quiet and only talks when she knows a person very well. She is clever in one sense, she comes top of her form. She is very reserved but once you get to know her she is exactly the opposite. It is very unusual to see her not attending the lessons. At sometime or another all of our minds wander but hers never seems to do so. One of the things I admire in her is she is very tidy. (girl, 14 years, 1 month)

These are three responses to a request to 'describe what sort of person' someone is, collected by Livesley and Bromley (1973, pp. 214–21). Everyone will respond differently to such a question, and each description gives quite different kinds of information about the people described. But they tell us even more about the people who wrote them – their idea of what 'personality' is, their cognitive skills, values, interests and social worlds. Accounts of personality can include concepts described in previous chapters – beliefs, desires, emotions, the distinction between appearance and reality – and more, because sometimes fleeting mental states must be integrated into a coherent and relatively stable whole. Knowing how someone feels now may help to explain their current behaviour, but it is usually not much use in predicting how they will behave tomorrow, or even in an hour's time. This chapter investigates the child as a naive personality theorist.

Naive psychology has witnessed a revival of interest, as this book shows, but this new interest is not simply a rediscovery of old questions. It has been influenced by work in philosophy and cognitive science, and in issues such as how children represent another person's representation of the world (see Chapter 2 above). While personality dispositions (traits) played a large role in the early research in naive psychology, and notably in implicit personality theory, they have played a lesser role so far in this revival. But people are fascinated by the question of personality – witness the popularity of biographies of the famous, whether authorized or not, and the desire to know what someone is 'really' like. When so much everyday behaviour is determined by social roles and rules, the question of a person's 'true', underlying character becomes especially intriguing. This chapter reviews work over the past twenty years on children's use of disposition terms, their understanding of the concept of a disposition, and their ideas about how traits are integrated into a personality. The area of trait understanding is particularly interesting, because several different kinds of theories have been applied in explaining its development, so it gives a good perspective of different theoretical approaches to development. It also gives us the opportunity to think about what we mean by a trait, a question which is all too easily taken for granted in studying the social psychology of adult thought.

The chapter is organized as follows: first, I look at how children describe people's personality spontaneously, and the kinds of words they use, focusing primarily on *traits*. Then I go on to some more experimental studies that are concerned with what lies behind the words children use – do they really understand traits as enduring internal states, in the way adults do, or do they use traits to refer to fleeting displays of behaviour? In the second main section, I go beyond the study of single traits to look at the broader issue of *personality*: how do children integrate different traits, and do they have 'implicit personality theories'? The third section looks at some of the important *consequences* of children's ideas of personality: how does it affect their thinking about stereotypes of gender differences in personality, and about the possibility for personal change? This section also brings us into more controversial waters: the question of why young children do not seem to use or understand trait terms. Some accounts stress the *cognitive* limitations of young children, while other accounts look at differences in the social and cultural worlds of adults and children. Finally, I consider theoretical debates and future directions. There are several previous reviews of early work in the area (Miller and Aloise, 1989; Shantz, 1983). In this review, as well as including more recent work, I have endeavoured to look beyond the use of trait terms, to consider their significance: What difference does your conception of personal attributes make to your conception of a person, to attitudes and stereotyping, and for personal change?

4.2 Traits

4.2.1 What is a trait?

In personality theory, 'trait' is a term that is laden with theoretical significance. Some psychologists, for instance, argue that traits express genetic predispositions (e.g. temperament); others that they are learned behaviour patterns; and yet others that they do not exist. The study of children's use of traits has not been committed to any of these theoretical frameworks, but we can identify two basic features underlying any coherent use of the concept: *temporal* – traits describe a series of actions over time – and *causal* – traits are used to explain the underlying causes of disparate actions. These two aspects are linked to the two primary functions of traits: *prediction* and *explanation* of action. Furthermore, they seem to reflect Western adults' intuitions. Chaplin, John and Goldberg (1988) examined these intuitions by asking adults to rate various descriptive terms, such as fiery, angry, aroused and nosey, as either 'traits' or 'states' (such as emotions), and to rate each term on various properties (for example, the extent to which the situation or the person is responsible for it). They identified three main distinguishing features: *stability*, *duration* and *locus of causation*. Traits are seen as stable over time, long-lasting and internal, whereas states are temporary, brief and caused by external circumstances. When we are considering children's understanding of traits, these features raise three questions: do children perceive traits as stable over situations, as consistent over time, and as internal factors explaining a range of actions? But I will begin by presenting some basic information about children's use of trait terms.

Before diving into the literature, it is worth putting the work on traits into the context of children as psychologists. Research on conceptions of personality has traditionally meant characterizing people as 'lay scientists' or (perhaps less flatteringly) 'naive psychologists', hence the term 'implicit personality theory' (see p. 96). However, attention was focused more on the *content* of adults' beliefs about traits than on their comprehension of the *nature* of the fundamental concept of a trait. Research on 'theory of mind', on the other hand, is concerned with comprehension of basic concepts such as belief and desire, not with their content (see Chapter 2 above). So far, theory of mind has had little to say about developing conceptions of personality. However, since traits are based on mental concepts such as desires, emotions, moods and preferences, children's theory of mind is obviously involved in their conceptions of traits. As we will see, we can make useful comparisons between children's understanding of emotions and traits (see also Yuill, in press, for links between traits and theory of mind).

4.2.2 Children's spontaneous use of trait terms

It would be naive to assume that there is a fixed list of 'trait terms' in a language. For example, I could say of someone that they are 'the sort of person who would sell their own grandfather'. Although I am not using a trait term, I might be attributing a stable disposition to that person that explains several disparate actions. It would be equally simplistic to think that use of a trait term necessarily means that the speaker has a conception of what a trait is. Saying of someone who gives you a present, 'That was kind', might be labelling the action rather than the person. However, the judicious study of children's spontaneous use of trait terms gives us a good *descriptive* base to which we can then address questions such as: Do age changes in children's use of such terms reflect cognitive growth, social experience, or – more likely – some combination of these?

One of the most thorough studies in this area is an investigation by Livesley and Bromley (1973), from which my introductory descriptions were taken. This study is ubiquitous in reviews of social cognition, simply because it is so comprehensive. They asked 320 7- to 15-year-old Liverpudlians first to write a description of 'the sort of person you are' and then to write eight descriptions of others: a girl, boy, woman and man whom they disliked, and four people in the same categories whom they liked. The children were given several examples of the sort of information that was *not* required, such as size, colouring and clothes. The resulting descriptions showed a marked increase with age in what the authors called 'central statements' – traits, habitual behaviour, motives and attitudes, with a corresponding decline in 'peripheral statements' – appearance, activities, incidents, possessions, factual information, tastes and social roles. The percentage of traits mentioned in the accounts increased from about 4 per cent in children just under 8 to 10–15 per cent in rising 9- to 15-year-olds. More recent research bears out the idea that younger children tend not to use trait terms. For instance, Bartsch and Wellman (1989), when asking each of 45 3- to 4-year-old children to explain characters' actions in nine vignettes, found only one 'trait' response.

This picture of children's infrequent use of traits is puzzling if we look at recent studies of children's vocabulary acquisition. Although these studies do not generally categorize trait terms as a distinct set, it is possible to derive these from the data available. As Chapter 3 above on emotions shows, 28-month-old children have a vocabulary of emotion terms (Bretherton and Beeghly, 1982), and some of these shade into trait terms – notably the evaluative labels nice, good, bad, naughty. Another relevant study looked at parental reports of vocabulary in children from 18 months to 6 years. Ridgeway, Waters and Kuczaj (1985) asked parents to report the age at which their children could understand and use a list of 125 adjectives. Ridgeway *et al.* describe these words as 'emotion-descriptors', but many of them could be used as personality descriptors, too. Thus, if children know these words, then they do at least have the potential to use them as traits. The words assessed include helpful and loving, known by most 2-year-olds; friendly, mean, gentle, lazy and shy, by most 3-year-olds; and cruel, stubborn, caring and nervous, used only by the oldest children. So it is not that children lack the vocabulary to describe personality. If we consider that they probably know other types of term, as well as just trait adjectives (e.g. scaredy-cat, cry-baby) that can be used to describe aspects of character, we can see that their potential linguistic repertoire for traits is large. Unfortunately, we do not know whether the children in this study could use these terms as *traits*.

So why don't children use these words when they are asked to describe people? There are two broad kinds of explanation we might offer. Either children are not capable of understanding the appropriate use of such terms – for instance, they use them to describe a single action, rather than an enduring trait – or they do not choose to use them in the context of a particular study. The first of these explanations can best be tested using experimental studies, which I discuss in the next main section. The second can be assessed by looking at the effects of varying instructions or experimental procedures, and hence the children's perceptions of what is expected of them.

It seems that the sorts of descriptions given do vary with the expectations and interests of the subjects. For instance, Craig and Boyle (1979) felt that children might be able to use more trait terms if prompted. They asked 5- to 10-year-olds to describe characters shown in short videotapes, and then posed forced-choice trait questions (e.g. Is she shy? Is she kind?) The use of these trait questions does seem to have encouraged trait use: 45 per cent of all 7-year-olds' descriptions included trait terms, and overall use of such terms doubled in frequency over the experiment. Furthermore, it would be a mistake to think that older children use primarily psychological descriptions: Honess (1981) argued that boys in particular put an increased emphasis on physical appearance from the ages of 8 to 13. These studies serve to remind us that a relatively open-ended task, 'describing a person', reveals as much about children's concerns and interests as it does about their abilities, and these concerns will vary according to one's social identity. An adolescent boy's query to his friend about a new girlfriend, 'What's she like?', will elicit a different kind of answer from the same question that I ask a colleague about my new boss.

The studies of spontaneous person-descriptions show fairly consistent findings: children's use of trait terms shows a sharp increase from the age of about 8, although younger children have many such terms in their vocabulary and can use them if prompted. These studies have a strength, in that they show the kinds of information that children of different ages consider informative about people, but they also have weaknesses. They tell us about the words children use, but do not tell us what *concepts* lie behind those words. There are several possibilities here. Perhaps children use trait terms but mean something different by them from adults. For instance, they may be describing the quality of a behaviour, rather than an enduring aspect of a person. Alternatively, they may be able to recognize the concept of a trait even before they begin to use trait terms frequently. From the experimental studies that have been done, we now know much more about these aspects.

4.2.3 Experimental studies of children's conception of traits

Stability and consistency: Tarzan meets the Bionic Woman
Do children think of people as having stable psychological attributes that can be used to predict their behaviour over time? It seems likely that even quite young children must be familiar with the personalities of their favourite TV and story characters. This is demonstrated in a study of children's memory for attributes of familiar TV characters by Ceci, Caves and Howe (1981). Seven- and 10-year-olds were told an entertaining story in which seven characters (e.g. Tarzan, the Bionic Woman, James Bond) behaved inconsistently with their known features. For example, the Six Million Dollar Man was too weak to pick up a can of paint. Asked to rate the story characters three weeks later, children tended to make the attributes more consistent with what they knew about the characters' usual behaviour, suggesting that they had strong pre-existing expectations about typical behaviour. It seems probable that younger children, too, have such expectations. Eder (1989) has shown that from 3 to 4 years of age, children can report memories about people's habitual behaviour – for example, that someone has been 'mostly good'; and she suggests that such general memories form the basis of later conceptions of dispositions.

One of the main studies to look systematically at children's conceptions of the stability of traits in an experimental context was by Heller and Berndt (1981; Berndt and Heller, 1985), who studied children's ability to generalize from one behaviour to others. They told 5-, 8- and 11-year-old children short stories about a character who behaved selfishly or generously on two occasions. The children were then asked to predict the same actor's behaviour in ten future situations. These new situations varied in how similar they were to the original behaviour. For example, children were asked whether an actor who had shared food on two occasions in the past would share food in the future (near-identical behaviour), whether they would help others, whether they would lie or tease, and whether they would do well academically. Children also rated the actor on traits that varied in terms of their similarity to the initial actions, such as selfish, nice and smart (clever). Even the youngest group predicted that an actor who had been generous in the past would be more likely to be generous in future than a selfish actor, and made similarly appropriate predictions for a selfish actor. Only from the age of 8, however, did children make significantly different predictions between one of the actors and a control condition (where they were given information only about a character's age and sex), and then only for the selfish actor. This means that even the youngest children expected some stability, but only in the rather general sense that a beneficient actor would be more likely than a maleficent one to do something good in the future. Even this is quite complex, as can be seen from the gradual development of children's ability to abstract general patterns from repeated events (see Chapter 7 below). As we shall see later, however, Heller and Berndt have provided evidence for only the broadest of 'personality theories' (that there are good people and bad people).

This ability to generalize was supported in a study by Bennett (1985–6), who found that there was no increase between the ages of 5 and 11 in the ability to make generalized predictions from an act of theft to future actions of sharing and helping: even the youngest children made generalized predictions. However, Rholes and Ruble (1984) found some evidence of a lack of generalization in young children's predictions. They found that 5- to 7-year-olds did not predict that a generous child would do something helpful as often as older children did. The authors argued that the source of the difference from other studies is that the prediction situations varied between studies. In the Heller and Berndt study, for example, denying oneself food on one day is used to predict whether one would deny oneself food on another day, compared to the Rholes and Ruble task of sharing lunch used to predict helping with a task. In addition, Ruble, Newman, Rholes and Altshuler (1988) argued that children might expect stability of behaviour in the *same situation over time*, because behaviour is controlled by the constant situational pressures, but that they may not expect stability in *different situations across time*. Thus, it seems that at least from 5 years of age, children can use trait terms to predict stability, but they seem to rely on rather general evaluations, following a simple rule that good behaviour follows good, and bad follows bad.

Ferguson, Olthof, Luiten and Rule (1984) looked in more detail at what kind of information children used to make attributions of personality dispositions. They told 5- to 11-year-olds stories about characters whose actions differed in covariation (consistency and distinctiveness) and frequency. In traditional attribution theory, these types of information are informative for dispositional attribution. If someone behaves similarly over time and across situations, the behaviour is *consistent*. If they show this behaviour to one target in particular, the behaviour is *distinctive*. So for example, if a girl shares sweets with six other children (low distinctiveness), has shared other possessions on three past occasions (high consistency), and often shares things (high frequency), then she is more likely to be labelled generous than a girl who always shares sweets with one other child (high consistency), but never shares anything with anyone else (high distinctiveness). Ferguson *et al.* (1984) pitted the different kinds of information against each other, and found that younger children used *frequency* information more than older children, while there was an increase with age in the use of *covariation* information. Even the youngest children, however, did use covariation information, indicating that they understand that people's behaviour shows stability over time and situations.

Traits as explanations

It is important not to forget that the experimental studies described so far look only at the *temporal* aspects of traits – that is, the repetition of particular types of action over time. Barenboim (1985, p. 63) points out forcefully the other main feature of traits:

> missing [from previous developmental research] is the top–down explanatory nature of these constructs ... the traditional view of personality traits is that they are a dynamic, causative force that explains why people behave the way they do. They are not simply labels of convenience or shorthand for summarising similar behaviour seen on different occasions.

If we think back to the work on understanding of emotions (Chapter 3 above) we can see that it is just this internal causal aspect which has proved to be of great interest in recent research. The view presented by Harris (1989) is that children of around 6 have a situational idea of emotion – that is, they link emotions to situations: people are happy at birthday parties, frightened in a haunted house. Older children understand emotions as inner mental states that produce behaviour. Once emotion is understood as internal, it is possible to see how it can be changed by 'thinking yourself out of' a particular mood, and how to deceive others about your 'real' internal feelings by putting on an external display of behaviour that suggests a different underlying feeling.

This account describes children's spontaneous accounts of emotion well (although there is evidence that even children of 3 to 4 can imagine individual differences in feelings in structured experimental situations: Harris *et al.*, 1989). If we accept this account, then we would expect that young children, just as they do not fully understand emotions as internal causes, do not spontaneously see traits as internal causes of behaviour. There is unfortunately much less research on the causal aspects of traits, but a study by Gnepp and Chilamkurti (1988) seems to support Harris's view. They argued that if traits are seen as internal states causing behaviour, they can be used to predict individual differences in emotional reactions to an event. For example, being chosen for the leading part in a play may produce excitement and delight if we are outgoing and extroverted, but dread and terror if we are more reserved and shy. Gnepp and Chilamkurti told children stories about characters with differing traits who found themselves in such situations. Even kindergarteners were influenced by trait information in predicting emotion, although this tendency was rather weak until the age of about 9. The results seem to suggest that a causal understanding of traits is achieved gradually, just as children slowly develop such a view of emotions.

So far, it seems that young children understand that behaviour may be stable over time, and later they also appreciate that an internal psychological construct (a trait) can explain why behaviour is stable: that is, someone is predictably inquisitive because they possess the internal disposition of nosiness. But how is the earlier, *predictive* use of traits augmented by the *explanatory* view? Barenboim (1981) tried to illuminate this question by positing a developmental sequence and testing it, partly using longitudinal data. He interviewed 6-, 8- and 10-year-olds, using a fairly typical free-response format, and then reinterviewed them a year later. Both longitudinal and cross-sectional data supported a sequence of views: first, children used *'behavioural comparisons'* – for example, 'Billy runs a lot faster than Jason', or 'she draws the best in our whole class'. Once such comparisons can be made, children are able to infer that there are stable attributes, or *'psychological constructs'* (such as traits or behavioural regularities) that account for behavioural stability within a person. Use of such constructs did increase around 7 to 8 years of age, as the use of behavioural comparisons declined at about the age of 10. Finally, children should be able to compare people on these psychological constructs, to create *'psychological comparisons'* (e.g. 'more shy . . . than most kids'). Again, the results supported the sequence: such comparisons increased at around 10 to 11 years old. Although this study does not show what motivates the change from one form of construct to another, it does give us some fairly clear descriptive evidence of a developmental change.

Again, we end up with a fairly clear picture of children's abilities: from the age of 3 or 4, they understand that people's behaviour tends to be stable, and can make very general predictions about behaviour by the age of about 5. However, these predictions are based on rather broad, evaluative assumptions, and they make less use of covariation information, which assesses consistency of behaviour despite changes in – for example – target or situation, than they do of frequency information. From about 5 to 7 years of age children begin to have an idea that traits can explain motivation behind behaviour, and this understanding may develop gradually, in line with causal understanding of mental states such as emotions. This development is accompanied by an apparently sudden increase in the spontaneous use of trait terms.

4.3 *Personality*

The issue of traits as explanations brings us back to the issue of what it means to understand personality. So far, we have dealt solely with the use and understanding of the concept of a personality trait, but there is more to understanding personality than this. The first description at the beginning of this chapter does not mention traits at all, except for the general term 'nice'. The second is a list of traits and habits that have a very general kind of connection (they are all unpleasant). The final description mentions traits that are superficially conflicting ('reserved ... exactly the opposite') but are presented as arising from a coherent inner person: for example, her apparently conflicting degrees of reserve really depend on how well she knows someone. We can discuss personality beyond single traits in terms of two main questions. First, how do children integrate specific traits into a general conception of a whole personality? Social psychologists use the term *implicit personality theory* to describe people's assumptions about how personality traits are clustered. For example, one very simple kind of theory is that some people have only good attributes and other people are all bad. The second question about personality integration is how children come to understand what it is to have a personality in the sense of a continuing personal identity. That is, we think of ourselves as having continuity in our psychological states from one moment to another, and as being unique and different from any other person.

4.3.1 Implicit personality theory

In the early social psychology literature, the issue of implicit personality theory was an important focus. Researchers were particularly interested in how we could use one characteristic to predict the existence of others, and the ways in which a single characteristic can affect our perception of the person as a whole. For example, if someone is witty, then we might also expect them to be imaginative and creative. If, however, we hear that they are also rather cold, we would get a very different overall impression than if we find that they are very warm: one cluster of traits suggests a cutting, sarcastic character to be treated with caution, while the other implies a person who is much less of a threat. Because we are concerned primarily with the understanding of personality, it is important to know not just which traits go together, but *why* children might infer that, say, a person who is fussy might also be neurotic and excitable. Snodgrass (1976) provides a useful list of the kinds of reasons why different characteristics might be viewed as related. *Evaluative consistency* is based on the idea mentioned above: that good behaviour goes with good, and bad goes with bad. Thus, someone who is judged clever might also be generous, because both of these are positively valued. *Descriptive consistency* concerns the meaning of two terms: for example, stealing and lying go together because both are dishonest. *Empirical association*, as the name suggests, is the idea that two characteristics go together simply because they have been observed to co-occur. For example, a child might perceive that the cleverest children in her class are also best at sport. *Causal attribution* involves a causal relation between two terms: either one trait causes the other (e.g. a boy who steals also lies in order to conceal his stealing) or two traits have a common underlying cause (e.g. both stealing and lying are caused by hidden hostility).

There is very little information about what kinds of relations children perceive between traits, but Snodgrass's study provides some indication. He asked second-to-sixth-graders to predict one trait from another and to explain the connection. For instance, they were asked whether someone who told lies would also be stingy, and why. In explaining conjunctions of traits, the children used causal attribution most frequently of these four categories. However, there is little information about the sorts of relations that kindergarteners and first-graders used, because so few of them articulated any reasons for the inferences they made. Because the technique was verbally demanding, other methods will be needed to work out why the younger children made the inferences that they did.

Many of the early studies of implicit personality theory cited the increase in complexity and integration of personality descriptions (see Shantz, 1983), but such an account is not very specific. Fortunately, the study by Livesley and Bromley provides an analysis of exactly how the organization of personality descriptions changes with age. They found that children's accounts became increasingly complex with age on several dimensions. Children increasingly gave *reasons* why someone had a particular characteristic: for example, 'he is nervous and this makes him shy at times'; 'he hates children only because he has none of his own'. There was also more evidence of acknowledgement of *trait combinations* that are often assumed to be conflicting, for example: 'he is very good at work but very slow'; 'she is always being kind but she is nosey'. Third, older children were more likely to describe *discrepancies between apparent* behaviour, or professed intention, *and actual behaviour*, e.g. 'although she professes to be your friend, when you are ill she doesn't visit you'; 'he is always showing off his car and pretends he knows all about them'; 'she is very reserved but once you get to know her she is exactly the opposite'. These results were similar to those found by Peevers and Secord (1973), who elicited free descriptions from American children. If you have read Chapter 3 on emotions, you may have noticed that some parallels can be drawn here with children's developing acknowledgement of mixed and conflicting emotions, and the distinction between emotional display and underlying reality.

There is also evidence from more constrained experimental studies that young children make use of a general evaluative consistency to link personal characteristics. Saltz and Medow (1971) described how children of 5 to 8 often did not acknowledge the coexistence of good and bad features in a single person (e.g. a liar cannot also be a good baseball player), but were much more likely to accept the coexistence of two good features (e.g. a mother can also be a good sales clerk).

A more detailed study of the kinds of inferences made from one attribute to another was carried out by Honess (1979). Using a repertory grid technique with 8- to 13-year-olds, he showed that children's patterns of inferences became considerably more differentiated with age, and were organized more hierarchically. It is interesting to note that the content of these children's implicit theories differed: boys at all ages tended to draw most implications from *activities* and *abilities* – that is, they could use information such as 'good at chess' and 'drops litter' to make other inferences – whereas girls increasingly used *personality traits* in making inferences.

A different angle on implicit personality theory is to study children's understanding of individual traits. For example, Yussen and Kane (1983) and Leahy and Hunt (1983) both investigated children's conceptions of intelligence, relating their results to a broadly Piagetian framework, while Baldwin and Baldwin (1970) studied in detail the prerequisites for attribution of kindness. The importance of studying a range of traits is emphasized by Reeder and Brewer (1979), who presented a conceptual analysis showing that different traits were structured in different ways; and by Yuill (1992), who reports evidence suggesting that children think of traits concerned with social interactions (such as kindness and helpfulness) differently from traits referring primarily to internal states (such as fearlessness and pessimism).

4.3.2 The concept of identity

We have gone from single traits to integration of traits, but have said nothing so far about the concept of personal identity. To a philosopher, this is a complex question that involves asking how we know that someone is 'the same person' even after transformations. This is relevant for the purposes of this chapter in so far as a stable and continuing personality is important in judging someone to be an individual. Most of the developmental research relevant to the issue of identity has been carried out to investigate children's conceptions of the self: while there are parallels between understanding of self and others, it is worth remembering that differences exist (see Damon and Hart, 1988).

In Piagetian theory, the concept of identity consists of appreciating that an object or person remains the same even if irrelevant properties are changed. For example, a girl remains a girl even if she puts on boys' clothes and cuts her hair in a typically boyish style. According to Keil's (1989) theory, children who do not understand this idea think of appearance as a defining feature of sex, rather than just a characteristic one. There are many features of a person that might be thought to contribute to their identity: gender is one particularly notable feature. Personality is another feature that is expected to remain reasonably constant, or at least to show continuity.

Anecdotal evidence suggests that pre-school children are happy to accept that pictures of themselves as babies are still 'me', but they find it difficult to understand that there was a time when they did not exist. For example, a friend's 3-year-old son insisted that photographs of his parents eight years ago could not have been taken before he existed: he was not in the picture, he argued, but was still in the house. Carey (1985, p. 66) notes her 3-year-old daughter grappling with the problem of identity: 'When I grow up, there won't be a little girl named Eliza around here any more'.

When children do grasp the idea that their identity is continuous, they show changes in the criteria for judging this continuity. Mohr (1978) asked children of 6 to 11 three questions about personal identity: what would you have to change about yourself to become your best friend, what will (not) change about yourself when you grow up, and what has (not) changed about you since you were a baby? The 6- to 7-year-olds mentioned external features – appearance, name, possessions; the 8- to 9-year-olds usually mentioned typical behaviour; and only the oldest children mentioned internal characteristics such as feelings, thoughts and knowledge. This is a picture that should be fairly familiar by now from the work on descriptions of personality. Damon and Hart (1988) have elaborated on these studies of identity understanding to produce a detailed stage model of self-understanding that is broadly consistent with work on the understanding of others.

The primacy of appearance over actual behaviour for young children is shown in a study by Hoffner and Cantor (1985), who investigated which attribute was seen as more predictive of future action. They showed children a cartoon depicting an old woman who either treated her cat well, stroking and feeding it, or mistreated it, yelling at it and throwing it down the stairs. The woman was depicted with typical witch-like features (bony, with a long nose, chin and fingernails, and so on) or as a typical cuddly grandmother, with more rounded features. Children of 3 to 5 judged the woman's behaviour on the basis of her appearance – they thought that when two children sneaked into the woman's house, she would grab them and put them in a cupboard more often for the 'witch' picture than for the 'grandmother' picture. Children of 6 and 10 years of age made their predictions on the basis of the character's previous behaviour rather than her appearance: the kind woman would ask the children to stay and would give them biscuits, regardless of her appearance.

4.4 The significance of changing conceptions of personality

4.4.1 Stereotypes

The study mentioned above should remind us that even though the older children seemed to be 'fair' in judging by behaviour rather than appearance, people of all ages can make attributions about personality on the basis of apparently quite irrelevant and inadequate information, such as gender, age and ethnic group. Such attributions are studied under the more general rubric of stereotypes. Typically, studies of stereotyping and prejudice have been carried out quite independently of research on conceptions of traits, but as this section will show, the two areas of study are closely related. Work on stereotypes in adults has concentrated on national characteristics and gender stereotypes, and shows that whether or not people actually subscribe to the stereotypes, they know many personality characteristics that are purported to go with particular kinds of people (e.g. Peabody, 1985).

Most of this work reports adults' beliefs, but Williams and Best (1982) have carried out fairly large-scale and varied surveys of children's gender stereotypes.[1] They developed a measure of gender-stereotyping consisting of a list of trait adjectives, with example 'stories' of typical behaviour. Children are shown two pictures, a silhouette of a man and a woman, and asked which person the story is about. For example: 'One of these people is emotional. They cry when something good happens as well as when everything goes wrong. Which is the emotional person?'

In the United States, where the original research was done, even 5-year-olds assigned many of the stories to the gender with which the trait is stereotypically associated. Evidence of similar stereotypes was also apparent in 5-year-olds from twenty-two other countries, including places in South America, Western Europe, Asia, Africa and Oceania. In the majority of these places, females were associated with the following traits: weak, gentle, appreciative, soft-hearted, meek, affected, emotional and affectionate. In contrast, males were associated with being enterprising, disorderly, boastful, severe, independent, loud, coarse, cruel, strong and aggressive. There were a further eight female and six male traits that these children did not reliably associate with one gender or the other, although older children and adults did, indicating the elaboration of gender stereotypes with increasing age.

One criticism that has been made of the results on gender-stereotyping is that children can only make a forced choice, and therefore have to display stereotyping (e.g. Etaugh, Levine and Mennella, 1984). This criticism, however, does not affect the fact that these young children knew what traits men and women are commonly supposed to show, even if they did not subscribe to the stereotypes themselves. The results do not tell us how children conceive of these attributes. Do they understand that such traits are stable attributes, and why do they think such stereotypes exist? We have already looked at children's understanding of the stability of traits, and the research so far suggests that stability is appreciated in only a very general evaluative way at 5, and is not understood more precisely until around the age of 7. The work on gender-stereotyping, however, should lead us to suspect, at least, that some aspects of personal identity – in this case gender-related traits – are perceived as stable by younger children. If children understand that gender is a stable attribute, then they may believe that traits commonly supposed to be associated with a particular gender will also remain stable. Rotenberg (1982) also drew this parallel between person-perception and gender constancy, and found that 'character constancy' developed in a similar way to gender constancy. More recent work (e.g. Bem, 1989) has questioned the findings on gender constancy, so this is an area where more research might be done.

Some data relevant to gender constancy and stereotyping, and an interesting extension of gender-stereotyping work to younger children, are presented by Kuhn, Nash and Brucken (1978). They asked 2- and 3-year-olds to assign various attributes (activities, traits and future roles) to a boy or a girl doll. They found agreed gender stereotypes on about half of the items. Although the different item types were not analyzed separately, it seems that most of these agreed items were activities rather than traits or roles. The second interesting feature of these results is that stereotyping was related to gender identity and constancy: the greater understanding children had about the stability of gender, the more they knew about conventional gender stereotypes. We cannot be sure why this correlation occurs, but Kuhn *et al.* present an interesting discussion of the possible roles of emotional self-evaluation and cognitive development in the acquisition of sex-role concepts.

The issue of why such stereotypes exist brings us to the second main question about traits: in what ways do children explain why certain traits are supposed to be characteristic of an entire group of people? Unfortunately, there is very little work in this area. Ullian (1976) reports a descriptive study that included an analysis of how children conceived of gender differences. Although she does not present data, but just a stage model which was apparently supported by her results, she argues that the basis on which children understand stereotypes changes with age. Around 6 to 8 years old children have a *biological orientation*: they view gender roles as based on physical differences such as size, strength, length of hair. For example, one child argued that 'a father can get more money . . . than the lady because . . . a lady has a delicate skin, a man has tougher skin' (*ibid.*, p. 35). The next level, *societal orientation*, sees gender-based traits as the prerequisite of a social system requiring differentiated roles. This is illustrated by a 10-year-old who attributed intelligence to men because of the social roles they were expected to fulfil: 'Men are smarter because they have to do . . . thinking. They have to work at their jobs' (*ibid.* p. 38). The final level is *psychological orientation*, where children distinguished individual identity and social roles. As one student explained, the difference in male and female power arises 'because society expects women to pretend they can't protect themselves and let the men do it. In fact, they are just as able as men to do it, but they're not supposed to' (*ibid.*, p. 41). As Ullian points out, these age differences suggest that even if children of different ages do show similar stereotypes, they may differ considerably in the reasons for such stereotypes and their views about whether such stereotypes are equitable. We should, of course, treat these results with caution, as Ullian's report was a preliminary one, and we would expect children's views of stereotypes to be influenced by wider social changes, as well as by their cognitive development.

4.4.2 The link between conceptions of personality and behaviour

We have already seen that children's understanding of gender identity seems to be related to their attribution of gender-stereotyped personality attributes.

This in turn might be expected to influence their perception of and behaviour towards others. In this section, I look at the implications of changing conceptions of personality for two areas: achievement motivation and the possibility of psychological change.

What difference might your conception of disposition make to your behaviour? This was the question posed by Rholes, Jones and Wade (1988), who tried to integrate research on traditional 'person-perception' with one aspect of behaviour which has been closely linked with attribution theory: motivation and performance. Cognitive theories of motivation (e.g. Weiner, 1985) propose that success or failure has its biggest effect on future motivation when the outcome is attributed to causes that are stable, because such an attribution leads the person to expect similar outcomes in the future. That is, if you attribute your good performance in an exam to your high ability, and you see ability as a relatively fixed trait, then you will expect to do well in your next exam, too. As we have already seen, young children may not generalize from a dispositional attribution as much as older children do. Rholes *et al.* reasoned that if that were so, there should be a relation between how much children perceive traits as stable, and their reactions to success or failure. They tested this idea by finding 7- to 8-year-old children who either did or did not have a stable conception of trait terms (using material from previous work by Rholes and Ruble), and giving these children puzzles on which the experimenters contrived that the children either succeeded or failed. The experimenters then measured the children's persistence on the tasks. The outcome, success or failure, had more influence on children who had a stable conception of dispositions than on those who did not: the former group showed relatively more persistence when they succeeded, and less when they failed. Rholes, Newman and Ruble (1990) provide a fuller account of the relation of disposition concepts to achievement motivation and self-evaluation.

Other predictions might be made about the behavioural effects of different conceptions of personality: for example, Leahy (1985) speculated that the conception of personality attributes as stable could contribute to a feeling of helplessness in those who believe they have personality 'defects'. The influence of one's conceptions of traits for personal change is further examined by Sparks (1989). Little work has been done in this area with children, although there is a substantial literature on locus of control and achievement, but a study by Maas, Marecek and Travers (1978) gives some interesting clues. They investigated 7- to 11-year-olds' perceptions of disordered behaviour by asking them about three characters who were described in short vignettes, exemplifying withdrawn, antisocial and self-punitive behaviour. Younger children more often thought that these disorders were caused by internal factors (being born that way, result of physical injury), whereas older children tended to mention social-environmental causes (e.g. treatment by others). Most of the children at all ages, however, said that the characters could change their behaviour. Younger children tended to say that this could be done just by trying, whereas older children also suggested changes in the environment (e.g. moving house, seeking help from friends).

Yuill (1991) interviewed 4- to 10-year-olds to assess their understanding of the nature, origin and time-course of four different aspects of character. Older children tended to cite cognitive rather than behavioural accounts of traits, and used interactionist models of personality development; whereas younger children were more often like trait theorists. The children also differed in their beliefs about how people could change. For the younger ones, characters could simply stop being the way they were. For example, Anthea (6) said that a grumpy person could change: 'If he turned his mouth round that way [i.e. into a smile instead of a scowl] he will be happy.' Older children more often cited the use of cognitive control over characteristics: Vicky (10) described how someone could stop being grumpy: 'They could [try] to forget about [bad things], and do a lot of other things that don't make them think about it, keep themselves busy all the time.'

It was interesting to note that children at all ages had a variety of different kinds of accounts of the development of different traits: the same child might see one trait as innate, and another as determined by situations or learned via imitation. Many of the children, for example, saw shyness in children as a function of their social situation: when you go to school, you are placed among strangers and face potentially embarrassing situations such as being asked difficult questions when you don't know the answer. For many children, adulthood is a blissful time at which you have control over these circumstances: Sean (10) noted: 'When you're grown up, there's no one telling you what to do, so you can do what you want, there's no teachers.' Such children were often quite taken aback at the very thought that an adult might be shy. Stephen (10), for example, says: 'I've never seen any shy grown-ups . . . perhaps 'cos they're getting older and more mature they don't really feel really shy, perhaps they haven't got any school bullies and as they get older they see more people who they know, work in offices and everything so they see more people and it just stops.' This result again underlines the fact that we may find a different picture for different traits.

4.4.3 Cognitive development and social ecology

I have hinted in various places in this review that the idea of 'personality' assumed by most of the studies is culturally relative. Proponents of the rapidly growing field of 'ethnopsychology' (a kind of cross-cultural study of naive psychology) have been at pains to point this out. We cannot assume that every child develops towards the same final conception of personality. For example, Miller (1984) has questioned the idea that the move from concrete to abstract, trait-based descriptions of people is culturally universal. She found that traditional Hindus in India described people in terms of the relationships between them rather than using psychological traits that distinguish between individuals, and that they explained actions with respect to social context rather than attributing behaviour to internal, personal dispositions. Miller relates these differences to culturally divergent conceptions of the person: Western cultures are thought to focus on the individual as an autonomous agent, whereas in non-Western cultures such as India, people are seen as being more interdependent. The fact that Western children show increasing use of traits with age, she argues, reflects the process of *enculturation* rather than changes in cognitive abilities or cultural differences in experience – e.g. of modernization or formal education. In a subsequent paper, however, Miller (1986) does acknowledge the role of both cultural and cognitive-developmental factors in the use of trait terms. She found that 8-year-olds in both Chicago and Mysore explained actions in terms of immediate situational influences – e.g. 'he got angry so he called me a name' – and suggests that episodic, or script-based, knowledge of this kind may be a universal basis for the development of more culturally specific modes of attribution. Miller's work underlines the importance of considering both cognitive development and cultural meaning in social explanation.

The idea that non-Western cultures are not orientated towards using personality characteristics is common in the literature on ethnopsychology. For example, Black (1985), in describing the folk psychology of the Tobians in Micronesia, says:

> In common with many people who live in small, close-knit communities, Tobians label actions much more than they label persons. . . . Perhaps because they understand one another well enough to know what complex, contradictory, and situationally-dependent people [they are] . . . Tobians do not talk extensively about 'personality' or 'character'. . . . This gives Tobian discussion of persons a concrete and highly specific character. (p. 275)

Black goes on to note that Tobians instead speak of the 'foibles' of others: 'These foibles were neither morally evaluated nor taken as a reflection of some deeper, truer, inner self. They were simply accepted as interesting attributes of the behaviour of certain people' (*ibid.*). It is interesting to note that Black's description of the social ecology of Tobians bears some similarity to the environment in which young Western children are usually reared. This suggests the hypothesis that use of trait terms is fostered by living conditions which are loosely knit, with many superficial relationships rather than a few close ones.

It is not only cross-cultural evidence that gives us an insight into different conceptions of the person. Historical research also illuminates such changes, and reminds us that the concept of the private individual is a fairly recent (and largely Western) construction. For example, the very idea of an autobiography, describing individual characteristics and idiosyncrasies, would have been alien to an English person in the Middle Ages: it was only from the sixteenth century that such writings became at all common. In medieval times, personal identity was defined primarily by social rank and family, and the idea that an individual personality exists separately from and prior to a social role became current only towards the beginning of the last century (see Baumeister, 1987).

4.5 *Theoretical debates and future directions*

There are two main classes of account that have been used to explain the developments reviewed in this chapter: cognitive-developmental and social-cultural. While much of the developmental literature tends to assume that age changes reflect developmental changes, several critics, notably ethnopsychologists, have suggested that these changes might also reflect enculturation processes. In this section, I examine the different accounts of each type that have been proposed: I have characterized these broadly as cognitive-developmental and social-ecological.

The first type of explanation is that younger children lack the cognitive abilities required to use trait terms or to integrate traits into a coherent personality. This lack has sometimes been explained in Piagetian terms, by arguing that attribution of enduring psychological properties requires the concept of invariance – the idea that essential qualities of an object (e.g. its volume) or of a person (e.g. their gender) remain the same despite superficial changes in form and appearance (e.g. Rholes and Ruble, 1984; Rotenberg, 1982). This account derives support from two main types of evidence: first, the ages at which changes occur correspond roughly to those commonly associated with Piagetian or Kohlbergian stages; second, some people have found correlations between cognitive-developmental measures of stage and aspects of person-perception (e.g. Kuhn *et al.*, 1978; Rotenberg, 1982).

Other accounts of the same general kind stress the development from global to specific evaluations and from concrete (behavioural) to abstract (dispositional) descriptions (Livesley and Bromley, 1973). This type of explanation is closer to Werner's account of the nature of developmental change as increasing differentiation. Another account reflecting cognitive-developmental concerns is the idea that young children are limited by their information-processing capacity or skills. For example, social psychologists have put forward the idea that traits are prototypes (Cantor and Mischel, 1977; Chaplin, John and Goldberg, 1988), and Bennett (personal communication) has suggested that trait terms are a superordinate category which develops later than the use of the 'basic' level of desires and beliefs in explaining actions. Yet another explanation in this category is provided by Ferguson, Olthof, Luiten and Rule (1984), who suggest that children of around 5 to 6 may use information about frequency of behaviour in judging character, rather than information about the conditions with which behaviour covaries. When these two types of information conflict, young children may be unable to form a coherent impression of character because of their limited information-processing abilities.

A second sort of account is related not to cognitive competence but to sociocultural factors. The argument here is that children may be *able* to use trait terms, but do not do so for some reason. One reason is a possible difference in orientation. Rogers (1978) suggests that younger children are not interested in long-term prediction, for which trait terms might be useful, and they therefore have little use for such terms. A similar speculation is made by Corsaro (1981) in an ethnographic study of children's friendships in nursery school. He suggests that the functions of friendship in this environment are concerned with social integration and are 'seldom based on the children's recognition of enduring personal characteristics of playmates' (p. 235). These suggestions are interesting speculations, but they have not as yet received clear empirical support. One additional clue comes to us from the field of 'ecological psychology'. Barker and Gump (1964) argue that fine classification of personality is a feature of heavily populated settings, because each person is less likely to have key functions that define them than they will in a smaller setting. Instead, they are differentiated from others only by the sort of person they are, rather than what functions they perform. Although there is no direct support for resulting differences in the use of traits, it was found that children in small schools did have more functions to perform than those in large schools. As we have seen, the cross-cultural literature also supports the idea that small communities may not need to think of peers in terms of personality traits. This social-ecological approach, as I have characterized it, although it is not identified as a 'school' or theory in the way that cognitive-developmental accounts are, has much in common with a Gibsonian approach.

In very general terms, the theoretical development in this field has been dominated by the established cognitive-developmental (and largely Piagetian-inspired) view, which assumes – implicitly, at least – that conceptions of the person are universal. The more recent work on cross-cultural views of the person has primarily been descriptive, relativistic and critical of the standard cognitive-developmental view. Because the cross-cultural work is generally focused on adult views of the person, there is little information about the extent to which the developments we have traced in this chapter are universal – as is also the case with other topics in this book. Miller's work, however, suggests that both culturally relative and developmentally common influences are at work.

A third position, which has not been articulated in any detail with respect to conceptions of personality, reflects post-Piagetian views of development that underlie some of the recent work on children as theorists. Two main strands can be identified. First, the structure of one's knowledge may change as that knowledge increases (see Chi, 1978). This is an important claim, because it means that children's understanding of personality could change not because of mainly intrinsic and global cognitive-developmental changes but as a result of increasing experience with and knowledge of people. Of course, age, experience and cognitive development are usually inextricably intertwined, creating a potential problem in distinguishing different accounts of growth (see Higgins and Parsons, 1983). Second, people may structure their knowledge according to different theories which may be specific to a particular domain of knowledge (e.g. Carey's [1985] account of the change from psychological to biological accounts of bodily functions, Keil's [1989] view of conceptual change). We have seen in this chapter that understanding of personality shares some of the concepts that are part of a 'theory of mind', and to that extent we would expect the major changes in children's conceptions of the mental to influence their ideas about personality. For instance, the development of the mentalistic concepts of belief and desire may permit children to append what I have called the explanatory view of traits to their earlier, predictive use of traits. As I pointed out above, however, trait terms can be used without any underlying understanding that traits play a causal role in behaviour. That is why we need to examine not just *whether* a child uses trait terms, but also *how* they are being used – to predict or to explain? As this book shows, work on theory of mind is both developing and controversial, and our views about children's conceptions of personality will change with the development of our ideas about the child as psychologist.

Notes

1. In common with recent usage, I use gender, rather than sex, to avoid the connotation that differences are assumed to be biological – similarly, I refer to ethnic rather than racial prejudice. However, much of the previous literature uses 'sex' and 'race'.

Acknowledgements

I am grateful to Mark Bennett and Sue Leekam for constructive criticisms of drafts, and to Jane Oakhill and Robin for providing examples. Preparation of this chapter, and my studies of traits, were supported by grant No. R000232886 from the Economic and Social Research Council (UK).

References

Baldwin, C.P. and Baldwin, A.L. (1970) 'Children's judgments of kindness'. *Child Development*, 41, 29–47.
Barenboim, C. (1981) 'The development of person perception in childhood and

adolescence: From behavioural comparisons to psychological constructs to psychological comparisons'. *Child Development*, **52**, 129–44.

Barenboim, C. (1985) 'A response to Berndt and Heller'. In S.R. Yussen (ed.) *The Growth of Reflection in Children*. Orlando, FL: Academic Press.

Barker, R.G. and Gump, P.V. (1964) *Big School, Small School: High school size and student behavior*. Stanford, CA: Stanford University Press.

Bartsch, K. and Wellman, H. (1989) 'Young children's attribution of action to beliefs and desires'. *Child Development*, **60**, 946–64.

Baumeister, R.F. (1987) 'How the self became a problem: A psychological review of historical research'. *Journal of Personality and Social Psychology*, **52**, 163–76.

Bem, S.L. (1989) 'Genital knowledge and gender constancy in preschool children'. *Child Development*, **60**, 649–62.

Bennett, M. (1985–6) 'Developmental changes in the attribution of dispositional features'. *Current Psychological Research and Reviews*, **4**, 323–9.

Berndt, J.J. and Heller, K.A. (1985) 'Measuring children's personality attributions'. In S.R. Yussen (ed.) *The Growth of Reflection in Children*. Orlando, FL: Academic Press.

Black, P.W. (1985) 'Ghosts, gossips and suicide: Meaning and action in Tobian folk psychology'. In G.M. White and J. Kirkpatrick (eds) *Person, Self and Experience: Exploring Pacific ethnopsychologies*. Berkeley, CA: University of California Press.

Bretherton, I. and Beeghly, M. (1982) 'Talking about internal states: The acquisition of an explicit theory of mind'. *Developmental Psychology*, **18**, 906–21.

Cantor, N. and Mischel, W. (1977) 'Traits as prototypes: Effects on recognition memory'. *Journal of Personality and Social Psychology*, **35**, 38–48.

Carey, S. (1985) *Conceptual Change in Childhood*. Cambridge, MA: MIT Press.

Ceci, S.J., Caves, R.D. and Howe, M.J.A. (1981) 'Children's long-term memory for information that is incongruous with their prior knowledge'. *British Journal of Psychology*, **72**, 443–50.

Chaplin, W.F., John, O.P. and Goldberg, L.R. (1988) 'Conceptions of states and traits: Dimensional attributes with ideals as prototypes'. *Journal of Personality and Social Psychology*, **54**, 541–57.

Chi, M.T.H. (1978) 'Knowledge structures and memory development'. In R. Siegler (ed.) *Children's Thinking: What develops?* Hillsdale, NJ: Erlbaum.

Corsaro, W.A. (1981) 'Friendship in the nursery school: Social organisation in a peer environment'. In S.R. Asher and J.M. Gottman (eds) *The Development of Children's Friendships*. Cambridge: Cambridge University Press.

Craig, G. and Boyle, M.E. (1979) 'The recognition and spontaneous use of psychological descriptions by young children'. *British Journal of Social and Clinical Psychology*, **18**, 207–8.

Damon, W. and Hart, D. (1988) *Self-Understanding in Childhood and Adolescence*. Cambridge: Cambridge University Press.

Eder, R.A. (1989) 'The emergent personologist: The structure and content of 3½, 5½, and 7½-year-olds' concepts of themselves and other persons'. *Child Development*, **60**, 1218–28.

Etaugh, C., Levine, D. and Mennella, A. (1984) 'Development of sex biases in children: 40 years later'. *Sex Roles*, **10**, 913–24.

Ferguson, T.J., Olthof, T., Luiten, A. and Rule, B.G. (1984) 'Children's use of observed behavioural frequency versus behavioural covariation in ascribing dispositions to others'. *Child Development*, **55**, 2094–105.

Gnepp, J. and Chilamkurti, C. (1988) 'Children's use of personality attributions to predict other people's emotional and behavioural reactions'. *Child Development*, **59**, 743–54.

Harris, P.L. (1989) *Children and Emotion: The development of psychological understanding*. Oxford: Blackwell.

Harris, P.L., Johnson, C.N., Hutton, D., Andrews, G. and Cooke, T. (1989) 'Young children's theory of mind and emotion'. *Cognition and Emotion*, **3**, 379–400.

Heller, K.A. and Berndt, T.J. (1981) 'Developmental changes in the formation and organisation of personality attributions'. *Child Development*, **52**, 623–91.

Higgins, E.T. and Parsons, J.E. (1983) 'Social cognition and the social life of the child: Stages as subcultures'. In E.T. Higgins, D.N. Ruble and W.W. Hartup (eds) *Social Cognition and Social Development: A sociocultural perspective*. Cambridge: Cambridge University Press.

Hoffner, C. and Cantor, J. (1985) 'Developmental differences in responses to a television character's appearance and behaviour'. *Developmental Psychology*, **21**, 1065–74.

Honess, T. (1979) 'Children's implicit theories of their peers: A developmental analysis'. *British Journal of Psychology*, **70**, 417–24.

Honess, T. (1981) 'Girls' and boys' perceptions of their peers: Peripheral versus central and objective versus interpretative aspects of free descriptions'. *British Journal of Psychology*, **72**, 485–97.

Keil, F.C. (1989) *Concepts, Kinds, and Cognitive Development*. Cambridge, MA: MIT Press/Bradford Books.

Kuhn, D., Nash, D.C. and Brucken, L. (1978) 'Sex-role concepts of two- and three-year-olds'. *Child Development*, **49**, 445–51.

Leahy, R.L. (1985) 'The costs of development: Clinical implications'. In R.L. Leahy (ed.) *The Development of the Self* (pp. 267–94). Orlando, FL: Academic Press.

Leahy, R.L. and Hunt, T.M. (1983) 'A cognitive-developmental approach to the development of the concept of intelligence'. In R.L. Leahy (ed.) *The Child's Construction of Social Inequality* (pp. 135–60). New York: Academic Press.

Livesley, W.J. and Bromley, D.B. (1973) *Person Perception in Childhood and Adolescence*. London: Wiley.

Maas, E., Marecek, J. and Travers, J. (1978) 'Children's conceptions of disordered behaviour'. *Child Development*, **49**, 146–54.

Miller, J.G. (1984) 'Culture and the development of everyday social explanation'. *Journal of Personality and Social Psychology*, **46**, 961–78.

Miller, J.G. (1986) 'Early cross-cultural commonalities in social explanation'. *Developmental Psychology*, **22**, 514–20.

Miller, P.J. and Aloise, R.R. (1989) 'Young children's understanding of the psychological causes of behaviour: A review'. *Child Development*, **60**, 257–85.

Mohr, D.M. (1978) 'Development of attributes of personal identity'. *Developmental Psychology*, **14**, 427–8.

Peabody, D. (1985) *National Characteristics*. Cambridge: Cambridge University Press.

Peevers, B.H. and Secord, P.F. (1973) 'Developmental changes in attribution of descriptive concepts to persons'. *Journal of Personality and Social Psychology*, **27**, 120–8.

Reeder, G.D. and Brewer, M.B. (1979) 'A schematic model of dispositional attribution in interpersonal perception'. *Psychological Review*, **86**, 61–79.

Rholes, W.S., Jones, M. and Wade, C. (1988) 'Children's understanding of personal dispositions and its relationship to behaviour'. *Journal of Experimental Child Psychology*, **45**, 1–17.

Rholes, W.S., Newman, L.S. and Ruble, D.N. (1990) 'Understanding self and other: Developmental and motivational aspects of perceiving persons in terms of invariant dispositions'. In E.T. Higgins and R.M. Sorrentino (eds) *Handbook of Motivation and Cognition, vol. 2: Foundations of Social Behavior* (pp. 369–407). New York: Guilford.

Rholes, W.S. and Ruble, D.N. (1984) 'Children's understanding of dispositional characteristics of others'. *Child Development*, **55**, 550–60.

Ridgeway, D., Waters, E. and Kuczaj, S.A. (1985) 'Acquisition of emotion-descriptive language: Receptive and productive vocabulary norms for ages 18 months to 6 years'. *Developmental Psychology*, **21**, 901–8.

Rogers, C. (1978) 'The child's perception of other people'. In H. McGurk (ed.) *Issues in Childhood Social Development* (pp. 107–29). London: Methuen.

Rotenberg, K.J. (1982) 'Development of character constancy of self and other'. *Child Development*, **53**, 505–15.

Ruble, D., Newman, L., Rholes, W. and Altshuler, J. (1988) 'Children's "Naive Psychology": The use of behavioral and situational information for the prediction of behavior'. *Cognitive Development*, **3**, 89–112.

Saltz, E. and Medow, M.L. (1971) 'Concept conservation in children: The dependence of belief systems on semantic representations'. *Child Development*, **42**, 1533–42.

Shantz, C.U. (1983) 'Social cognition'. In J.H. Flavell and E.M. Markman (eds) *Cognitive Development*, vol. 3 of P.H. Mussen (series ed.) *Handbook of Child Psychology* (4th edn) (pp. 495–555). New York: Wiley.

Snodgrass, S.R. (1976) 'The development of trait inference'. *Journal of Genetic Psychology*, **128**, 163–72.

Sparks, P. (1989) 'The interpretation of dispositions: Social psychological perspectives'. Unpublished D.Phil. thesis, University of Oxford.

Ullian, D.Z. (1976) 'The development of conceptions of masculinity and feminity'. In B. Lloyd and J. Archer (eds) *Exploring Sex Differences* (pp. 25–47). London: Academic Press.

Weiner, B. (1985) 'An attributional theory of achievement motivation and emotion'. *Psychological Review*, **92**, 548–73.

Williams, J.E. and Best, D.L. (1982) *Measuring Sex Stereotypes: A thirty-nation study*. Beverly Hills, CA: Sage.

Yuill, N. (1991) 'Children as implicit personality theorists: Definitions of trait terms and their use in explaining individual differences in personality' (Working Papers in Psychology no. 3). Psychology Group, University of Sussex.

Yuill, N. (1992) 'Children's production and comprehension of trait terms'. *British Journal of Developmental Psychology*, **10**, 131–42.

Yuill, N. (in press) 'Children's conception of personality traits: A critical review and analysis'. *Human Development*.

Yussen, S.R. and Kane, P.T. (1983) 'Children's ideas about intellectual ability'. In R.L. Leahy (ed.) *The Child's Construction of Social Inequality* (pp. 109–33). New York: Academic Press.

Chapter 5

Understanding of social rules
Judith G. Smetana

5.1 Introduction

Developing an understanding of social rules is one of the major tasks of childhood. Children encounter a wide variety of social rules and expectations in different social settings, and an understanding of these rules is necessary if one is to be a competent member of society. Social rules may be articulated explicitly by parents and teachers ('Don't hit!', 'Use your fork, not your fingers') or the law ('You must be 16 years old to drive in New York'); or they may be implicit in children's social interactions (other children may laugh when sex-role expectations are violated). Social rules may govern social regularities that seem unimportant or are taken for granted ('Say please when you ask for something'), as well as expectations whose violations have serious consequences ('It's wrong to kill'). This chapter considers children's understanding of all these different types of social rules. It should be noted that although the focus is on children's rule understanding, most of the research to be discussed is on children's understanding of social rule *violations* (that is, transgressions). This is because it is typically assumed that the social rules that organize behaviour may be most accessible to study in situations where they are violated.

The chapter begins with a description of a conceptual model for categorizing different types of social rules. Next, the development of children's rule knowledge is examined, focusing both on what develops and on the processes that account for development. Then, children's understanding of social rules in different social contexts, including the family, schools and culture, is considered. Finally, an understanding of social rules in special populations, including rejected children, deaf children, retarded children and abused and neglected children, will be discussed.

5.2 Domains of social rules

How should social rules be conceptualized? Do children treat all social rules alike? Or are there systematic differences in the way children think about the types of social rules they experience? Researchers and theorists have taken different positions on these questions. One assumption has been that children have a unitary concept of social rules, and treat all social rules alike (Piaget, 1932/1965; Kohlberg, 1969). For instance, Piaget (1932/1965) studied children's understanding of the rules of the game of marbles. From his interviews with young children, he attempted to generalize from children's concepts of game rules to their concepts of moral rules. Piaget, as well as Kohlberg (1969), maintained that young children treat all rules in the same way because they stem from the commands of authority. With age, children progress from viewing rules as fixed and unalterable to viewing them as changeable by general agreement or mutual consent.

The assumption guiding this chapter, in contrast, is that children have varied social experiences, including experiences with different types of social rules, and that these lead to the development of a differentiated conception of social rules. The primary distinction to be addressed here is between children's concepts of *moral* and *social-conventional* rules. Consider the following examples, both observed during the course of observations in daycare centres:

Event A: Lisa, Michael and David are all rocking in the rocking boat. Jenny, who has been waiting nearby for a turn, finally approaches. As the rocking slows down, she bites Lisa in the arm. Lisa screams and then cries.

Event B: It is a hot day, and the teachers decide to take the children outside to play in the baby pool. Jason has forgotten his bathing suit, so the teachers tell him to pick one from the box of discarded bathing suits. He picks a pink suit. The teachers tell him he can't wear that one because it's a girl's bathing suit. He persists and says that that is the one he wants to wear today. The teachers repeatedly attempt to dissuade him. After prolonged discussion among themselves, they decide to let him wear it. He proudly puts it on. The other toddlers are oblivious to this breach of social convention.

Both are social events; both were prohibited in the child's classroom. From the child's perspective, however, they differ in important ways. Consider Event A. Lisa does not need to be told that it is wrong to bite; she can infer it from the pain or injury she experienced. Similarly, so can Jenny, Michael and David, as observers to the event. Now consider Event B. There is no intrinsic basis for knowing that it is wrong for boys to wear pink. This understanding comes from knowledge of accepted uniformities, or prohibitions within specific social systems. In fact, it is totally arbitrary that in American culture little boys wear blue (and rarely wear pink), whereas little girls wear pink (and rarely wear blue). In other settings or other cultures, the reverse could be equally acceptable.

Event A is an example of a *moral* transgression. Moral rules pertain to issues such as others' welfare (harm), trust, or the fair distribution of resources. For example, moral rules may pertain to issues such as hitting or hurting another (an extreme example is killing another) or how property should be shared. Moral knowledge is thought to be constructed from the intrinsic consequences of acts for persons. Because moral events have consequences for others' rights and welfare, moral rules are hypothesized to be obligatory, non-alterable, and applicable across situations, and the wrongness of moral acts is thought to be non-contingent on specific social rules or authority dictates (Turiel, 1979, 1983).

In contrast, Event B is an example of a *social convention*. Conventional knowledge is constructed from an understanding of the social system and refers to the arbitrary and consensually agreed-upon behavioural uniformities that structure social interactions within social systems. For example, all cultures have rules governing modes of address (titles, greetings), acceptable dress, manners and sex roles. The exact form of each of these conventions may differ – some individuals eat with forks and others with chopsticks – but despite these differences in form, conventions serve the same function: they provide members of a social unit with shared expectations about how to behave. In doing so, conventional rules regulate social interactions. Because they are agreed-upon, they can be changed (Smetana, 1983; Turiel, 1983). In contrast to moral rules, conventional rules are hypothesized to be contextually relative, arbitrary and changeable, and the wrongness of conventional acts is hypothesized to be contingent on the rules and dictates of authority. Morality and social convention are hypothesized to be distinct types of social knowledge that develop in parallel out of different types of social interactions (Turiel, 1979, 1983; Turiel and Davidson, 1986). This distinction between moral and conventional rules is also one that has been made by many moral philosophers (Dworkin, 1978; Gewirth, 1978; Mill, 1863/1968; Rawls, 1971).

In addition to moral and conventional rules, other types of social rules have been described. For instance, based upon Black's (1962) formal analysis, Much and Shweder (1978) further differentiate moral and conventional rules from instructions (techniques, recipes or 'know-how') and truths (beliefs). However, their observations in pre-schools and kindergartens indicate that violations of conventional and moral rules account for almost all (90 to 95 per cent) breaches observed at these ages. Given this finding, and that these additional rule categories have received little research attention, they will not be considered further in this chapter, although it is useful to keep these distinctions in mind.

Children also encounter many rules that regulate acts that involve safety, harm to the self, comfort and health (for instance: 'Wear a helmet when riding a bicycle'; 'Stoves are hot'; 'Wear your mittens when you go outside in the snow'). These rules have been referred to as *prudential* rules, and research indicates that children distinguish between prudential and moral rules (Shweder, Turiel and Much, 1981; Tisak and Turiel, 1986). Both moral and prudential rules regulate acts that have physical consequences to persons. Moral rules, however, pertain to interactions between people, whereas prudential rules pertain to acts that have negative consequences to the self (for instance, harm occurring through carelessness). Those consequences are immediate and directly perceptible to the actor (Shweder, Turiel and Much, 1981). Relatively less research has examined the development of children's understanding of prudential rules than moral or conventional rules, but this research will be mentioned when relevant. The criteria distinguishing moral, conventional and prudential rules are presented in Table 5.1.

5.2.1 Methods of assessing children's rule knowledge

A great deal of research has examined children's understanding of social rules. In this research, children's rule knowledge has been assessed in two ways. First, children have been asked to make judgements along a set of dimensions that are hypothesized to differentiate moral and conventional

Table 5.1 Domains of social rule understanding

Moral	
Definition:	Prescriptive, categorical judgements of right and wrong
Structured by:	Concepts of justice
Examples:	Issues of welfare, rights, fair distribution of resources, trust
Criteria:	Impersonality, generalizability, obligation, independence from rules and authority, unalterable
Conventional	
Definition:	Behavioural uniformities that structure social interactions within social systems
Structured by:	Concepts of social organization
Examples:	Modes of address, dress, sex roles, manners
Criteria:	Rule contingency, alterability, contextualism, relativity, subject to rules and authority jurisdiction
Prudential	
Definition:	Acts that have negative consequences for the self
Structured by:	Concepts of the person
Examples:	Acts involving safety, comfort, health – for instance, wearing mittens in the winter, not touching electrical outlets
Criteria:	Rule utility, generalizability, rule contingency

rules. The questions (referred to as *criterion judgements*) are drawn from formal definitions of the domains and are used to assess subjects' classification of social issues as moral or conventional. For example, children have been asked to judge whether it would be all right to commit the acts if there were no rules about them in school, assessing the acts' contingency on rules. They have also been asked whether it would be all right to commit the acts at home or in another school, and whether it would be permissible to change the rule, assessing the acts' generalizability and the alterability of rules pertaining to them, respectively. Another question that has been used widely in research pertains to whether the acts would be permissible if an authority (for instance, the teacher) permitted them. This question assesses children's judgements regarding the acts' contingency on authority.

In addition, assessments have also been made of children's *justifications* for their judgements (for instance, 'Why it is wrong to break a promise?'). Children typically justify the wrongness of moral transgressions by appealing to fairness ('I don't think it would be fair'), others' welfare ('Because somebody could have gotten hurt'), or obligation ('Because my conscience would bother me'); whereas they typically justify the wrongness of conventional transgressions by appealing to the rules or commands of authority ('Because if they make the rules, you should abide by them'), desires to avoid punishment ('It's not OK because she could get into trouble'), the disorder created by the act ('It would be a mess'), references to norms or expectations ('Because you always do it when you marry'), or the need for social coordination ('Everyone needs to do their part so that the work gets done').

5.2.2 Supporting research evidence

Moral and conventional rules
A great deal of research has been conducted on children's understanding of moral and social rules. This research has focused on a number of issues, including the age-related differences in children's rule knowledge, the contexts or conditions that affect children's judgements of social rules, and children's judgements about more complex social issues. In general, this research has indicated that children across a wide age range distinguish between moral and social-conventional rules and transgressions in their reasoning and judgements (see Turiel, Killen and Helwig, 1987, for a review of research). Let us now turn to a study of young children's social judgements (Smetana, 1981) which illustrates both the research methods that have typically been used and the pattern of findings that have been obtained.

The subjects in this research were middle-class pre-school children (both boys and girls) divided into two age groups. The younger group ranged from 30 to 42 months of age; and the older group from 44 to 57 months of age.

Children were shown drawings depicting familiar moral and conventional transgressions. The moral items pertained to hitting, not sharing, shoving, throwing water at another child, taking another child's apple; the conventional items pertained to rules that were enforced at the nursery schools, including not participating in show-and-tell, not sitting on the rug during story time, not saying grace before snack, not putting a toy away in the correct place, and not putting belongings in the designated place.

For each transgression, children were asked to make judgements regarding rule contingency ('Would it be all right to commit the act if there was no rule about it in the pre-school?') and generalizability ('Would it be all right to commit the act at home or in another school?'), as well as the seriousness of the acts and the amount of punishment the transgressor deserved. (Children's justifications for their judgements were not assessed in this study, owing to the limited verbal abilities of very young children.)

The results indicated that pre-school children as young as 2½ distinguish between moral and conventional rule violations. Children judged moral transgressions to be more wrong in the absence of rules, more serious, more deserving of punishment, and less contextually relative than conventional transgressions. Furthermore, with one exception, no age differences were found in these judgements; all children maintained the distinction between the domains, although their judgements of moral transgressions were more clearly differentiated than their judgements of conventional transgressions.

In this study, as well as in most other studies of children's judgements about social rules, children have been asked to evaluate rules and transgressions that are presented hypothetically, in the form of pictures or stories. In a recent study, however, pre-school children's judgements about hypothetical transgressions were compared to their judgements about actual transgressions they witnessed in their pre-school (Smetana, Schlagman and Adams, 1993). In this study, hypothetical transgressions were evaluated in the same way as in the aforementioned study. Judgements about actual events were obtained by interviewing children immediately after they witnessed (but were not directly involved in) actual moral and conventional transgressions in their pre-school classrooms. Few differences in judgements about hypothetical and actual transgressions were observed, but there was some evidence that children made clearer distinctions between moral and conventional rules when judging hypothetical than actual transgressions. This result may seem surprising; for instance, one could hypothesize that actual events would be more vivid than hypothetical transgressions, and therefore easier to evaluate. The authors hypothesized, however, that when transgressions become contextualized in specific situations, other considerations – such as children's relationships to the victim and transgressor, as well as extenuating circumstances surrounding the event – may influence their judgements.

Although the aforementioned studies indicate that moral transgressions may be judged to be more serious than conventional transgressions, the severity of the transgression is not considered to be a formal criterion for distinguishing moral and conventional rules and transgressions. For instance, it is possible to think of examples where a conventional violation could be more serious than a moral transgression. Therefore, Tisak and Turiel (1988) specifically manipulated the seriousness of hypothetical transgressions to determine whether distinctions in children's judgements of moral and conventional rules merely reflect their evaluations of the seriousness of the events, or whether, as is claimed, children are making distinctions between qualitatively different types of social rules. These researchers asked children to compare a moral transgression with minor consequences (stealing an eraser) with a moral transgression with major consequences (hitting someone) and a major conventional transgression (wearing pyjamas to school). A pilot study conducted before the actual study had indicated that children considered this to be a very serious transgression because it could result in much ridicule to the child and disruption in school. When forced to choose, the majority of children stated that a person would be more likely to commit the minor moral transgression rather than the major conventional act. Asked what one should do, however, children chose the major conventional transgression over either the major or minor moral transgression. Furthermore, children judged the major conventional transgression to be less wrong than either of the moral transgressions. These last two judgements were both justified on the grounds that the moral transgressions would result in negative consequences for others (that is, others' welfare). Thus, these findings suggest that differences between morality and social convention are not solely quantitative and based on the seriousness of the transgressions, but rather are made on the basis of fundamental differences between the acts.

So far, these studies have focused on children's judgements about transgressions, but a study by Weston and Turiel (1980) clarifies the relations between children's evaluations of acts and rules. In this study, children either evaluated specific acts (for instance, a child taking his clothes off on the playground because it was too warm, or a child hitting another child) with no reference to rules, or they evaluated the same events described in the context of school rules that either permitted or prohibited the acts. When children were asked to evaluate the acts independent of any information regarding school policy, the majority negatively evaluated the acts, and negative evaluations of the conventional acts increased with age. However, children considered the nature of the act when evaluating acts in relation to rules. The majority stated that it was all right for the schools to permit the conventional acts, but not the moral acts, and rules regarding moral acts were evaluated on the basis of the negative consequences of each act. Likewise, when schools were described as permitting the acts, children evaluated actors described as engaging in conventional acts (but not moral acts) positively, and the majority predicted that the teacher would not respond to the conventional acts because of school policy. When evaluating hitting, however, children were evenly divided between those who stated that the teacher would not respond (in accord with school policy) and those who stated that the teacher would reprimand the child, in spite of school policy. Thus, children's evaluations of conventional acts were contingent on the presence or absence of rules, whereas moral transgressions were negatively evaluated, whether or not the acts were socially regulated.

To summarize these important results: children are rule-orientated when they think about conventional acts, but they focus on the negative consequences of the acts for persons when they think about moral rules. This stands in contrast to Piaget's (1932/1965) and Kohlberg's (1969) theories. They hypothesized that young children believe that all rules should be maintained because they stem from the commands of authority. With age and increasing social experience, children focus more on the consequences of acts for others. The research by Weston and Turiel, however, demonstrates that children's rule orientation depends on the type of act under consideration.

Prudential rules

In the research discussed thus far, we have focused on distinctions in children's judgements of moral and conventional rules. But a recent study by Tisak (in press) examined pre-school children's judgements regarding moral and prudential rules. Pre-school children evaluated stories concerning violations of pre-school rules. The violations pertained to similar issues and had similar consequences, but differed in whether the violation resulted in consequences to persons other than the actor. For instance, one moral act pertained to a child pushing another child off the swing, whereas the matched prudential act pertained to a child purposely jumping off the swing. Children judged that moral transgressors (like children pushing other children off a swing) deserved more punishment than prudential violators (like children harming themselves). Although the consequences of the events were the same, children judged that peers violating moral rules should get more punishment than children who violated the prudential rules. Furthermore, when the degree of harm was varied, children judged that peers who caused minor physical harm to others (minor moral transgressions) deserve more punishment than peers who caused more serious physical consequences to themselves (major prudential transgressions). Finally, children judged moral rule violations to be more wrong than prudential rule violations, even when the consequences of the prudential rule violations were more severe than the consequences of the moral rule violations. Thus, this study demonstrates that pre-school children have a clear understanding of rules that are designed to protect physical safety, but they evaluate those rules as less important, and rule violations as less serious, than violations of moral rules.

5.2.3 Issues of rule overlap

The examples and research discussed thus far suggest that all rules are clearly distinguishable as strictly moral, conventional or prudential. In fact, the social world is more complex than this, and many rules or events can be seen as multifaceted, entailing components of different rule domains. For instance, the law specifying that drivers in the United States must drive on the right-hand side of the road can be seen as a primarily conventional regularity: the law is arbitrary, it is alterable by consensus, and a different conventional arrangement (such as driving on the left-hand side of the road) would serve the same function of organizing social behaviour. At the same time, however, violations of the law can clearly cause great harm to others. There are many other examples of issues that entail overlaps between two domains.

The proposition that children differentiate among different types of social rules does not preclude the possibility that in some instances, rules or events may overlap the different domains, and children will need to consider different components of the situation in making judgements about them. Turiel (1983) has suggested that such multifaceted situations may take three forms: (1) those in which conventional concerns for social organization entail injustices (such as in a caste system); (2) second-order events in which a violation of a convention results in psychological or physical harm to others adhering to the convention (such as in the driving example just given); and (3) ambiguous multidimensional events, where individuals make different domain attributions about the same event. For instance, many hotly debated social issues such as abortion or homosexuality can be seen as examples of such multifaceted issues, and research indicates that reasoning about multifaceted events entails the coordination (or failure to coordinate) moral, conventional or personal features of the situations (Smetana, 1982; Turiel, Hildebrandt and Wainryb, 1991). Although issues of domain overlap in children's rule knowledge will not be given further consideration in this chapter, it is important to acknowledge the complexity of the social world and children's understanding of it.

These studies demonstrate a surprisingly sophisticated awareness of social rules. The findings discussed in this section indicate that very young (i.e. pre-school) children make distinctions between different types of social rules, and that children distinguish between acts and rules. Finally, research indicates that children recognize and distinguish acts that overlap different social knowledge domains. These findings lead to two questions about the development of children's rule understanding: What develops? and What processes account for this understanding? We consider each of these questions in turn in the next sections.

5.3 Development of children's rule knowledge

5.3.1 What develops?

The finding that young children make distinctions in different types of social rules raises two questions: First, if social rule understanding is differentiated by the pre-school period (ages 3 to 5), when does this awareness develop? And second, do these results indicate that pre-school children's rule understanding is as sophisticated as adults' rule knowledge? In this section we consider several studies that provide some answers to these questions.

Smetana's study (1981) suggests that by 3½ years of age, children distinguish between familiar moral and conventional rules and transgressions. The results of this study, therefore, suggest that even younger children must be studied to trace the origins of children's rule understanding. In a more recent study, Smetana and Braeges (1990) examined 2- and 3-year-old children's judgements to determine when distinctions in judgements of moral and conventional transgressions differed, and the effects of language development on those judgements.

The children in this study were divided between boys and girls at three ages: 2 years, 2 months; 2 years, 10 months; and 3 years, 6 months. In individual interviews, children judged the permissibility, seriousness, generalizability, and rule and authority contingency of ten familiar moral and conventional transgressions (depicted using pictures), as well as the amount of punishment the transgressors deserved. With age, children increasingly distinguished between moral and social-conventional transgressions. The youngest children in the study (the 2-year-olds) did not distinguish moral from conventional transgressions on any of the dimensions. Children's judgements that acts are wrong in different contexts appeared to be the earliest-developing criterion for distinguishing social rules; children who were nearly 3 years old judged moral transgressions to be more generalizably wrong than conventional transgressions, but they did not make distinctions on any of the other dimensions included in this study. In contrast, 3½-year-old children judged moral transgressions to be significantly more independent of rules and authority, more generalizably wrong, and more serious than conventional transgressions.

Furthermore, children with more advanced language development distinguished moral rule violations from conventional rule violations at earlier ages than did children with less advanced language development. Children who responded correctly to the language items distinguished the transgressions on the basis of whether acts were generalizably wrong (or contextually relative) at 2 years of age (as compared to nearly 3 years of age for the sample as a whole) and on the basis of authority contingency at nearly 3 years of age (as compared to 3½ years of age for the sample as a whole). Nevertheless, these findings raise an important question regarding the relations between language and thinking. Thus, it is unclear whether children 'know more than they can say' – that is, whether their knowledge of social rules develops before language – or whether language development is necessary for the acquisition of an understanding of social rules. Rudimentary distinctions between familiar moral and social-conventional transgressions are made during the third year of life, and are more consistently made and firmly established by the fourth year of life. As might be expected, children's ability to make differentiated social judgements is related to more advanced language development. This study clearly demonstrates that the ability to distinguish between moral and conventional rules develops in early childhood.

Another study by Davidson, Turiel and Black (1983) points to aspects of rule understanding that develop during middle childhood. In this study, 6-, 8- and 10-year-old children made judgements and provided justifications for moral and conventional transgressions that were classified as either familiar or unfamiliar issues. Familiarity was assessed by whether the child knew anyone personally who experienced the act or had actively considered and thought about the event. For instance, one of the moral events that was judged to be familiar by a majority of children pertained to a boy who bullies a group of children in the playground, pushing one of them off the top of the slide. One of the moral events that was judged to be unfamiliar by a majority of children pertained to an emergency-room surgeon who leaves his post due to boredom, although there is no one to relieve him.

Three results are of interest here. As would be expected, children distinguished between moral and conventional acts, and the types of reasons children at all ages gave differed for moral and conventional issues. Justifications pertaining to fairness, others' welfare and obligation were used in connection with moral issues. In contrast, justifications pertaining to appeals to authority, punishment avoidance, and customs or traditions were used in connection with conventional issues. Thus, the results of this study are consistent with the other studies in demonstrating that children distinguish social events as moral or conventional in terms of justifications and identifiable criteria.

In addition, however, children distinguished the domains more for familiar than for unfamiliar issues, and the unfamiliarity of the issue had more of an effect on the responses of younger than older children. That is, the youngest children (the 6-year-olds) distinguished between moral and conventional events more sharply on familiar than on unfamiliar issues. Thus, with age, children are able to apply criteria to a broader and broader range of social events. Development proceeds from a reliance on specific personal experiences to an ability to abstract or generalize to unfamiliar events.

Also, there were age differences in the types of justifications used, suggesting that reasoning, or level of conceptual understanding, develops within a given domain and becomes more sophisticated with age. Although younger and older children were equally likely to explain that moral transgressions are wrong because they cause harm, older children were much more likely to refer to fairness in condemning these transgressions. So, in the moral domain, reasoning develops from a focus primarily on others' welfare to reasoning which also includes a notion of reciprocity between individuals' rights. In the conventional domain, in contrast, there was a decrease with age in children's appeals to authority and the avoidance of punishment. Thus, conventional reasoning develops from a focus on the expectations of authority and the avoidance of punishment to a focus on the functions of convention in coordinating social interactions.

Similar age differences were found in the study by Tisak and Turiel (1988) on children's judgements of the seriousness of transgressions described above. They found that the distinctions between morality and convention were made more comprehensively by older children. This finding suggests that whereas young children have developed the competence to distinguish moral from conventional events, there are situations in which the distinction is not clearly applied. Furthermore, Tisak and Turiel (1988) found similar age differences in reasoning as those described by Davidson, Turiel and Black (1983). That is, they found that with age, children's moral reasoning shifted from a focus on others' welfare to a focus on fairness and rights. Children's conventional reasoning showed age-related increases in responses focusing on the role of conventions in structuring social interactions.

The studies discussed in this section suggest that although children distinguish between different types of social rules at very early ages (that is, during the pre-school years), with age they apply these distinctions to a broader range of social events, including more abstract and unfamiliar social events. Furthermore, level of conceptual understanding within a domain changes with age.

5.3.2 Origins of social rule understanding

There are several potential explanations that might account for the development of children's rule understanding. One possibility is that an awareness of social rules is a biological given – that is, that it is somehow 'hard-wired' into individuals. Another possibility is that an awareness of different types of social rules is socialized through the explicit or implicit teaching of adults.

The third possibility – the one that is advanced here – is that children's rule understanding is actively constructed through their social interactions. Children have different types of social experiences, and it has been proposed that moral and conventional judgements are constructed from the different features of their social interactions (Turiel, 1979, 1983). To return to the example given at the beginning of this chapter: Lisa did not need to be told that it is wrong to bite. She could infer it from the pain she experienced. Similarly, so could Jenny, David and Michael, as observers to the event. The hypothesis is that from their experiences as victims and observers of transgressions, children develop prescriptive judgements of right and wrong. (This is not to say that instructions from adults are not important for moral rule understanding. Rather, feedback from adults can be seen as providing one type of information about the wrongness of acts.) In contrast, children's experiences with regulations in specific social contexts lead to the construction of conventional concepts. For instance – to return to the second example given at the beginning of the chapter – Jason's experience with adult reactions to his breach in convention leads to an understanding of the norms expected for his behaviour.

To test these hypotheses, researchers have looked for systematic patterns of differentiated social interactions that parallel hypothesized distinctions in social concepts. Correspondences between social interactions and social judgements are seen as demonstrating that social interactions provide the experiential basis for the construction of social knowledge (Turiel, Smetana and Killen, 1991). Children's responses to naturally occurring violations of moral and conventional rules have been examined in a series of observational studies; responses to violations of prudential rules have also been examined, although to a lesser extent. In these studies, children have ranged in age from infants and toddlers (Smetana, 1989a, 1989b) and pre-school children (Much and Shweder, 1978; Nucci and Turiel, 1978; Smetana, 1984; Tisak, Nucci, Baskind and Lamping, 1991) to school-age children (Blumenfeld, Pintrich and Hamilton, 1987; Nucci and Nucci, 1982a, b). Furthermore, children have been studied in different contexts, including the home (Dunn and Munn, 1987; Smetana, 1989a, 1989b), daycare centres and nursery schools (Much and Shweder, 1978; Nucci and Turiel, 1978; Smetana, 1984; Tisak *et al.*, 1991), school classrooms (Blumenfeld *et al.*, 1987; Nucci and Nucci, 1982a) and playgrounds (Nucci and Nucci, 1982b). The purpose of these studies has been to determine whether moral and conventional interactions differ qualitatively. To examine these questions (and in contrast to the research discussed thus far), researchers have conducted observational studies of naturally occurring moral and conventional (and less frequently, prudential) interactions in different contexts.

The results of these studies demonstrate that social interactions in the context of moral, conventional and prudential transgressions differ – in terms of who responds to transgressions, as well as the *type* of response that occurs. Both adults and children (primarily the victims) respond to moral trans-gressions in ways that provide feedback about the effects of acts for others' rights or welfare. For instance, adult responses to moral disputes (such as hitting, pushing and not sharing objects) typically focus on requests to take the victim's perspective ('How would you feel if he did that to you?') and evaluations of rights ('She had it first – give it back!'). From very early childhood on, children initiate responses to moral transgressions, and their responses also focus on the consequences of the acts. For instance, they respond with statements of injury or loss ('Ouch – you hurt me!'), emotional reactions (cries, shrieks, screams, etc.) and evaluations of rights ('That's mine!'), as well as with physical retaliation and commands to cease the offending behaviour ('Stop that right now!'). These responses are consistent with the notion that children's moral understanding can be derived from the acts themselves rather than from the rules that regulate the acts.

In contrast to moral transgressions, the research demonstrates that until middle childhood, adults primarily respond to children's conventional transgressions. This suggests that adults are more concerned with regulating social conventions and maintaining social order than are young children, at least when the conventions that are studied are generated by adults. One intriguing study (Killen, 1989) suggests that even young children respond when the conventions are generated by the children themselves. Furthermore, researchers (Much and Shweder, 1978; Nucci, Turiel and Gawrych, 1983) who have distinguished between cultural conventions and school regulations have found that only adults responded to regulations but that pre-school children responded to other children's breaches of cultural conventions. With age, children become increasingly likely to respond to school conventions, with the greatest increase occurring between the second and fifth grades (Nucci *et al.*, 1983).

Adult responses to children's conventional transgressions generally focus on commands to cease the behaviour and statements focusing on aspects of social organization, such as statements regarding the disorder the act creates, rules and sanctions. By about the age of 7, children respond to other children's conventional transgressions with sanctions and statements of ridicule (Nucci and Nucci, 1982a, b). Thus, responses to conventional transgressions focus on the expected regularities in the social system (that is, information about what is acceptable in different contexts and what is not), leading to the development of an understanding of cultural, social group and familial conventions. These results are suggestive, but further research needs to test more directly the hypothesis that these social interactions provide the experiential basis for the development of children's understanding of moral and conventional rules.

Two observational studies have been conducted on social interactions regarding prudential rule violations. In one study, mothers' and peers' responses to toddlers' prudential transgressions (as well as moral and conventional transgressions) were examined in the home (Smetana, 1989a). The other study focused more specifically on young children's moral and prudential interactions in the pre-school (Tisak *et al.*, 1991). This research indicates that moral transgressions are much more frequent among young children than are prudential transgressions, and reveals that adults respond to violations of prudential rules, whereas children do not (Smetana, 1989a; 1989b; Tisak *et al.*, 1991). Furthermore, responses to moral transgressions typically focus on the harm that has actually occurred, whereas with prudential transgressions, teachers respond in the face of potential harm (Tisak *et al.*,

1991). Finally, adult responses to prudential rule violations typically focus on rationales for why the acts are wrong (Smetana, 1989a, 1989b).

Much and Shweder (1978) propose that an understanding of social rules can also be obtained from a more fine-grained analysis of speech behaviour. They argue that cultural rules and expectations are continually tested, employed, clarified and negotiated in moments of everyday life, which they refer to as situations of accountability. Adults' and children's speech provide tacit messages about the expectations of particular social contexts. For instance, they describe an example of some nursery-school children who have got their clothes wet and are changing into spare clothes kept by the school. The children are in a dressing area with a double door that opens separately above and below. Two boys attempt to peek over the top as the girls change. The girls' comments ('Don't look!' 'Keep the doors locked!') can be expanded to provide the cultural message that one should not watch while others undress. Much and Shweder argue that such situations of accountability provide a series of cultural control messages, and that children's understanding of social rules is socially transmitted in such encounters.

Another study focusing on the inference process children use to make domain distinctions (Smetana, 1985) provides further clues as to how social rule understanding develops. In this study, a methodology was developed that separated the content of familiar transgressions from associated features hypothesized to distinguish moral and conventional actions. Children were presented with stories that varied different features of moral and conventional interactions, but in which the content of the events themselves was un-specified (by using nonsense words instead of actual words). Thus, the features of interactions that generate differentiated judgements were examined independent of children's knowledge of the content of specific events.

Children heard either stories describing transgressions that were familiar and enforced in their pre-schools, or stories where the events themselves were not specified. In these stories the events were depicted by nonsense words, and the stories described attributes associated with the moral and conven-tional domains (the consistency of the prohibitions regarding the events and the types of responses to the actions). In some stories, for example, events were depicted as prohibited in two contexts (home and pre-school), whereas in others events were depicted as prohibited only in pre-school. This manipulation varied the consistency of prohibitions. Some of the stories described 'moral' reactions to the unspecified transgressions (for instance, another child cried); whereas other stories depicted teachers issuing com-mands to stop the behaviour.

As expected, pre-school children differentiated between familiar moral and conventional transgressions. As in other studies, children reasoned that moral transgressions are wrong because they affect others' welfare, whereas social-conventional transgressions are wrong because they create disorder. Although the results of this study are complex, they indicate that pre-school children focus on the nature of the acts when they reason and make judgements about events that affect others, whereas they focus on the presence of rules in the absence of apparent harm or violation of rights. Thus, the basis for the differentiation between morality and convention in early childhood appears to lie in children's ability to infer different features of moral and conventional actions.

5.4 Children's understanding of social rules in different contexts

Children encounter rules in a variety of different contexts, including the family, daycare, schools and the broader society. In this section, we consider children's rule understanding in these different contexts.

5.4.1 The family

Children's earliest experiences of social rules typically occur in the context of the family. Although a great deal of research has examined mothers' child-rearing strategies (e.g. Kuczynski, 1984; Maccoby and Martin, 1983), considerably less research has considered how children's awareness of social rules develops in the context of the family. (Although there has been a great deal of research on young children's compliance to maternal commands, this research typically does not make distinctions among the types of commands mothers make, or consider the implications of mothers' behaviour for children's developing social rule knowledge.)

The results of several observational studies in the home suggest that children begin to be concerned about adult standards during the end of the second year of life. In two studies, Dunn and Munn (1985, 1987) examined 14- to 36-month-old infants' interactions with their mothers and siblings to illuminate how toddlers' understanding of social rules develops in the context of family interactions. Dunn and Munn (1985) found that none of the mothers of 14-month-olds explicitly referred to social rules, except by referring to acts as 'naughty' or 'good'. However, from observations of children's non-verbal reactions to their siblings' rule violations (for instance, looking and smiling at the mother, observer or sibling while such transgressions were being carried out, or drawing the attention of the mother or sibling to these events), these researchers inferred that children were aware of social rule violations by 16 to 18 months of age. They also noted a significant increase between 18 and 24 months of age in the number of conflict incidents in which mothers referred to social rules in addressing the child. As children grew older, mothers also offered increasingly sophisticated justifications to their children, and correspondingly, children offered more sophisticated reasons to explain their misbehaviour. Furthermore, in a study examining differences in 2- and 3-year-old toddlers' interactions with mothers and familiar peers, Smetana (1989) observed an age-related increase in the frequency of conventional transgressions in the home. Although it is possible that the absolute number of these violations increases during these years, it is more probable that these differences represent mothers' increasing demands for conventionally appropriate behaviour; by 3 years of age, children are expected to understand and remember familiar conventional rules.

In all three studies, differences were also found in mothers', children's, siblings' and peers' interactions regarding moral and conventional transgressions. For instance, Dunn and Munn (1987) found that conflicts with siblings occurred chiefly over issues of rights, possessions and property, whereas children argued with mothers over a wide range of topics. Similarly, Smetana (1989) found that conflicts with peers occurred primarily over possessions, rights, taking turns and hurting, aggression and unkindness (all moral issues), whereas conflicts with mothers occurred primarily over manners and politeness, rules of the house and cultural conventions (all conventional issues). This finding is consistent with the notion that an understanding of moral rules develops primarily from children's interactions with peers (Damon, 1977; Piaget, 1932/1965), whereas an understanding of social conventions develops from experiences of regularities in different social settings.

Furthermore, the results of these studies provide some explanations as to why children's understanding of moral rules appears to be more advanced than their understanding of conventional rules during the pre-school years. Mothers were more likely to offer justifications for disputes over rights than over other topics, and children were more likely to show anger or distress in rights disputes than in disputes over other topics (Dunn and Munn, 1987). Mothers were more likely to provide commands to cease the behaviour without providing explanations for why the acts were wrong for conventional transgressions than for moral transgressions (Smetana, 1989). Thus, children appear to receive information about the consequences of their moral violations for others' rights and welfare from two sources: first, they receive feedback in the form of directly experienced or observed negative reactions from the victims of moral transgressions; and complementarily, adults also provide explanations as to why the acts are wrong. In contrast, the wrongness of conventional events cannot be inferred directly from the acts themselves, and adults provide fewer explanations regarding these acts.

Another series of studies have examined children's concepts of parental authority for different types of social rules. For instance, a study by Tisak (1986) examined children's conceptions of the jurisdictional boundaries of parental authority. Almost all 6- to 11-year-old children in this study judged that parents had the legitimate authority to make rules about stealing (a moral issue) and doing family chores (a conventional issue). Almost all children, however, judged that parents did not have the authority to legislate friendships. Furthermore, whereas almost all children (about 98 per cent) judged that children have an obligation to adhere to the rules about stealing and doing family chores, the majority (about 65 per cent) judged that one does not have an obligation to adhere to a rule pertaining to friendship. Their reasoning about friendship was based primarily on concerns with individual preferences and prerogatives, and this reasoning about personal choice increased with age. Thus, children appear to draw boundaries to legitimate parental authority, and these boundaries depend on the type of action under consideration.

Another study examining conceptions of parental authority among adolescents and their parents (Smetana, 1988) demonstrates that parental authority decreases during adolescence for some types of issue, but not for others. In this study, both adolescents and parents were found to believe that parents have legitimate authority to make rules regarding moral transgressions that occur in the context of the family (such as lying to parents or hitting brothers and sisters) as well as conventional misbehaviour in the home (such as not doing assigned chores or calling parents by their first names). Their reasons for these judgements were based on moral and conventional concerns. Furthermore, these judgements did not change across adolescence; even older adolescents judged that parents should retain authority over these issues. With age, however, adolescents were more likely to treat issues such as their choice of activities, personal appearances, friendship choices, and keeping their room clean as under their personal jurisdiction and outside the bounds of legitimate parental authority. Furthermore, children at all ages were more likely to see these issues as legitimately within their own authority (and outside parents' jurisdiction) than did parents, although with adolescents' increasing age, parents granted them more jurisdiction over these issues. These differences may account for the parent–child conflict that is typically observed during adolescence.

5.4.2 Daycare

There has been increasing interest in the effects of daycare on children's social development (Clarke-Stewart, 1989; Phillips, McCartney, Scarr and Howes, 1987). One study (Siegal and Storey, 1985) has examined the effects of social experience in daycare on children's social rule knowledge. In this study, daycare veterans (pre-school children who had been in daycare at least 18 months and on average 2½ years) were found to differentiate moral and conventional rule violations more sharply than did daycare newcomers, who had been enrolled in the same daycare centre as the veterans for the past three months. Daycare veterans and new enrollees did not differ in their evaluations of moral transgressions, but they did differ in their evaluations of conventional transgressions, which pertained to conventions of the daycare setting and were therefore largely unfamiliar to the new enrollees. New enrollees judged conventional transgressions to be significantly naughtier, more deserving of punishment, and more wrong contingent on teachers' authority than did daycare veterans. Thus, this study demonstrates that social experience in a new setting (in this case, daycare) is necessary to acquire an understanding of the conventional rules of that setting, although an understanding of moral rules appears to transcend the specific context. Further research needs to examine the effects of daycare on younger children's understanding of social rules.

5.4.3 Schools

Although most of the research on children's conceptions of social rules has been conducted in schools, there has been surprisingly little research examining children's conceptions of school rules. Two exceptions are studies by Blumenfeld, Pintrich and Hamilton (1987) and Nucci and Nucci (1982a). Blumenfeld and her colleagues examined first-through-fifth-grade children's reasoning about classroom norms, including moral, conventional and academic issues. In addition, they distinguished between conventions which are social and pertain to interpersonal issues (such as talking in class) and conventions which are academic and pertain to work (for instance, preparedness). Children reasoned about both academic conventions and academic achievement primarily in terms of prudence, including statements about the external consequences of actions to the self ('You'll have to do it over'), the internal consequences to the self ('It shows you're smart when you get all the answers right') and attributions focused on goals for the self ('It means you learned when you get your math right'). To a lesser extent, children reasoned about these acts in terms of external sanctions or grades. In contrast, children reasoned about moral and conventional norms primarily in terms of others' welfare.

Although the prevalence of reasoning about others' welfare in reference to social-conventional violations is surprising, several of the events chosen as examples of classroom social conventions, such as lining up properly and talking in class, are what others (Smetana, 1983; Turiel, 1983) have referred to as second-order conventions, or conventions that may have moral consequences. Indeed, in their study of second-, fifth- and seventh-grade classrooms, Nucci and Nucci (1982a) distinguished between these different types of conventional violations and found differences both in children's judgements and in teachers' responses to the events. For instance, in the simple conventional cases (such as talking in class when it did not affect others), teachers responded with commands, reminders and rules, and children treated the transgressions as conventions. In the case of second-order conventional violations (for instance, talking in class that prevented students from hearing a movie), however, teachers responded with requests to take others' perspectives (a typically moral response), and children treated the events as moral.

Hamilton, Blumenfeld, Akoh and Muira (1989) replicated the study by Blumenfeld and her colleagues in Japan to compare American and Japanese children's reasoning about academic, moral and procedural conventional rules. They found similar distinctions in both cultures: children were more likely to reason about others' welfare in relation to moral than conventional or academic issues. Japanese children, however, gave significantly more internal reasons for academic performance than did American children. For instance, Japanese children were more likely to reason that they should adhere to academic rules ('Because I want to learn new things'), whereas American children were more likely to reason that 'the teacher expects it'. Thus, both these studies demonstrate that children differentiate among different types of classroom norms, but they also demonstrate cross-cultural differences in reasoning about academic conventions.

Geiger and Turiel (1983) studied the relationship between the developmental level of children's reasoning about social conventions and disruptive school behaviour. Their subjects were seventh- and eighth-grade students, half of whom had a record of disruptive school behaviour and half of whom were non-disruptive, as indicated by school records and school counsellors. When the students were first tested, all of them (except one) in the disruptive group were at a developmental level in their understanding of conventional concepts involving a rejection of the necessity for many conventions and rules, a critical orientation to the dictates of those in authority, and a view that conventions are the arbitrary expectations of others. Students in the non-disruptive group, however, were typically at a more advanced developmental level. These children affirmed the importance of conventions because they had developed systematic concepts of social organization. They viewed adherence to conventions and rules as necessary if they were to be part of the social system, and regarded conventions as serving necessary societal functions.

Children in the disruptive group were reinterviewed one year later. The school records indicated that slightly less than half of this group were still classified as disruptive, whereas the remainder were now classified as non-disruptive. Children's developmental level of understanding of conventional concepts was reassessed. Those who were still classified as disruptive had not progressed in their thinking regarding social conventions; their thinking still entailed a critical attitude towards the role of conventions as part of the rule system and a rejection of organizational rules. In contrast, those who had become non-disruptive over the year had developed a more systematic understanding of conventions as regulation within hierarchical social systems. Thus, this study indicates that the school-related social behaviour of adolescents is related to changes in developmental levels of thinking. Furthermore, students' disruptive behaviour did not generalize across social rules or situations. Disruptive students did not engage in delinquent or criminal behaviour; the disruptive behaviour was limited to rules and conventions related to the social-organizational aspects of school life. Rejection of school conventions was not related to a rejection of moral rules. Thus, these findings demonstrate that social behaviour is related to children's developmental level of reasoning about social rules.

5.4.4 Public versus private settings

Miller and Bersoff (1988) argue that children's and adults' acceptance of conventional rules depends on their perceived social utility, as well as the social setting in which they apply. That is, they propose that rules are likely to be regarded as legitimate social conventions to the extent that they are seen as functional in meeting interests common to all members of a social group. Furthermore, they propose that rules would also be accepted as legitimate conventions if they were set in contexts in which access was a matter of privilege rather than rights. To test these hypotheses, they asked some subjects (7- and 11-year-olds, and adults) about social rules that were described as applying in various public settings entered voluntarily by individuals (for instance, a public park); whereas they asked other subjects (at the same ages) about the same rules now described as applying to various private settings entered voluntarily as a discretionary privilege (for instance, a private health club). Furthermore, they compared subjects' understanding of rules that were either high in social utility (for instance, involving issues of order maintenance and efficiency) or low in social utility (for instance, involving issues of etiquette and propriety).

Their results suggest that rules about actions that are seen as having low social utility tend to be categorized in conventional terms in private settings and in personal terms in public settings. This suggests that children's and adults' orientation to rules depends in part on the context in which a rule is enforced. Children and adults view conventional rules as more legitimate in private than in public contexts, and when they pertain to acts that are important for regulating social interactions.

5.4.5 Culture

A number of studies have examined children's rule understanding in different cultures. One purpose for much of this research has been to test the notion, found in both popular and social scientific writings, that Western culture is individualistic in contrast to other cultures – for instance, Eastern cultures – which are described as collectivistic and interdependent. The research discussed in this chapter suggests, however, that children's conceptions of social rules are differentiated across cultures. Because moral rules govern behaviour that has consequences for others' rights and welfare, it would be expected that for the most part, moral rules would be cross-culturally generalizable. In contrast, the definition of social conventions as arbitrary and agreed-upon uniformities that are contextually relative suggests that social conventions are culturally specific.

The coexistence of moral and conventional rules has been studied in a number of cultures, including Ijo children and adolescents in Nigeria (Hollos, Leis and Turiel, 1986), children in Zambia (Zimba, 1987), children and adolescents in Korea (Song, Smetana and Kim, 1987), secular urban Jews, secular kibbutz Jews, and traditional Arab villagers in Israel (Nisan, 1987), pre-school children in St Croix (the Virgin Islands), and children and adults in India (Shweder, Mahapatra and Miller, 1987). It is important to note that the purpose of these studies was *not* to delineate the sets of social acts or issues that are classified as moral or conventional in different cultures. (As Shweder and Levine [1984] have argued, cataloguing these differences is tantamount to reducing cultural anthropology to a travelogue.) Rather, their purpose was to determine whether children in different cultures make similar distinctions among different types of social rules. The moral transgressions examined in these studies are generally events that are considered wrong in most cultures (for instance, harming another or stealing). The conventional transgressions, however, are culturally specific. In the study in Nigeria, for instance, one of the items pertained to eating with the left hand (Hollos, Leis and Turiel, 1986); whereas in Korea, the conventional items included taking shoes off before entering a room and eating with fingers instead of using chopsticks (Song, Smetana and Kim, 1987). In these studies, children and adolescents have been asked to evaluate acts using the same criteria employed in previous research.

The distinction between moral and conventional rules has been found in almost all the cultures studied, although some cultural differences have been found, primarily in the types of justifications children use. Korean children and adolescents, for instance, make much greater use of justifications pertaining to social status, social roles, appropriate role behaviour and courtesy, whereas these concerns are not commonly observed in American children's reasoning (Song, Smetana and Kim, 1987). Ijo children and adolescents in Nigeria (Hollos, Leis and Turiel, 1986) and Arab children in Israel (Nisan, 1987) affirm the importance of customs and tradition to a greater degree than American children typically do. Thus, rather than finding collectivistic versus individualistic orientations across cultures, the results of these studies suggest that there is a mixture of social judgements, actions and concerns of persons within cultures. Individuals may uphold personal rights or freedoms in certain situations, and they may subordinate individual goals to the welfare of the group in other situations.

There is some dispute, however, over the interpretation of the cross-cultural findings. For instance, based on research in New Delhi, Miller and Luthar (1989) argue that Indian children's and adults' moral reasoning is not based solely on justice considerations, as is the case for American children and adults. They argue that Indians apply their moral code in a more contextual manner than do Americans, and that in India, moral reasoning about justice coexists with a focus on role-based interpersonal responsibilities (duty). Furthermore, Miller, Bersoff and Harwood (1990) argue that Indian culture has a broader and more stringent view of one's social responsibilities to others than does American culture. Therefore, the debate about the role of culture in children's understanding of social rules is far from resolved. The research provides evidence that there is cross-cultural applicability of distinctions between moral and social-conventional rules, although the conventions are culturally variable. However, research needs to focus more specifically on how children's experiences in different social contexts lead to the development of their understanding of social rules and the social world.

5.5 Rule understanding in special populations

A number of studies have examined rule understanding among children with disabilities. These studies have been conducted to elucidate rule understanding in children who have different social experiences by virtue of their special status as a child with a disability (or a different level of social skills). Such comparative studies can also be used to shed light on development in normal children. For instance, abused and neglected children have been studied to test hypotheses about the role of social experience in the development of social judgements (Smetana, Kelly and Twentyman, 1984). As moral judgements have been hypothesized to be constructed from children's experiences with the consequences of actions for others, it was hypothesized that children who have extended experiences with abuse or neglect would be more sensitive to justice or welfare issues, and treat these events as less permissible than other children.

In this study, maltreated children were divided between those who had primarily been abused and those who had primarily been neglected. Their judgements were compared to those of a control group of non-maltreated children who were matched in age, sex, race and IQ. In this study, the moral items pertained to physical harm, psychological distress and unfair resource distribution. Few differences between maltreated and non-maltreated children's judgements were found, but those differences were consistent with the nature of the maltreatment. Abused children considered psychological distress to be more universally wrong than neglected children, whereas neglected children considered the unfair distribution of resources to be more universally wrong than abused subjects. As denial of access to physical resources has been defined as one aspect of neglect, and psychological distress is an aspect of abuse, these results suggest that maltreated children's social experiences are related to their increased sensitivity to the wrongness of related moral transgressions. Thus, abused and neglected children differ from non-maltreated children only in moral judgements that may be seen as most closely related to their own experiences of maltreatment.

Another study by Rachford and Furth (1986) examined rule understanding in profoundly and pre-lingually deaf children living in residential schools. These authors were interested in determining whether profoundly deaf children who do not have ready access to the verbal system of communication would develop different ideas about interpersonal interactions and social rules than would hearing children. Nine- to 18-year-old children who were deaf before the age of 2, and had a minimum hearing loss of 85 decibels Pure Tone Average, were compared to a group of same-aged hearing subjects from the local schools. Children were asked about a game rule, a school conventional rule (no running in the hall), and a societal conventional rule (the law specifying 16 as the legal age for driving). Children were asked whether the rule could be changed, whether the rule must be obeyed, and the purpose of the rule.

With age, all children were more likely to view all three types of rules as changeable. Deaf students, however, were more likely than hearing students to say that rules cannot be changed. Moreover, for each rule at each age, deaf children lagged behind hearing children, and deaf children were less advanced in their social understanding of school and societal rules than game rules. This slower development in deaf children may be due to the greater incidence of socio-emotional behaviour problems and lower social maturity. However, deaf children's less mature understanding of school and societal rules than game rules may be due to the fact that these children have less opportunity actively to manipulate these rules. Thus, the findings argue powerfully for the role of social experience in the development of social understanding.

Another study by Schmidt, Nucci and Kahn (1991) examined retarded adolescents' understanding of social rules. Based upon previous research which indicates that cognitive development in retarded children follows the same sequence and pattern – albeit at a slower rate – than in non-retarded individuals, this study examined the hypothesis that retarded adolescents' reasoning and judgements would be consistent with the patterns observed among non-retarded children of similar mental age. Subjects in this study were twelve retarded adolescents who ranged in age from 16 to 21, but their mental age ranged from 4 to 11.

Several findings are of interest here. First, as was expected, retarded adolescents discriminated between moral and conventional rule violations using a variety of criteria. However, these subjects judged a higher proportion of conventional items as wrong in the absence of rules than has generally been found in studies using non-retarded subjects. The researchers proposed that this might be because retarded children typically experience a highly structured and rule-orientated classroom environment. Consistent with this explanation, retarded adolescents' justifications were highly dependent on appeals to authority or the absence of rules themselves. Indeed, as was hypothesized, their justifications were consistent with the types of justifications given by young children in previous research (Davidson *et al.*, 1983). Also, the developmental maturity of their reasoning about social conventions was more consistent with their mental age than with their chronological age. Thus, the results of this study indicate that retarded adolescents make distinctions between moral and social rules, although they do so in a way that is consistent with young children's judgements.

Finally, Sanderson and Siegal (1988) examined relationships between peer status and pre-school children's conceptions of moral and social rules. To classify children's peer status, each child was asked to name the three children with whom they most liked to play and the three children with whom they least liked to play. On the basis of these peer nominations, children were classified as controversial, popular, average, neglected or rejected. The popular group consisted of children who received many nominations as a child others most like to play with. These children were rarely nominated as someone with whom others did not want to play. Controversial children were those who received many nominations in both categories – that is, others nominated them in the categories of both highly desirable and undesirable playmate. Rejected children were highly nominated as children with whom others did not want to play. Neglected children were seen as having low social impact – that is, they were rarely nominated in either category.

Regardless of peer status, all children judged moral transgressions to be more serious, more generalizably wrong, and more independent of rules than conventional transgressions. Children's judgements of the deservedness of punishment, however, differed according to their peer status. All four non-rejected groups (controversial, popular, average and neglected children) rated moral transgressions as deserving more punishment than social-conventional transgressions, but rejected children did not discriminate between the punishment due to perpetrators of moral and conventional rule violations. Conceptions of punishment due to perpetrators of rule transgressions may be a more salient feature of social acceptance in the pre-school than other judgements. Furthermore, controversial children rated moral transgressions as deserving significantly more punishment than did their popular counterparts, regardless of how long children had attended the daycare centres. Interestingly, the rule conceptions of popular and average children did not differ. Thus, a knowledge of distinctions between moral and social rules may be an important but insufficient condition for popularity in pre-schoolers.

These studies suggest that there are some differences in both the rate of acquisition and the types of social judgements made by children with disabilities or poorer social skills. These findings illuminate the role of social experience in the development of children's understanding of social rules.

5.6 Summary and directions for future research

To summarize: these studies indicate that both normal and atypical children distinguish between different types of social rules, including moral, conventional, prudential and academic rules; and that these distinctions are made by children both in Western and in non-Western cultures (although the specific conventions may vary). Although children's understanding of social rules has been assessed primarily in the context of interviews that focus on hypothetical rules and transgressions, similar distinctions are found when children make judgements about actual transgressions they witnessed (Nucci and Turiel, 1978; Smetana, Schlagman and Adams, 1993). Observations in the family suggest that an understanding of social rules develops during the second year of life (Dunn and Munn, 1985, 1987). These distinctions can be assessed by the third year of life and are related to children's language development (Smetana and Braeges, 1990). An understanding of social rules does not appear to be obtained solely through the learning of specific prohibitions, but is constructed out of children's social interactions.

Thus, the research discussed in this chapter suggests that children actively interpret their social worlds, and that even at very early ages they have differentiated conceptions of social rules. The evidence indicates that children distinguish between rules that are prescriptive and pertain to others' welfare and rights, and rules that are arbitrary, contextually relative, and function to structure social interactions in different social settings. This view of children's social understanding stands in contrast to earlier theorizing by Piaget (1932/1965) and Kohlberg (1969), who proposed that young children are orientated solely towards the rules and commands of authorities, and that a differentiated conception of social rules develops out of a global confusion between morality and social convention.

The findings from the research discussed here do have practical implications. The research suggests, for instance, that to facilitate development, parents and teachers need to respond to children's transgressions in domain-differentiated ways. That is, they should respond to moral transgressions in ways that focus the transgressor on the harm or violation of rights caused by their behaviour, whereas they should respond to conventional transgressions by focusing on the effects on the social system (for instance, the disorder created). Previous research also suggests that children prefer responses to transgressions that are domain-consistent to those that are domain-inconsistent or undifferentiated (Nucci, 1984).

It should be noted that the focus of this chapter has been on children's *thinking* about social rules, not on their rule-following *behaviour*. Although the emphasis on children's conceptions is in keeping with the focus of this volume, it is also consistent with the proposition (Blasi, 1980; Turiel and Smetana, 1984) that thinking guides behaviour, and that an understanding of children's thinking is necessary to understand their social behaviour. According to this view, judgements and behaviour are related, although not always straightforwardly (Turiel and Smetana, 1984). A variety of factors may attenuate relationships between judgements and behaviour, but it would be expected that these would affect behaviour in systematic and specifiable ways.

Although a great deal of evidence in support of the views described here has been obtained, there are a number of unanswered questions. For instance, relationships between children's understanding of social rules and their social and moral behaviour would bear further investigation. Also, the connections between children's differentiated social interactions and the development of their social rule understanding needs to be examined directly, preferably through longitudinal research. In addition, the research has concentrated primarily on children's judgements regarding prototypical items in different domains. This has been a deliberate strategy to establish that children distinguish different types of social rules, events and transgressions, and to determine the ages and conditions in which these differentiated social judgements occur. However, there is a need for more research on everyday judgements. This includes greater attention to issues of domain overlap – for instance, in children's and adults' judgements regarding controversial social issues, as well as how aspects of situations affect social judgements. In addition, future research needs to consider the effect of children's social relations on their social judgements. For instance, we do not know whether social judgements vary when the victim or transgressor is a friend or family member. Another related area that has received little attention from researchers from this perspective is the role of affect in children's social judgements (Harris, 1989; for some recent exceptions, see Arsenio, 1988; Arsenio and Kramer, 1992). Finally, as noted above, the debate over cultural determinants and differences in children's social rule understanding is far from resolved and deserves further research.

The research discussed in this chapter indicates that with age, children apply their knowledge of social rules to an increasingly wide range of social events and social issues, including those that are ambiguous, controversial and complex. Further research will be needed to map the conditions and factors that transform young children's differentiated (but rudimentary) understanding of simple prohibitions and rules to adults' social and moral judgements regarding the complex dilemmas facing society.

References

Arsenio, W.F. (1988) 'Children's conceptions of the situational affective consequences of sociomoral events'. *Child Development*, **58**, 1611–22.
Arsenio, W.F. and Kramer, R. (1992) 'Victimizers and their victims: Children's

conceptions of the mixed emotional consequences of moral transgressions'. *Child Development*, **63**, 915–27.

Black, M. (1962) *Model and Metaphors*. Ithaca, NY: Cornell University Press.

Blasi, A. (1980) 'Bridging moral cognition and moral action: A critical review of the literature'. *Psychological Bulletin*, **88**, 1–45.

Blumenfeld, P.C., Pintrich, P.R. and Hamilton, V.L. (1987) 'Teacher talk and students' reasoning about morals, conventions, and achievement'. *Child Development*, **58**, 1389–401.

Clarke-Stewart, K.A. (1989) 'Infant day care: Maligned or malignant?' *American Psychologist*, **44**, 266–73.

Damon, W. (1977) *The Social World of the Child*. San Francisco, CA: Jossey-Bass.

Davidson, P., Turiel, E. and Black, A. (1983) 'The effect of stimulus familiarity on the use of criteria and justifications in children's social reasoning'. *British Journal of Developmental Psychology*, **1**, 49–65.

Dunn, J. and Munn, P. (1985) 'Becoming a family member: Family conflict and the development of social understanding in the second year'. *Child Development*, **56**, 480–92.

Dunn, J. and Munn, P. (1987) 'Development of justification in disputes with mother and sibling'. *Developmental Psychology*, **23**, 791–8.

Dworkin, R. (1978) *Taking Rights Seriously*. Cambridge, MA: Harvard University Press.

Geiger, K.M. and Turiel, E. (1983) 'Disruptive school behavior and concepts of social convention in early adolescence'. *Journal of Educational Psychology*, **75**, 677–85.

Gewirth, A. (1978) *Reason and Morality*. Chicago, IL: University of Chicago Press.

Hamilton, V.L., Blumenfeld, P.C., Akoh, H. and Miura, K. (1989) 'Japanese and American children's reasons for the things they do in school'. *American Journal of Educational Research*, **26**, 545–71.

Harris, P.L. (1989) *Children's Understanding of Emotion*. Cambridge: Cambridge University Press.

Hollos, M., Leis, P.E. and Turiel, E. (1986) 'Social reasoning in Ijo children and adolescents in Nigerian communities'. *Journal of Cross-Cultural Psychology*, **17**, 352–74.

Killen, M. (1989) 'Context, conflict, and coordination in early social development'. In L.T. Winegar (ed.) *Social Interaction and the Development of Children's Understanding* (pp. 114–36). Norwood, NJ: Ablex.

Kohlberg, L. (1969) 'Stage and sequence: The cognitive-developmental approach to socialization'. In D. Goslin (ed.) *Handbook of Socialization Theory and Research* (pp. 347–480). Skokie, IL: Rand McNally.

Kuczynski, L. (1984) 'Socialization goals and mother–child interaction: Strategies for long-term and short-term compliance'. *Developmental Psychology*, **20**, 1061–73.

Maccoby, E.E. and Martin, J.A. (1983) 'Socialization in the context of the family: Parent–child interaction'. In P.H. Mussen (series ed.) *Handbook of Child Psychology, vol. 4: Socialization, Personality and Social Development* (pp. 1–102). New York: Wiley.

Mill, J.S. (1863/1968) *Utilitarianism*. New York: Washington Square Press.

Miller, J.G. and Bersoff, D.M. (1988) 'When do American children and adults reason in social conventional terms?' *Developmental Psychology*, **24**, 366–75.

Miller, J.G., Bersoff, D.M. and Harwood, R.L. (1990) 'Perceptions of social responsibilities in India and the US: Moral imperatives or personal decisions?' *Journal of Personality and Social Psychology*, **58**, 33–47.

Miller, J.S. and Luthar, S. (1989) 'Issues of interpersonal responsibility and accountability: A comparison of Indians' and Americans' moral judgments'. *Social Cognition*, **7**, 237–61.

Much, N. and Shweder, R.A. (1978) 'Speaking of rules: The analysis of culture in breach'. In W. Damon (ed.) *New Directions for Child Development, vol. 1: Moral Development* (pp. 19–40). San Francisco, CA: Jossey-Bass.

Nisan, M. (1987) 'Moral norms and social conventions: A cross-cultural comparison'. *Developmental Psychology*, **23**, 719–25.

Nucci, L.P. (1984) 'Evaluating teachers as social agents: Students' ratings of domain-appropriate and domain-inappropriate teacher responses to transgressions'. *American Educational Research Journal*, **21**, 367–78.

Nucci, L.P. and Nucci, M.S. (1982a) 'Children's social interactions in the context of moral and conventional transgressions'. *Child Development*, **53**, 403–12.

Nucci, L.P. and Nucci, M.S. (1982b) 'Children's responses to moral and social-conventional transgressions in free-play settings'. *Child Development*, **53**, 1337–42.

Nucci, L.P. and Turiel, E. (1978) 'Social interactions and the development of social concepts in preschool children'. *Child Development*, **49**, 400–7.

Nucci, L.P., Turiel, E. and Gawrych, G. (1983) 'Children's social interactions and social concepts: Analyses of morality and convention in the Virgin Islands'. *Journal of Cross-Cultural Psychology*, **14**, 468–87.

Phillips, D.A., McCartney, K., Scarr, S. and Howes, C. (1987) 'Selective review of infant day care research: A cause for concern'. *Zero to Three*, **7**, 18–21.

Piaget, J. (1932/1965) *The Moral Judgment of the Child*. New York: Free Press.

Rachford, D. and Furth, H.G. (1986) 'Understanding of friendship and social rules in deaf and hearing adolescents'. *Journal of Applied Developmental Psychology*, **7**, 391–402.

Rawls, J. (1971) *A Theory of Justice*. Cambridge, MA: Cambridge University Press.

Sanderson, J.A. and Siegal, S. (1988) 'Conceptions of moral and social rules in rejected and nonrejected preschoolers'. *Journal of Clinical Child Psychology*, **17**, 66–72.

Schmidt, M.F., Nucci, L. and Kahn, J.V. (1991) 'Development of conventional reasoning in trainable mentally retarded adolescents'. Unpublished manuscript, University of Illinois at Chicago.

Shweder, R.A. and Levine, R.A. (1984) *Culture Theory: Essays on mind, self, and emotion*. Cambridge, MA: Cambridge University Press.

Shweder, R.A., Mahapatra, M. and Miller, J.G. (1987) 'Culture and moral development'. In J. Kagan and S. Lamb (eds) *The Emergence of Morality in Young Children* (pp. 1–82). Chicago, IL: University of Chicago Press.

Shweder, R.A., Turiel, E. and Much, N. (1981) 'The moral intuitions of the child'. In J.H. Flavell and L. Ross (eds) *Social-Cognitive Development: Frontiers and possible futures* (pp. 288–305). Cambridge: Cambridge University Press.

Siegal, M. and Storey, R.M. (1985) 'Day care and children's conceptions of moral and social rules'. *Child Development*, **56**, 1001–8.

Smetana, J.G. (1981) 'Preschool children's conceptions of moral and social rules'. *Child Development*, **52**, 1333–6.

Smetana, J.G. (1982) *Concepts of Self and Morality: Women's reasoning about abortion.* New York: Praeger.

Smetana, J.G. (1983) 'Social-cognitive development: Domain distinctions and co-ordinations'. *Developmental Review*, 3, 131–47.

Smetana, J.G. (1984) 'Toddlers' social interactions regarding moral and conventional transgressions'. *Child Development*, 55, 1767–76.

Smetana, J.G. (1985) 'Preschool children's conceptions of transgressions: The effects of varying moral and conventional domain-related attributes'. *Developmental Psychology*, 21, 18–29.

Smetana, J.G. (1988) 'Adolescents' and parents' conceptions of parental authority'. *Child Development*, 59, 321–35.

Smetana, J.G. (1989a) 'Toddlers' social interactions in the context of moral and conventional transgressions in the home.' *Developmental Psychology*, 25, 499–508.

Smetana, J.G. (1989b) 'Toddlers' social interactions in the context of harm'. Unpublished manuscript, University of Rochester.

Smetana, J.G. and Braeges, J.L. (1990) 'The development of toddlers' moral and conventional judgments'. *Merrill-Palmer Quarterly*, 36, 329–46.

Smetana, J.G., Kelly, M. and Twentyman, C.T. (1984) 'Abused, neglected, and nonmaltreated children's conceptions of moral and conventional transgressions'. *Child Development*, 55, 277–87.

Smetana, J.G., Şchlagman, N. and Adams, P. (1993) 'Preschoolers' judgments about hypothetical and actual transgressions', *Child Development*, 64.

Song, M.J., Smetana, J.G. and Kim, S.Y. (1987) 'Korean children's conceptions of moral and conventional transgressions'. *Developmental Psychology*, 23, 577–82.

Tisak, M.S. (1986) 'Children's conceptions of parental authority'. *Child Development*, 57, 166–76.

Tisak, M.S. (in press) 'Preschool children's judgments of moral and personal events', *Merrill-Palmer Quarterly*.

Tisak, M.S., Nucci, L.P., Baskind, D.E. and Lamping, M.G. (1991) *Preschool children's social interactions: An observational study.* Paper presented at the annual meeting of the American Psychological Association, San Francisco, August.

Tisak, M.S. and Turiel, E. (1986) 'Children's conceptions of moral and prudential rules'. *Child Development*, 55, 1030–9.

Tisak, M.S. and Turiel, E. (1988) 'Variation in seriousness of transgressions and children's moral and conventional concepts'. *Developmental Psychology*, 24, 352–7.

Turiel, E. (1979) 'Distinct conceptual and developmental domains: Social convention and morality'. In C.B. Keasy (ed.) *Nebraska Symposium on Motivation* (pp. 77–116). Lincoln, NB: University of Nebraska Press.

Turiel, E. (1983) *The Development of Social Knowledge: Morality and convention.* Cambridge: Cambridge University Press.

Turiel, E. and Davidson, P. (1986) 'Heterogeneity, inconsistency, and asynchrony in the development of cognitive structures'. In I. Levin (ed.) *Stage and Structure: Reopening the debate* (pp. 106–43). Norwood, NJ: Ablex.

Turiel, E., Hildebrandt, C. and Wainryb, C. (1991) 'Children's reasoning about complex social issues'. *Monographs of the Society for Research in Child Development*, 56, No. 2 (Serial #224).

Turiel, E., Killen, M. and Helwig, C. (1987) 'Morality: Its structure, functions, and vagaries'. In J. Kagan and S. Lamb (eds) *The Emergence of Morality in Young Children* (pp. 155–243). Chicago, IL: University of Chicago Press.

Turiel, E. and Smetana, J.G. (1984) 'Social knowledge and social action: The coordination of domains'. In J.L. Gewirtz and W.M. Kurtines (eds) *Morality, Moral Development, and Moral Behavior* (pp. 261–82). Hillsdale, NJ: Erlbaum.

Turiel, E. Smetana, J.G. and Killen, M. (1991) 'Social contexts in social cognitive development'. In J.L. Gewirtz and W.M. Kurtines (eds) *Handbook of Moral Behavior and Development* (pp. 307–32). Hillsdale, NJ: Erlbaum.

Weston, D. and Turiel, E. (1980) 'Act–rule relations: Children's concepts of social rules'. *Developmental Psychology*, 16, 417–24.

Zimba, R.F. (1987) 'A study on forms of social knowledge in Zambia'. Unpublished doctoral dissertation, Purdue University.

Chapter 6

Understanding events: the development of script knowledge
Judith A. Hudson

6.1 Introduction

Young children experience the world as a series of ongoing events – daily events such as eating breakfast, going to school and getting ready for bed in the evening, as well as less frequently experienced events such as going to a birthday party or going on a family vacation. What do young children understand about these different kinds of events? Can they remember the different experiences they are exposed to, the varied kinds of activities, places and people involved? Can they learn to predict future occurrences based on their past experience? How do they draw on their knowledge of events in everyday social interactions? These are fundamental questions for developmental psychology; understanding how children organize their knowledge of everyday events is a first step in understanding how children make sense of their world.

6.1.1 The script concept

Research over the last fifteen years has shown that children and adults represent their knowledge of recurring events in the form of general event schemas, referred to as scripts (Abelson, 1981; Schank and Abelson, 1977) or generalized event representations (Nelson, 1986; Nelson and Gruendel, 1981). Scripts are mental structures which organize information about the sequence of predictable actions, locations, roles and props that constitute events. For example, most adults have well-developed scripts for what happens when you go to a restaurant. (A diagram of a script representation for going to a restaurant is shown in Figure 6.1.) When you enter, you expect to be seated and to be given a menu; then you expect that someone will take your

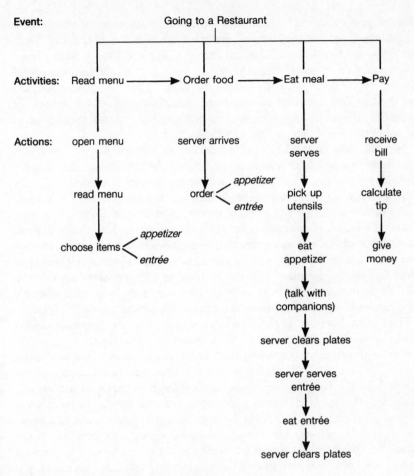

Figure 6.1 Script representation: Going to a restaurant.

order; next, your meal should be served; and finally, you pay for your meal and leave.

Because scripts are schematic knowledge structures, they share properties in common with other kinds of schemas such as scene and story schemas (Mandler, 1979, 1983). Mandler (1979) describes a schema as:

> an organized representation of a body of knowledge ... a spatially and/or temporally organized cognitive structure in which the parts are connected on the basis of contiguities that have been experienced in time or space. A schema is formed on the basis of past experience with objects, scenes, or events and consists of (usually unconscious) expectations about what things look like and 'what goes with what.' (p. 236)

Several important characteristics of schematic knowledge structures have implications for the way scripts are used in cognitive processing. First, schemas are *holistic* knowledge structures: a single reference to the event implies the entire event structure. So, if you know that someone ordered dinner from a menu, you can assume that all the other component activities involved in eating a meal at a restaurant also occurred. Thus, scripts are powerful inferential structures; one can predict all the necessary components of an event even if they are not explicitly stated.

Second, like other kinds of schemas, scripts are *general* knowledge structures, derived from real-world experiences but not simply collections of individual episodes. They organize knowledge of what is expected to occur whenever the event is experienced such as 'you order food', instead of representing this activity in terms of specific examples: 'at Luigi's, you order pasta; at the Fish House, you order seafood', and so on. Knowledge of these kinds of variations can be represented in a generalized event representation, but not as lists of different episodic experiences. Instead, scripts include open slots (i.e. entrée, appetizer) that can be filled by different slot-filler items in any single instantiation of the event. In this way, knowledge of predictable alternatives is represented within the general framework.

Third, as Mandler (1979) emphasized, schemas are *temporally and/or causally organized*. When you go to a restaurant, you expect each of the component actions to occur in a fixed order as indicated by the directional arrows in Figure 6.1. However, different events may vary in terms of the strength of the temporal and causal links between component actions and activities. Abelson (1981) drew a distinction between strong and weak event scripts as reflecting differences in the organization of events in the real world. Strong scripts are formed for events with a high degree of temporal and causal structure. Going to a restaurant is an example of an event with many temporal and causal links. You have to read the menu before you order your food; you cannot eat your food until you have ordered and you have been served; you must pay before you leave; and so on. In contrast, children's birthday parties have relatively few temporal and causal links. You can play games before or after you eat the cake, and you can open birthday presents at any time during the party. Consequently, children's scripts for going to a restaurant are more causally constrained than their scripts for birthday parties (see Slackman, Hudson and Fivush, 1986).

Fourth, scripts are *hierarchically organized*. As Figure 6.1 shows, the overall *event* is composed of *activities* which, in turn, consist of various *actions* upon *objects*. As stated above, these levels are organized in a holistic structure, so that the action of looking at a menu implies the entire event structure. Although they are not shown in this example, an event hierarchy can also include *optional* and *alternative* paths. For example, you may form an optional subscript for checking your coat that is invoked only in certain kinds of restaurant. The activity of paying for your meal can be represented as alternative action paths for paying for dinner at a fancy French restaurant or paying for lunch in a coffee shop. Thus, the entire event representation includes both general and specific event information embedded in different levels in the hierarchy, as well as information about variable and invariant actions and activities.

We call on script knowledge in many different kinds of context. Your restaurant script helps to guide your behaviour whenever you go out to eat, but it also helps you to understand what a friend is talking about when she relates an amusing story of not having enough money to pay the bill when she went out to dinner last night. When you read a story that refers to a character entering a restaurant, your general knowledge about going to a restaurant provides you with information to understand the character's behaviour in that context. Furthermore, you can use this knowledge when you are planning an evening's activities. Knowing the sequence of actions involved in eating at a restaurant, you can make decisions about when to make reservations in order to catch an eight o'clock movie. Thus, we do not use event knowledge only when we are actually enacting events; scripts are essential for discourse, for text comprehension, and for planning. This leads us to the fifth and final important characteristic of script knowledge: scripts are *activated automatically* whenever an event is encountered in the real world or referred to in text or conversation. As we shall see later, once children form scripts for familiar events, they have a well-organized knowledge base that is available to them for understanding stories, communicating with others, planning for future events, and organizing their knowledge of the world. Because this knowledge is accessed automatically, children do not need to develop sophisticated strategies for drawing inferences from event knowledge. Scripts provide children with an early-developing form of mental representation which can support their early cognitive activities such as comprehension and planning.

How do young children form scripts, and how does their event knowledge develop? These questions are the focus of the next section. The final section will discuss research on how children use scripts in various kinds of cognitive and social activities.

6.2 The acquisition and development of event knowledge

Scripts are essentially cultural knowledge – they are necessary for understanding everyday events as experienced within particular cultures and communities. According to Nelson (1986):

> Scripts primarily represent culturally defined events as a consequence of the fact that virtually all the events we take part in are culturally defined. Scripts, therefore,

are necessarily learned, the product of experience. Adults inevitably guide and direct such learning, implicitly or explicitly teaching children how to take their part. Children in turn, through the process of participatory interaction, learn the script even as they act within the scripted event. (p. 15)

The process of script acquisition is therefore both a social and a cognitive achievement, a product of children's cognitive efforts to understand their world that is guided by adults who direct children's participation in everyday social events (French, 1985; Nelson, 1981).

6.2.1 Children's script reports during early childhood

In the initial research on the development of children's scripts, Nelson and her colleagues (Nelson, Fivush, Hudson and Lucariello, 1983; Nelson and Gruendel, 1981) simply asked children from 3 to 8 years old to report 'what happens' in familiar events – for example: 'What happens when you bake cookies?' and 'What happens when you go grocery shopping?' In response to the simple question, 'What happens when you . . . ?' children as young as 3 are able to provide coherent script reports that are general in form, sequentially organized, and with a high level of commonality in the information they include in their reports. The finding that young children can report coherent verbal scripts for what happens in familiar events has since been replicated in numerous studies of children's general event knowledge (Bearison and Pacifici, 1990; Fivush, 1984; Fivush, Kuebli and Clubb, 1992; Hudson, 1990; Hudson and Nelson, 1986; Hudson and Shapiro, 1991; Hudson, Shapiro and Sosa, 1992). Examples of children's script reports for going to a birthday party and going to the doctor's office for a check-up are shown in Table 6.1.

There are several noteworthy characteristics of children's script reports. First, children tend to include general-level information about the events in question (e.g. 'you get toys') instead of reporting details from specific episodes (e.g. 'I got a toy airplane at my birthday party'). Second, children report information in a general format using the impersonal pronoun 'you' and the timeless present tense – for example: 'you buy things'. Again, this indicates that children are reporting general, not episodic information. Finally, the sequence of actions children report tends to be highly accurate (see also French and Nelson, 1982). For example, when reporting what happens when you go to the doctor's office (see Table 6.1), children always report sitting in the waiting room before they mention that the doctor checks them. They frequently mark the temporal sequence using terms such as 'first', 'then' and 'when'. This finding is surprising, given that past research has found that preschool children's concept of time is not well developed (Piaget, 1969). Despite the fact that young children may not have a well-articulated concept of time in the abstract, their script reports indicate that they understand the temporal

Table 6.1   Examples of children's script reports

Birthday party

You get to sing. / You get cake. / You eat ice cream. (4-year-old)

You get toys. / And you get bags of candy and toys. / Yeah, and you get stuff to eat. And they give you cake. And you get to watch the person open up presents. / There could be magic men coming to show you a show. (6-year-old)

Well, you just go to the party and you have fun times. You have cake, play games, and have a lot of fun. / Kids get gifts. And people give you cards for your birthday. You play on your birthday and you play all the games that you get sometimes. / Some kids, if they are at your party, they would want to play, too. (8-year-old)

Check-up at the doctor's

You have to wait until your turn. / When they say your name then you go in. / He checks you out. (4-year-old)

You get a needle and then they put a patch over your eye and say ABC's. And then do the other eye. And then say your ABC's again. And check your heart. / I think that's about it. (6-year-old)

Well, you go in and wait in the waiting room. And then the doctor probably calls your name and you go in. They might give you a shot or medicine. First you have to tell them what's wrong with you or if it was your yearly check-up you would probably get a shot. / Well, then you say that you got a good check-up and then you go. / If you got a bad check-up, um, then you would have to go to the hospital or something. (8-year-olds)

/ indicates non-directive prompts from experimenter (e.g. 'Anything else?')

Source: Hudson and Shapiro (1991)

---

sequencing of familiar events quite well. These characteristics of children's script reports provide support for the notion that children as young as 3 are accessing schematically organized, general event knowledge when reporting 'what happens' (see also Slackman, Hudson and Fivush, 1986).

The discovery of children's script knowledge generated questions about how children acquire general event knowledge. Do they collect memories of specific episodes and then generalize over many episodes, or are they able to form an event script after a single encounter? Interestingly, research indicates that children are able to provide general script reports even after the first experience (Fivush, 1984; Nelson and Gruendel, 1986; Hudson and Nelson, 1986), suggesting that they form scripts based on a single encounter. Of course, children are also able to recall specific details of a single, novel event (Fivush, 1984; Hudson and Nelson, 1986). It appears that after only one experience, children are able to remember specific details of that experience, but they also assume that future occurrences will be consistent with the first experience (see also Hudson and Fivush, in press). For example, when asked to provide a script report for 'what happens when you go to Disneyland' after a single visit, one 5-year-old reported: 'You go in a hotel. You go on rides. You see Mickey Mouse and Goofy . . .' (Hudson and Nelson, 1986).

6.2.2 Effects of age and experience on the development of event knowledge

Although children are able to provide script reports after a single experience, their event knowledge does become more elaborate (they report more of the component activities) and more complex (they report more conditional and optional activities) with increasing age and experience (Fivush and Slackman, 1986). Note that these two factors, age and experience, are often confounded. That is, not only are older children more cognitively advanced than younger children, but they have also had more opportunities to experience events. For example, 5-year-olds have attended more birthday parties, baked more batches of cookies, and had more annual check-ups at the doctor's than have 3-year-olds.

In the examples of children's script reports for what happens in familiar events in Table 6.1, you can see that older children's reports are longer and tend to include more complex information than younger children's. In particular, older children are more likely to report optional and conditional information – for example: 'there could be magic men coming to show you a show', and 'if it was your yearly check-up you would probably get a shot' (Fivush and Slackman, 1986). Do these age differences mean that older children are able to form more complex event representations because there are differences in the ways in which older and younger children *think* about events? Or do children's event representations become more complex with increasing *experience*? A third explanation is that older children may possess more sophisticated verbal skills; age differences in length and complexity of children's script reports may simply reflect language development, not script development.

Two research strategies have been used to address these issues. First, various studies have relied on measures other than the verbal report to assess children's event knowledge (Fivush *et al.*, 1992; Fivush and Mandler, 1985; Hudson, 1988). Second, several studies have investigated the development of children's scripts for novel events to control the level of experience for children at different ages (Fivush, 1984; Fivush *et al.*, 1992; Price and Goodman, 1990); these studies are discussed in the next section.

One way of assessing children's event knowledge without relying on verbal reports has been to ask them to sequence pictures of familiar events. Fivush and Mandler (1985) found that 4-, 5- and 6-year-old children easily sequenced six pictures of familiar events (going grocery shopping, going to McDonald's) in their correct temporal order. Thus, even though 4-year-olds may not always mention as many as six actions in their verbal reports, they do possess knowledge of at least this many actions, as is indicated by their ability to place all the actions in the correct order.

A different method was used by Hudson (1988) to assess whether younger children were aware of optional and conditional actions even if they did not report them in their verbal scripts. In this study, children were asked to provide frequency judgements for actions that might or might not occur in two familiar events, going grocery shopping and eating at McDonald's. Children at 4 and 7 years of age were asked to rate how often various actions occurred – for example, how often do you stand in a check-out line, buy orange juice, or put on your pyjamas when you go grocery shopping? Children at both ages agreed that you always stand in line, you sometimes buy orange juice, and you never put on your pyjamas. Thus, even though 4-year-olds rarely mention optional and conditional actions in their event reports, they are able to state that these actions do sometimes happen when they are asked to rate their frequency of occurrence. Together with the findings from Fivush and Mandler's (1985) picture-sequencing study, these findings indicate that younger children's (i.e. 4-year-olds') script knowledge is more complex than what they are able to report verbally.

6.2.3 Acquisition of new scripts

How does children's event knowledge develop over increasing experience with a novel event? Fivush (1984) investigated this issue by following a class of young children (mean age 5 years 1 month) in their first ten weeks of kindergarten. Children were asked to report 'what happens' in kindergarten on their second day of school, after two weeks, four weeks and ten weeks. One very striking characteristic of their reports was that even on the second day of school, children reported the school day in a general form that followed the temporal organization of the kindergarten routine. This result provided further evidence that young children can form a temporally organized script after just one experience with an event. Over the ten-week period, children's reports included more actions and more conditional statements (e.g. 'then I do art project if I have time'), indicating that their script knowledge became more elaborate and more complex with increasing experience. The results from this study indicate that even though children are able to form event scripts after a single experience, increasing experience does lead to more complex event knowledge.

Fivush (1984) was able to show the effects of increasing experience with an event on children's event knowledge independent of age effects. The question remains, however, whether there are age differences in how children initially represent event knowledge. Although 5-year-olds are able to report general event knowledge after a single exposure, how would their reports differ from those of older or younger children? This issue was addressed in two recent studies (Fivush *et al.*, 1992; Price and Goodman, 1990).

Price and Goodman (1990) examined children's knowledge of a novel event, 'visiting the wizard'. Children aged 2 years 5 months, 4 years, and 5 years 5 months visited a laboratory playroom where they were led through various kinds of activities by a 'wizard', actually a bearded man wearing a colourful robe. The activities included saying a special 'magic hello' greeting, putting on a special robe, playing with a large jack-in-the-box, and so on. The children visited the wizard four times over a five-day period. Before the final session, they were asked to tell an unfamiliar experimenter 'what it's like' to visit the wizard. Next, they were shown a scale model of the wizard's room and asked to show the experimenter what it's like to visit the wizard using a child doll and miniature props (the prop condition). Finally, the children entered the wizard's room and reenacted the activities, but before starting each activity they were asked 'Where do we go next?' (the familiar context condition).

Not surprisingly, children reported more activities with increasing age. At all ages, however, they recalled proportionally more information in the prop and familiar context conditions than during free production without support. Thus, relying solely on verbal script measures taken out of context under-estimated children's knowledge, but using non-verbal measures did not eliminate age differences. The finding that children's ability to demonstrate their event knowledge was affected by the elicitation context suggested that young children do not draw on scripts as fixed structures; rather, the display of children's event knowledge should be viewed as an interaction between mental structures, response mode and external physical cues.

Another study by Fivush *et al.* (1992) also found that younger children need more external support to demonstrate their developing script knowledge. In this study, the effects of increasing experience on children's script knowledge were examined with 3- and 5-year-old children. They were taught three new events in a laboratory playroom: making 'fundough', making a shape collage, and playing with different toys in a sandbox. Half the children participated in the events four times over a two-week period; the other half participated in the events only in a single visit to the laboratory. At the end of each session, children returned to a waiting room and were asked to 'tell Mom what we do in the playroom' while an experimenter recorded their event reports. Then each child returned for a final visit (the fifth visit for children who participated in four exposures; the second visit for children exposed to the events only a single time). In this last visit, children were taken into the playroom and asked to show an experimenter 'what we do in the playroom'. Thus, Fivush *et al.* obtained both verbal and non-verbal measures of script knowledge after either one experience or four experiences with a novel event.

In verbal recall, the 5-year-olds seemed to benefit more from increasing experience than did the 3-year-olds. They reported more actions after four experiences than after one, whereas 3-year-olds recalled the same number of actions (fewer than the number reported by the 5-year-olds) after one experience or four experiences. When children were allowed to reenact the events physically, however, a very different pattern of results emerged: 3-year-olds enacted as many actions as 5-year-olds, regardless of their amount of experience. Thus, 3-year-olds acquired a great deal of event knowledge after even a single experience with a novel event, but their event knowledge was apparent only in behavioural reenactment with extensive contextual cues (i.e. when they were in the actual room with all the props available). In contrast, after a single experience, 5-year-olds were able to provide fairly extensive verbal reports of what happens and, over increasing experiences, reported even more information.

This line of research indicates that young children are capable of forming very complete and well-organized general event representations after a single experience, but that increased experience with events leads to more complex verbal script reports. An important finding is that age differences in the amount of information children report after either one experience or multiple experiences are diminished or even eliminated using non-verbal assessment of event knowledge. Thus, younger children's event knowledge is best displayed non-verbally and with contextual support, but by the age of 5, children are able to report event knowledge verbally. Even at this age, however, verbal measures may underestimate the extent of children's event knowledge.

6.2.4 The development of hierarchical structure

Are children able to form an event hierarchy after a single experience? Are there age differences in the way children hierarchically organize event knowledge? In Price and Goodman's (1990) study of children's event representations for 'visiting the wizard' described above, each of the component activities included a main or nodal action that subsumed several subactions. For example, the nodal action of putting on a robe included the subactions of standing in a specific location, putting on the robe, facing the mirror, holding out arms, noticing an animal picture on the robe, and naming the animal. With age, children mentioned more of the nodal actions, indicating that they 'parsed' the overall event in terms of nodal activity units. Thus, there were age differences not only in the number of actions children reported but also in the way those actions were hierarchically organized.

Ratner and Smith (Ratner, Smith and Dion, 1986; Smith, Ratner and Hobart, 1987) have also examined the degree to which 5-year-old children can organize events hierarchically by teaching children a novel clay-making event organized in a hierarchy of activity- and action-level components. After participating in the event, the children were shown pictures of the component actions to sort into piles according to 'what goes together'. Most of them grouped pictures in terms of the specific actions or the objects associated with each action – for example, placing all the pictures that showed flour together because they shared a common element (Smith *et al.*, 1987). In contrast, adults produced activity-level groupings in this task – for example, grouping the actions of measuring and pouring salt, flour and cinnamon together because all these actions involved adding dry ingredients. Thus, as compared to adult performance, 5-year-olds showed less evidence of grouping a novel event according to an event hierarchy such as the one displayed in Figure 6.1.

However, when adults rated the actions in terms of which were most important to the overall goal of making clay-dough, these ratings predicted children's verbal recall of the event even after just two experiences (Ratner *et al.*, 1986). For example, adults rated adding flour as more important than adding cinnamon, and children recalled adding flour more frequently than they recalled adding cinnamon. These findings indicate that pre-school children are more sensitive to actions' centrality to the overall event goal than hierarchical structure of actions and activities after limited experience with novel events.

6.2.5 The very early development of script knowledge

Most of the research reviewed so far has focused on children from 2 years 5 months to 8 years of age. The fact that children as young as 2 years 5 months are able to form event scripts suggests that children start to develop script knowledge at a very early age, perhaps in infancy. Recent research has investigated how 1- and 2-year-olds understand events.

Because this line of research has necessarily relied on non-verbal indices of event knowledge, an action–imitation paradigm has emerged as the 'classic' methodology for assessing toddlers' scripts (Bauer and Mandler, 1989, 1990; Bauer and Shore, 1987; O'Connell and Gerard, 1985; Ungerer, 1985). The method is fairly straightforward. First a baseline measure of children's behaviour with a set of objects is obtained; then an experimenter models a simple action sequence with the objects; finally, children are given the props and encouraged to reproduce the action sequence. In delayed or deferred imitation, children are presented with the objects again after a delay of one day to six weeks. This time their actions before modelling serve as a measure of deferred imitation. To assess children's use of existing event scripts to encode and reproduce the actions, sequences are designed to incorporate predictable actions in scripted events such as taking a bath (remove teddy bear's clothes, put teddy in the tub, wash teddy). Children's success in reproducing the modelled sequences are interpreted as evidence that the sequences match their internal event representations. To mimic the process of learning a new script, children are presented with unfamiliar action sequences in order to see what kinds of events very young children are capable of learning.

Using this method, Ungerer (1985) found that children from 18 to 30 months of age were able accurately to reproduce the sequences of actions consistent with familiar event sequences, but had considerable difficulty reproducing a random sequence of unrelated actions. Research by Bauer and her colleagues (Bauer and Mandler, 1989, 1990; Bauer and Shore, 1987) has further shown that children from 16 to 20 months old are able to imitate familiar action sequences both immediately after viewing and up to six weeks later in deferred imitation. As in Ungerer's (1985) study, children reproduced the familiar event sequences in the correct temporal order, providing clear evidence that at least by 16 months of age, children's scripts are temporally organized.

In order to test whether temporal and causal relations are represented in very young children's initial event representations, Bauer and Mandler (1989, 1990) also presented children with novel event sequences that were either causally or arbitrarily sequenced. An example of a causal sequence is 'making a rattle'. The experimenter places a ball in one of two graduated nesting cups, covers it with a second cup, and then shakes the 'rattle'. An example of an arbitrary sequence is 'making a picture'. The experimenter attaches a sticker to a small chalkboard, leans the chalkboard against an easel, and scribbles on the chalkboard. Both 16- and 20-month-old children reproduced the novel–causal sequences in order, but had difficulty reproducing the order of the novel–arbitrary sequences. Thus, even in their initial exposure to new event sequences, children as young as 16 months are sensitive to causal relations between action components.

6.2.6 Summary

Research on the development of children's event knowledge indicates that there are developmental differences in their scripts for both familiar and novel events. Older children tend to report more actions in events than do younger children; but using non-verbal measures or extensive prompting significantly diminishes these age differences (Fivush *et al.*, 1992; Fivush and Mandler, 1985; Hudson, 1988; Price and Goodman, 1990). From the first experience with an event, the temporal–causal structure is well represented in children's script representations at all ages studied, but younger children may be less able than older children to organize event knowledge into a hierarchical structure (Price and Goodman, 1990; Ratner *et al.*, 1986; Smith *et al.*, 1987). Action–imitation studies with toddlers have shown not only that children as young as 16 months already possess well-organized knowledge about the sequence of everyday events, but that causal relations between actions are represented in their script knowledge even after a single exposure to a novel event.

6.3 How children use script knowledge

Research reviewed so far indicates that scripts are a very powerful form of mental representation which children acquire at a very early age and after a single experience with a novel event. What motivates children's script acquisition? What do children do with these representations? Nelson and Gruendel (1981) proposed that scripts provide young children with 'the basic building blocks' of cognitive development. That is, children acquire scripts in order to understand and mentally represent their world. These mental representations then serve the function of providing children with a well-organized knowledge base to support a variety of cognitive processes that are involved in understanding stories, remembering past events, conversing and playing with other children, and planning for future events. Thus, event knowledge is involved in all aspects of children's cognitive functioning. We turn now to research in these areas to examine the role of scripts as cognitive building blocks.

6.3.1 Story comprehension

Because scripts are accessed automatically whenever a familiar event is referred to, they can serve as powerful comprehension guides for understanding stories about familiar events. Once the appropriate event representation is invoked, children are able to anticipate the unfolding event sequence and draw inferences about unstated information based on script knowledge. In recalling script-based stories, children can rely on their generalized event representations to serve as retrieval guides, resulting in well-organized and exhaustive story recall (Hudson and Fivush, 1983; Hudson and Nelson, 1983; McCartney and Nelson, 1981).

Children's use of scripts to guide story memory is also evident from the pattern of errors they produce in recalling script-based stories. Whenever schematic knowledge structures are used to guide story comprehension, certain kinds of distortions in memory can occur because the listener has difficulty distinguishing those elements of the story that were actually presented in the text from relevant information that can be inferred from schematically organized knowledge (Bartlett, 1932; Mandler, 1983). When recalling script-based stories, both children and adults erroneously recall information that is consistent with their script knowledge but was not actually stated in the story test (Bower, Black and Turner, 1979; Hudson and Nelson, 1983; Slackman and Nelson, 1984). Central script actions are recalled more frequently than peripheral details, and typical script actions are recalled better than atypical information (Adams and Worden, 1986; Graesser, Woll, Kowalski and Smith, 1980; McCartney and Nelson, 1981; Slackman and Nelson, 1984; Smith and Graesser, 1981). Story information may also be altered or transformed to conform to the listener's script representation. For example, if a story includes misordered actions that violate the typical event sequence, subjects tend to reorder the story sequence in recall to conform to the typical script sequence (Hudson and Nelson, 1983). As time goes by, schematic processing plays an ever greater role in memory, so that delayed recall of script-based stories becomes less reproductive and more reconstructive; distortions of text material increase as recall becomes ever more script-like (Bartlett, 1932; Hudson, 1988; Hudson and Nelson, 1983; Slackman and Nelson, 1984; Smith and Graesser, 1981).

In most cases, distortions in memory for script-based stories reflect the fact that subjects infer typical event information that was not explicitly stated. To examine children's ability to draw inferences based on general event knowledge more directly, Hudson and Slackman (1990) examined 4- and 7-year-olds' responses to inference questions after listening to short stories about familiar events. Even 4-year-olds were able to draw inferences about unstated story information based on script knowledge. After listening to a story in which a little girl and her mother went to the grocery store for candy and ice cream, for example, children were able to infer that they paid the cashier in order to purchase the groceries, although this information was not stated in the story. However, they had difficulty drawing inferences about story information that was not already represented in their event scripts. In the grocery store study, 4-year-olds had difficulty inferring that the candy and ice cream were purchased for the little girl's birthday, even though the fact that the next day was her birthday was stated in the story. Thus, children were able to draw inferences based on script knowledge before they were able to use inductive and deductive reasoning strategies necessary for drawing inferences from text premisses.

Summary

Children's use of scripts in story comprehension and recall generally enhances their memory performance by increasing the amount and organization of recall. This line of research has shown that pre-school children are able to organize their recall in directed memory tasks if the material to be remembered is structured in a way that is meaningful to them. Their recall of script-based stories contrasts sharply with their relatively poor performance when asked to recall less meaningful material such as lists of words (Hudson and Fivush, 1983; Nelson and Hudson, 1988). This discrepancy in performance has led to a reexamination of the development of memory processes in young children, suggesting that memory development may, to a large extent, reflect the development of knowledge structures rather than the development of deliberate strategies for remembering material (see Bjorklund, 1985; Chi and Ceci, 1987). In addition to supporting early memory skills, scripts may also support children's early inferential skills (Hudson and Slackman, 1990).

6.3.2 Remembering past events

Do scripts guide children's memory for episodes of familiar events in the same way that they guide their story recall? If so, children should produce distortions in recall as details of specific episodes are confused with general event knowledge. To some degree, these effects have been found in children's memory of specific episodes of familiar events (Hudson, 1986; Hudson and Fivush, in press). In one study (Hudson and Nelson, 1986) pre-school children had difficulty recalling 'what happened' at snack and dinner yesterday, and more easily reported 'what happens' in general for these highly routine events. This suggested that their memory of yesterday's snack and dinner had become fused into their general event knowledge, and could not be retrieved as separate, distinct episodes. When children from 3 to 7 years of age were asked to recall 'what happened one time' for events that varied in terms of familiarity, their recall included more general information and fewer episodic details as a result of increasing experience with an event. For example, one 3-year-old recalling a day at summer camp which he had experienced many times reported: 'In summer you go to camp. Play. And play. Play in the sandbox.' Again, this finding suggests that episodes of familiar events become fused into a general event representation.

When children do report details from specific episodes of familiar events, they tend to confuse similar episodes in memory (Farrar and Goodman, 1990; Hudson, 1990; Hudson and Nelson, 1986; Kuebli, 1990). For example, one 5-year-old from Hudson and Nelson's (1986) study had trouble distinguishing between separate but very similar trips to the zoo: 'I remember only a time that I went to the Israel one. There was a wolf there, I think . . . . No, that was another zoo. There was no wolf. . . . There was a duck. There wasn't no zebras . . . I think there *was* zebras, but I'm not sure.' This suggests that details of individual episodes (such as which animals you see at the zoo) may be represented in memory as variations or slot-fillers in a script representation, not as distinct episodes. When recalling a specific episode, the slot is filled with an appropriate action or activity, but this reconstruction may not accurately reflect the particular episode in question.

Further support for this interpretation comes from a study by Hudson (1990) where pre-school children participated in four creative movement workshops and were asked to recall individual episodes four weeks later. Although they were able to remember specific songs that were sung and particular games, they were often confused as to which song or game was experienced in which workshop. Their confusion suggested that their memory of the workshops was represented as a general script that included the activities of singing songs and playing movement games with open slots for 'songs' and 'games' that could be filled with different items on separate occasions. When recalling (or reconstructing) a memory of a particular workshop, children mentally filled in the song and game slots with appropriate fillers, but these were not necessarily the correct ones. Interestingly, difficulties in recalling individual episodes and confusions about details of similar episodes occur after as few as two experiences with a novel event, providing further evidence that scripts are formed in the very first encounters with new events (Farrar and Goodman, 1990; Fivush, 1984).

Although episodes of familiar events that conform to the general script sequence are difficult to reconstruct as distinct episodes, episodes of highly novel or distinctive experiences are more easily recalled (Hudson, 1986;

Hudson and Fivush, in press). Experiences that violate one's expectations based on script knowledge tend to 'stand out' in memory. For example, kindergarten children who participated in an unusual class field trip to an archaeology museum were able to recall details of the visit event six years later (Fivush, Hudson and Nelson, 1984; Hudson and Fivush, 1991a). What made this trip so distinctive was that it contrasted with their scripts for what typically happens when you go to a museum. Asked to report what happens when you go to a museum two weeks before going on the field trip, children generally reported that you looked at things and you couldn't touch anything (Fivush *et al.*, 1984). During their visit, however, they were allowed to pretend they were archaeologists, and they dug for artifacts in a sandbox. Then they were given clay to make clay models of the artifacts they had found to take home with them. Six weeks after the visit, the children's recall of this experience was as extensive and detailed as their memories on the day of the experience. One year later, all but one child was able to recall the trip when reminded of the most distinctive activity, digging in the sandbox (Fivush *et al.*, 1984). Six years later, when they were shown photographs taken of children digging in the sand and working with the clay, twelve out of thirteen children interviewed remembered additional details about this experience (Hudson and Fivush, 1991a).

Thus, a highly distinctive episode that did not conform to children's scripts was retained in memory over six years. Interestingly, even though the children were able to recall some of the more routine aspects of the experience after a year (e.g. walking to the museum, talking to the museum guide), these activities dropped out of recall after six years, when children focused almost exclusively on the distinctive features of the experience in their recall. This suggests that it was the distinctive features of the experience that were retained in memory, not the entire episode.

Summary
Research on children's memory for episodes of recurring events indicates that their recall of real-world events is also influenced by general event knowledge. Distortions in recalling specific episodes occur as what *actually* happened is confused with what *typically* happens based on script knowledge (see also Linton, 1982; Neisser, 1981; Reiser, 1986, for similar findings in research with adults). In addition, details of similar episodes can become confused with one another because episodic variations are represented in memory as alternative slot-fillers or optional paths in the general script representations, not as completely separate and distinct experiences. Whereas routine experiences are difficult to recall as distinctive episodes (and, in fact, may become permanently irretrievable, fused into the general event script), unusual or distinctive episodes are retained in memory over long periods of time and can serve as 'tags' for retrieval of episodic information.

6.3.3 Social interactions and play

As stated above, scripts guide not only memories of past events but also social interactions in the present. Scripts provide the basis for shared knowledge between individuals about routine events that is necessary for communication in social interactions. Although shared knowledge of cultural scripts is important for communication among all members of a culture, it may be especially important for young children who have difficulty assessing others' knowledge states and recognizing signs of failed communication. In analyzing dialogues between pre-school children, Nelson and Gruendel (1979) proposed that shared script knowledge is essential in order for young children to communicate effectively:

> to sustain a dialogue the participants must each assume a shared topic context within which that dialogue is structured. This shared context determines such things as what is expressed and what is left to inference, the particular answers that follow from a given question, and the particular semantic and syntactic links that will be established between utterances. (p. 76)

When children attempted conversations about topics based on shared script knowledge, they were able to sustain a topic across multiple utterances and provided appropriate responses to each other's questions and comments. For example, two children engaged in an extended pretend phone conversation about making plans for dinner:

Gay:	Uhmmm. Where're we going at dinnertime?
Daniel:	Nowhere. But we're just gonna have dinner at 11 o'clock.
Gay:	Well, I made a plan of going out tonight.
Daniel:	Well, that's what we're gonna do.
Gay:	We're going out.
Daniel:	The plan ... it's goin be ... that's gonna be ... we're going to McDonald's.
Gay:	Yeah, we're going to McDonald's. And ... ah ... ah ... ah ... what they have for dinner tonight is hamburger.

In contrast, conversations that were not based on shared script knowledge could hardly be considered dialogues and more closely resembled what Piaget (1955) called 'collective monologues':

Brian:	I'm playing with this.
David:	A what's ... a what's ...
Brian:	Oh nut, oh nuts.
David:	Doodoodoo, round up in the sky. Do you like to ride in a [toy] helicopter?
Brian:	OK. I want to play in the sandbox.

In this excerpt, there is no connection between utterances. Each child seems to be in his own private world, talking aloud, but not taking into account what the other person is saying. It contrasts sharply with the previous exchange based on shared scripts for dinner and McDonald's.

The role of shared script knowledge in supporting and sustaining children's peer interactions has since been investigated in several observational and experimental studies (Duveen and Lloyd, 1988; French, 1985; French, Lucariello, Seidman and Nelson, 1985; Furman and Walden, 1990; Nelson and Seidman, 1984; Sachs, Goldman and Chaille, 1985; Seidman, Nelson and Gruendel, 1986). In general, children's dialogues about script-related topics are longer and more coherent than non-scripted topics – for example, negotiating toy ownerships (Duveen and Lloyd, 1988; French, 1985; French et al., 1985; Nelson and Seidman, 1984; Seidman et al., 1986). Knowledge of scripted events is also necessary for children to engage effectively in sociodramatic play; each child involved in the interaction needs to understand the overall event structure in order to generate ideas for actions that are compatible with the play theme. Children's sociodramatic play is more complex – that is, they include more elaborate role play and more complex themes – when they are enacting scripted play scenarios such as going to the doctor (Sachs et al., 1985) or having a birthday party (Seidman et al., 1986). With age, children's script-based play becomes increasingly complex as they coordinate aspects of different scripts into their thematic play. Whereas 3-year-olds might focus on pretending to bake a cake while playing in the sandbox, older children might make a cake, decorate it, add candles, and sing 'Happy Birthday'.

Most studies of script knowledge in peer interaction have involved well-acquainted peers. However, a study by French and Boynton (reported in French et al., 1985) found that previously unacquainted children from 2 years 5 months to 5 years of age who were observed in the first two weeks of nursery school were able to engage in coherent play conversations while enacting script routines for food preparation and mealtime interactions in the kitchen corner. Thus, pre-school children who do not have shared experiences with one another to serve as a basis for communication are nevertheless able to tap into their shared knowledge of routine events to support their thematic play.

Finally, a direct relationship between level of script knowledge and coherence in interactive thematic play has been demonstrated by Furman and Walden (1990). Pairs of children from 3 to 5 years old were observed during thematic play with props associated with a very familiar event (grocery store or McDonald's) and a less familiar event (aeroplane trip or train trip). Children's knowledge of these events was assessed independently in a script interview with each child. Children were more effective in communicating with one another in the situations for which they had greater script knowledge – that is, their conversations were longer and they were more responsive to each other in the more familiar script context. However, effects of shared script knowledge interacted with age; increased script knowledge resulted in longer topic-related conversations for younger children and fewer communication failures in older children (e.g. a child fails to respond appropriately to the other child's utterance) – perhaps because children at different ages were able to bring a different set of conversational skills to the situation. This finding suggests that shared script knowledge facilitates different aspects of communication depending on children's developmental level. For younger children, script knowledge may support the emergence of rudimentary skills (e.g. turntaking, maintaining a topic), but for older children it provides the basis for more complex skills (e.g. providing appropriate responses, supporting more complex thematic play).

Summary
Both observational and experimental research indicate that children's ability to converse with peers and to establish joint play interactions is facilitated by shared script knowledge. With age, children's script-related play becomes increasingly communicative and structurally more complex.

6.3.4 Planning for future events

Knowing what typically happens in a given event should provide a child with a good knowledge base to plan and predict future occurrences. Until recently, little research had been devoted to this topic. This is particularly surprising if one contemplates why children would be motivated to form scripts in the first place. Despite the fact that children rely on scripts in organizing memory for stories and past experiences, their script acquisition is motivated by the need to make sense of their world and to predict behaviour in current and future interactions (Nelson, 1985, 1990).

One recent study (Hudson *et al.*, 1992) investigated whether pre-school children could use scripts in constructing verbal plans for familiar events, and if so, whether their verbal plans were different from script reports for the same events. Children from 3 to 5 years of age were asked to report either a verbal script or a verbal plan for going grocery shopping and going to the beach. These events were selected because they were familiar to the children and they typically included some preparation activities. They differed, however, to the extent that going to the beach was a more child-orientated activity than going grocery shopping.

Not surprisingly, children's scripts and plans for these events were highly similar. However, children at all ages include more information about the preparation phases of the events when providing plans than when reporting scripts. Thus, even 3-year-olds were able to use script knowledge in formulating event plans and included preparatory planning activities (e.g. making a shopping list, packing their swimsuit) in formulating event plans.

After giving their script or plan reports, children were also asked two 'what if' questions for each event to assess their ability to form *remedy plans* for what happens if something goes awry (e.g. What could you do if you forgot to bring your shopping list to the grocery store?). Although the children's ability to construct remedy plans increased with age, even the youngest subjects were able to come up with adequate remedy plans for the more child-orientated event, going to the beach; children at all ages were less successful in providing remedy plans for the grocery shopping event than for going to the beach. Asked, for example, what you could do if you forgot to bring your lunch to the beach, children reported that you could go back home to get some food, or you could eat lunch in a restaurant.

Finally, after the remedy plan question, children were also asked: 'What could you do to make sure that didn't happen the next time?', to test their ability to formulate *prevention plans* for familiar events. Although 3- and 4-year-olds were generally unsuccessful in this task, 5-year-olds were able to generate adequate prevention plans. Asked, for example, what you could do to make sure you did not forget your shopping list the next time you went to the grocery store, one 5-year-old reported: 'Check around the house and take that list and put it on the dresser because Daddy always has to get money from his dresser.' These results indicate that pre-school children could construct plans to remedy common mishaps, although they were more successful in doing so for the more child-orientated event, but only 5-year-olds were able to backtrack in their scripts in order to figure out what to do to prevent mishaps.

This study showed that young children can use script knowledge to construct plans for future events. But can they carry out those plans? Psychologists studying planning behaviour have drawn a distinction between constructing plans and executing plans (Friedman and Scholnick, 1987). In order to construct a plan you must be able to think ahead, anticipate situations, and form a mental representation of actions to be taken to accomplish a goal. In executing a plan you must keep the plan in mind, execute the actions in sequence, and monitor where you are in the sequence. Thus, plan execution involves more memory and plan-monitoring skills than plan construction.

Results of two recent studies suggest that young children run into difficulties in executing event plans. Hudson and Fivush (1991b) found that 3- and 4-year-olds had difficulty remembering their original event plans when they were asked to plan a trip to a pretend grocery store to select items needed for a birthday party or for breakfast. Their performance improved significantly when they were reminded of the event goal while selecting items in the store, or when the items were arranged on the shelves so that all the birthday party items were together on one shelf and all the breakfast items were together on another shelf. As found in studies of children's script knowledge, younger children seemed to rely more on external support in executing their event plans.

Finally, Shapiro and Hudson (1991) found that 4-year-olds were quite good at constructing plans for novel events, but ran into difficulties in executing plans. Children were taught how to make two new art projects over two training sessions. Even with this limited experience, the children's verbal plans were good and they were able to select the supplies they needed from shelves of various art supplies. They ran into trouble, however, if they made any mistakes in their plan execution. In particular, they frequently failed to diagnose errors and backtrack during execution. For example, one project involved ironing two sheets of wax paper together. If the children forgot this step, they ran into trouble when they tried to trace a shape on the paper and cut it out, because the sheets of paper would fall apart. A simple solution to this problem would be to retrace one's steps to complete the omitted step. However, the children seemed incapable of this kind of backtracking and simply blundered on, producing a very different end result. When they were allowed to view an example of a completed project during plan execution they made fewer errors, indicating that a reminder of the final goal state helped them to organize their actions in the correct sequence.

This last study shows that in complex real-world planning tasks there are often consequences for failure to plan ahead adequately. Children may be unaware of any deficiencies in their event knowledge until they are actually faced with the challenge of executing an event plan. Although script knowledge may be ideally suited for representing the order of actions to be executed sequentially, if any errors are made during execution, children may have to invoke problem-solving skills that go beyond 'running off' one's script knowledge. This is precisely where 4-year-old children ran into difficulties when executing their plans for the two novel art projects and when they were asked to think of prevention plans in the interview study discussed above (Hudson *et al.*, 1992).

Summary

Script knowledge provides young children with a foundation for planning that allows them to formulate fairly complete plans for familiar events long before they show evidence of planning in novel contexts. However, planning also requires the ability to 'debug' plans gone awry in execution. Both of these skills develop between ages 3 and 5. Children's skill in translating scripts into plans also depends on the degree of external support provided by the physical and social environment. Finally, the type of event being planned for – for example, the degree to which the event is child- or adult-centred – affects children's ability to translate scripts into plans.

6.4 Scripts and cognitive development: conclusions and new directions

Research over the last fifteen years has shown that scripts are a powerful form of mental representation for organizing children's knowledge of the world.

This research indicates that children's representations of experiences such as going to a restaurant are not just episodic or 'one-off' representations of *particular* events. Rather, these sorts of experiences are represented in a *general* form. It is now clear that very young children have a remarkable ability to form temporally and causally organized general event representations from the first exposure to an event, and with increasing age and experience their knowledge becomes even more complex and accessible. From a very early age, children make use of their scripts in remembering past events, planning future events, interacting with parents and peers, and understanding stories. Research not reviewed in this chapter also indicates that script knowledge influences children's language acquisition (French and Nelson, 1985; Lucariello *et al.*, 1986), conceptual development (Lucariello and Nelson, 1987; Lucariello and Rifkin, 1986) and narrative skills (Shapiro and Hudson, 1991).

As discussed above, Nelson and Gruendel (1981) proposed that scripts can be considered the 'basic building blocks' of cognitive development. They support the early emergence of basic cognitive processes and provide a representational foundation for the development of more complex conceptual systems underlying knowledge of social roles, object categories, discourse procedures, word meanings and problem-solving strategies. These more abstract systems are all derived from the initial representation of experience in the form of scripts. The research reviewed in this chapter overwhelmingly supports Nelson and Gruendel's original building-blocks metaphor, showing that scripts support cognitive development by providing children with a cognitive or *representational context* for cognitive processing. Thus, pre-school children who typically fail in cognitive tasks in which the task or topic is unfamiliar are nevertheless able to remember, plan, draw inferences and communicate effectively in scripted event contexts.

Now that the link between script representation and the early emergence of cognitive skills has been established, we need to learn more about how increasing complexity in script knowledge (e.g. hierarchical organization) supports increasingly more complex cognitive processes. In addition, research on children's use of scripts in memory, play and planning suggests that older children may use script knowledge more flexibly than younger children (Farrar and Goodman, 1990; Hudson and Fivush, 1983; Hudson and Fivush, 1991b; Hudson *et al.*, 1992; Seidman *et al.*, 1986; Slackman and Nelson, 1984). That is, although younger children (3 to 4 years of age) can draw on script knowledge in complex cognitive tasks such as drawing inferences, supporting complex role play, and constructing event plans, older children (aged 5 to 6) can do more with their script knowledge; they can carry out even more complex inference and planning tasks and seem to rely less on the event structure to support their cognitive activities. Thus, over a relatively short period of time, cognitive operations that are first displayed in scripted contexts become generalizable to novel task situations. Understanding more about this process whereby cognitive operations become disembedded from familiar situations and existing knowledge structures is the key to understanding the process of cognitive development in the pre-school years.

References

Abelson, R.P. (1981) 'Psychological status of the script concept'. *American Psychologist*, **36**, 715–29.

Adams, L.T. and Worden, P.E. (1986) 'Script development and memory organization in preschool and elementary school children'. *Discourse Processes*, **9**, 149–66.

Bartlett, F.C. (1932) *Remembering: A study in experimental and social psychology*. Cambridge: Cambridge University Press.

Bauer, P.J. and Mandler, J.M. (1989) 'One thing follows another: Effects of temporal structure on 1–2-year-olds' recall of events'. *Developmental Psychology*, **25**, 197–206.

Bauer, P.J. and Mandler, J.M. (1990) 'Remembering what happened next: Very young children's recall of event sequences'. In R. Fivush and J.A. Hudson (eds) *Knowing and Remembering in Young Children* (pp. 9–29). New York: Cambridge University Press.

Bauer, P.J. and Shore, C.M. (1987) 'Making a memorable event: Effects of familiarity and organization on young children's recall of action sequences'. *Cognitive Development*, **2**, 237–338.

Bearison, D.J. and Pacifici, C. (1990) 'Children's event knowledge of cancer treatment'. *Journal of Applied Developmental Psychology*, **10**, 469–86.

Bjorklund, D. (1985) 'The role of conceptual knowledge in the development of organization in children's memory'. In C. Brainerd and M. Pressley (eds) *Basic Processes in Memory Development: Progress in cognitive development research*. New York: Springer-Verlag.

Bower, F.H., Black, J.B. and Turner, T.J. (1979) 'Scripts in memory for text'. *Cognitive Psychology*, **11**, 177–220.

Chi, M.T.H. and Ceci, S. (1987) 'Content knowledge: Its role, representation, and restructuring in memory development'. In H.W. Reese (ed.) *Advances in Child Development and Behavior* (vol. 10, pp. 91–142). Orlando, FL: Academic Press.

Duveen, F. and Lloyd, B. (1988) 'Gender as an influence in the development of scripted pretend play'. *British Journal of Developmental Psychology*, **6**, 89–95.

Farrar, M.J. and Goodman, G.S. (1990) 'Developmental differences in the relation between scripts and episodic memory: Do they exist?' In R. Fivush and J.A. Hudson (eds) *What Young Children Remember and Why*. New York: Cambridge University Press.

Fivush, R. (1984) 'Learning about school: The development of kindergarteners' school scripts'. *Child Development*, **55**, 1697–709.

Fivush, R., Hudson, J. and Nelson, K. (1984) 'Children's long-term memory for a novel event: An exploratory study'. *Merrill-Palmer Quarterly*, **30**, 303–16.

Fivush, R., Kuebli, J. and Clubb, P. (1992) 'The structure of events and event representations: A developmental analysis'. *Child Development*, **63**, 188–201.

Fivush, R. and Mandler, J.M. (1985) 'Developmental changes in the understanding of temporal sequence'. *Child Development*, **56**, 1437–46.

Fivush, R. and Slackman, E.A. (1986) 'The acquisition and development of scripts'. In

K. Nelson (ed.) *Event Knowledge: Structure and function in development* (pp. 71–98). Hillsdale, NJ: Erlbaum.

Friedman, S.L. and Scholnick, E.K. (1987) 'The planning construct in the psychological literature'. In S.L. Friedman, E.K. Scholnick and R.R. Cocking (eds) *Blueprints for Thinking: The role of planning in cognitive development* (pp. 2–29). New York: Cambridge University Press.

French, L.A. (1985) 'Real-world knowledge as the basis for social and cognitive development'. In J.B. Pryor and J.D. Day (eds) *The Development of Social Cognition* (pp. 179–209). New York: Springer-Verlag.

French, L.A., Lucariello, J., Seidman, S. and Nelson, K. (1985) 'The influence of discourse content and context on preschoolers' use of language'. In L. Galda and A. Pellegrini (eds) *Play Language and Story: The development of children's literate behavior* (pp. 1–27). Norwood, NJ: Ablex.

French, L.A. and Nelson, K. (1985) 'Taking away the supportive context: Preschoolers talk about the "then and there" '. *The Quarterly Newsletter of the Laboratory of Comparative Human Cognition*, 4, 1–6.

Furman, L.N. and Walden, T.A. (1990) 'Effect of script knowledge on preschool children's communicative interaction'. *Developmental Psychology*, 26, 227–33.

Graesser, A.C., Woll, S.B., Kowalski, D.J. and Smith, D.A. (1980) 'Memory for typical and atypical actions in scripted activities'. *Journal of Experimental Psychology: Human Learning and Memory*, 6, 503–15.

Hudson, J.A. (1986) 'Memories are made of this: General event knowledge and the development of autobiographic memory'. In K. Nelson (ed.) *Event Knowledge: Structure and function in development* (pp. 97–118). Hillsdale, NJ: Erlbaum.

Hudson, J.A. (1988) 'Children's memory for atypical actions in script-based stories'. *Journal of Experimental Child Psychology*, 46, 159–73.

Hudson, J.A. (1990) 'Constructive processes in children's event memory'. *Developmental Psychology*, 2, 180–7.

Hudson, J.A. and Fivush, R. (1983) 'Categorical and schematic organisation and the development of retrieval strategies'. *Journal of Experimental Child Psychology*, 36, 32–42.

Hudson, J.A. and Fivush, R. (1991a) 'As time goes by: Sixth graders remember a kindergarten experience'. *Applied Cognitive Psychology*, 5, 347–60.

Hudson, J.A. and Fivush, R. (1991b) 'Planning in the preschool years: The emergence of plans from general event knowledge'. *Cognitive Development*, 6, 393–415.

Hudson, J.A. and Fivush, R. (in press) 'Scripts and episodes: The development of event knowledge'. *Applied Cognitive Psychology*.

Hudson, J.A. and Nelson, K. (1983) 'Effects of script structure on children's story recall'. *Developmental Psychology*, 19, 625–35.

Hudson, J.A. and Nelson, K. (1986) 'Repeated encounters of a similar kind: Effects of familiarity on children's autobiographic memory'. *Cognitive Development*, 1, 253–71.

Hudson, J.A. and Shapiro, L.R. (1991) 'From knowing to telling: Children's scripts, stories, and personal narratives'. In A. McCabe and C. Peterson (eds) *Developing Narrative Structure*. Hillsdale, NJ: Erlbaum.

Hudson, J.A., Shapiro, L.R. and Sosa, B.B. (1992) 'Planning in the real world: Preschool children's scripts and plans for familiar events'. Submitted manuscript.

Hudson, J.A. and Slackman, E.A. (1990) 'Children's use of scripts in inferential text processing'. *Discourse Processes*, 13, 375–85.

Kuebli, J. (1990) *This way or that way: Complexity in children's event knowledge*. Paper presented at the Southeastern Conference on Human Development, Richmond, VA, March.

Linton, M. (1982) 'Transformations of memory in everyday life'. In U. Neisser (ed.) *Memory Observed* (pp. 77–89). San Francisco, CA: W.H. Freeman.

Lucariello, J., Kyratzis, A. and Engel, S. (1986) 'Event representations, context, and language'. In K. Nelson (ed.) *Event Knowledge: Structure and function in development* (pp. 137–60). Hillsdale, NJ: Erlbaum.

Lucariello, J. and Nelson, K. (1987) 'Remembering and planning talk between mothers and children'. *Discourse Processes*, 10, 219–35.

Lucariello, J. and Rifkin, A. (1986) 'Event knowledge as the basis for categorical knowledge'. In K. Nelson (ed.) *Event Knowledge: Structure and function in development* (pp. 189–203). Hillsdale, NJ: Erlbaum.

Mandler, J.M. (1979) 'Categorical and schematic organization in memory'. In C.R. Puff (ed.) *Memory Organization and Structure* (pp. 259–99). New York: Academic Press.

Mandler, J.M. (1983) 'Representation'. In J.H. Flavell and E.M. Markman (eds), P.H. Mussen (series ed.), *Handbook of child psychology: Vol. 3. Cognitive development* (4th edn, pp. 420–94). New York: Wiley.

McCartney, K.A. and Nelson, K. (1981) 'Children's use of scripts in story recall'. *Discourse Processes*, 4, 59–70.

Neisser, U. (1981) 'John Dean's memory: A case study'. *Cognition*, 9, 1–22.

Nelson, K. (1981) 'Social cognition in a script framework'. In J. Flavell and L. Ross (eds) *Social Cognitive Development: Frontiers and possible futures* (pp. 97–118). New York: Cambridge University Press.

Nelson, K. (1985) *Making Sense: Development of meaning in early childhood*. New York: Academic Press.

Nelson, K. (ed.) (1986) *Event Knowledge: Structure and function in development*. Hillsdale, NJ: Erlbaum.

Nelson, K. (1988) 'The ontogeny of memory for real events'. In U. Neisser (ed.) *Remembering Reconsidered: Ecological and traditional approaches to the study of memory* (pp. 244–76). New York: Cambridge University Press.

Nelson, K. (1990) 'Remembering, forgetting, and childhood amnesia'. In R. Fivush and J.A. Hudson (eds) *Knowing and Remembering in Young Children* (pp. 301–16). New York: Cambridge University Press.

Nelson, K., Fivush, R., Hudson, J. and Lucariello, J. (1983) 'Scripts and the development of memory'. In M.T.H. Chi (ed.) *What is Memory Development the Development of?* Basel: S. Karger.

Nelson, K. and Gruendel, J. (1979) 'At morning it's lunchtime: A scriptal view of children's dialogues'. *Discourse Processes*, 2, 73–94.

Nelson, K. and Gruendel, J. (1981) 'Generalized event representations: Basic building blocks of cognitive development'. In M.E. Lamb and A.L. Brown (eds) *Advances in Developmental Psychology* (vol. 1, pp. 21–46). Hillsdale, NJ: Erlbaum.

Nelson, K. and Gruendel, J. (1986) 'Children's scripts'. In K. Nelson (ed.) *Event Knowledge: Structure and function in development* (pp. 231–47). Hillsdale, NJ: Erlbaum.

Nelson, K. and Hudson, J.A. (1988) 'Scripts and memory: Functional relationships in development'. In F.E. Weinert and M. Perlmutter (eds) *Memory Development: Universal changes and individual differences* (pp. 147–67). Hillsdale, NJ: Erlbaum.

Nelson, K. and Seidman, S. (1984) 'Playing with scripts'. In I. Bretherton (ed.) *Symbolic Play: The development of social understanding* (pp. 45–71). New York: Academic Press.

O'Connell, B. and Gerard, A. (1985) 'Scripts and scraps: The development of sequential understanding'. *Child Development*, 56, 671–81.

Piaget, J. (1955) *The Language and Thought of the Child*. New York: World Publishing.

Piaget, J. (1969) *The Child's Conception of Time*. London: Routledge & Kegan Paul.

Price, D.W.W. and Goodman, G.S. (1990) 'Visiting the wizard: Children's memory for a recurring event'. *Child Development*, 61, 664–80.

Ratner, H.H., Smith, B.S. and Dion, S.A. (1986) 'Development of memory for events'. *Journal of Experimental Child Psychology*, 41, 411–28.

Reiser, B.J. (1986) 'The encoding and retrieval and memories of real-world experiences'. In J.A. Galambos, R.P. Abelson and J.B. Black (eds) *Knowledge Structures* (pp. 71–99). Hillsdale, NJ: Erlbaum.

Sachs, J., Goldman, J. and Chaille, C. (1985) 'Narratives in preschoolers' sociodramatic play: The role of knowledge and communicative competence'. In L. Galda and A. Pellegrini (eds) *Play, Language, and Stories: The development of children's literate behavior* (pp. 45–61). Norwood, NJ: Ablex.

Schank, R. (1982) *Dynamic Memory: A theory of reminding and learning in computers and people*. New York: Cambridge University Press.

Schank, R. and Abelson, A. (1977) *Scripts, Plans, Goals, and Understanding*. Hillsdale, NJ: Erlbaum.

Seidman, S., Nelson, K. and Gruendel, J. (1986) 'Make believe scripts: The transformation of ERs in fantasy'. In K. Nelson (ed.) *Event Knowledge: Structure and function in development* (pp. 161–78). Hillsdale, NJ: Erlbaum.

Shapiro, L.R. and Hudson, J.A. (1991) *From start to finish: What it takes for preschool children to plan a novel event*. Paper presented at the Conference on Human Development, Atlanta, April.

Slackman, E.A., Hudson, J.A. and Fivush, R. (1986) 'Actions, actors, links, and goals: The structure of children's event representations'. In K. Nelson (ed.) *Event Knowledge: Structure and function in development* (pp. 47–69). Hillsdale, NJ: Erlbaum.

Slackman, E.A. and Nelson, K. (1984) 'Acquisition of an unfamiliar script in story form by young children'. *Child Development*, 55, 329–40.

Smith, B.S., Ratner, H.H. and Hobart, C.J. (1987) 'The role of cuing and organization in children's memory for events'. *Journal of Experimental Child Psychology*, 44, 1–24.

Smith, D.A. and Graesser, A.C. (1981) 'Memory for actions in scripted activities as a function of typicality, retention interval, and retrieval task'. *Memory and Cognition*, 9, 550–9.

Ungerer, J.A. (1985) *The development of script knowledge in children from 18 to 30 months of age*. Paper presented at the Society for Research in Child Development, Toronto, April.

Chapter 7

The child as sociologist:
the childhood development of implicit theories of role categories and social organization
Nicholas Emler and Julie Dickinson

7.1 Introduction: the requirements for interactive competence

Both authors of this chapter are psychologists by profession; their thesis here is that in common with all our fellow human beings, we are also amateur sociologists by necessity. Between our waking in the morning and settling down to work in our offices, a number of interactions and transactions will have taken place between ourselves and other people – exchanges, perhaps, with other family members, other parents, school staff, shopkeepers, other motorists, cyclists and pedestrians, ticket clerks and ticket collectors, secretaries, students and other staff. As is discussed in the other chapters in this volume, our own and others' competent participation in these exchanges is predicated upon our possession – and ability to make use – of various kinds of knowledge. We must have a theory of mind, knowledge about wishes and intentions, an understanding of mood and emotions, beliefs about character and personality, and communicative competencies. In many of these respects we are making use of psychological knowledge. But must we also be sociologists?

Notice that the references to our early-morning encounters do not identify particular individuals; they refer instead to social roles and categories. The implication is that some part of these transactions – perhaps the major part, if not the entirety – is predicated upon the roles we occupy in relation to one another – husband–wife, father–daughter, customer–shopkeeper, motorist–pedestrian, parent–teacher – and not upon our respective personal identities. Our encounters are governed by the rules and expectations particular to the role-relationships between us. We react as we do not just because we have interpreted others' wishes and intentions, identified their current mood, or predicted their emotional responses, but because we possess some intuitive understanding of social structure and the social roles it contains (see Chapter 5 by Judith Smetana).

However, there are yet other and more general kinds of knowledge which lie behind our actions and are perhaps more implicit in any particular interaction, but none the less structure our behaviour and social relationships in the longer term. These will include some knowledge of social structure, beliefs about the ways in which people and positions are ordered in terms of status, prestige, wealth and power.

In contemporary society, the status order is closely related to occupation and related ideologically to the links between occupation and income. In this chapter we shall examine children's developing knowledge and beliefs about social structure, and in particular about the occupational structure of society and the connections between work, status and pay. We shall in effect be examining the development of the child as a lay social theorist, and as one who theorizes about the origins of social inequalities. In so far as these inequalities reflect variations in income, we need to examine the three areas of knowledge which must be integrated in judgements about incomes: knowledge of inputs (i.e. what different kinds of jobs involve and what they require of the people who do them), knowledge of outcomes (i.e. the scale of reward or remuneration associated with different jobs) and principles of distributive justice (i.e. principles for the fair distribution of rewards). In seeking to explain observed developments, we shall contrast two major theoretical positions: cognitive constructivism (Piaget, 1953) and genetic social psychology (cf. Moscovici, 1976, 1983; Doise and Mugny, 1984). Our general aim is to show that theoretical accounts based on constructivism are by themselves insufficient to make sense of the process by which children develop social theories; a more complete account also requires the perspective provided by genetic social psychology. This provides an analysis of the social mechanisms through which knowledge is generated and transmitted, and thus of the influence of the social environment on the child's developing knowledge.

7.2 *Background to research*

7.2.1 Exchange relations

The daily life of adults in contemporary societies is likely to involve participation in a number of economic exchange systems. Many will be members of a household economy, contributing their labour and perhaps income, and receiving a variety of benefits. They will almost certainly participate in the commercial system, as consumers if not as suppliers, exchanging commodities for money. Next, there is a less well recognized system of informal exchanges in which money is seldom involved and the resources are seldom explicitly valued in money terms by those concerned.

The exchanges might involve occasional help of various kinds, advice, 'favours' or loans of equipment (Boissevain, 1974). Finally, there is the system of employment relations in which people exchange labour for a wage. The employment relation has a number of distinctive features, but the central premiss is a more or less explicit contract the terms of which involve one person surrendering specified periods of time to another person or organization which then directs their activities during this period in exchange for agreed benefits, most obviously in the form of a wage or salary.

It is this last exchange system which is most directly relevant to social structure and stratification, and in this context the relation between work and income is pivotal in the development of knowledge and beliefs about social stratification. It is pivotal for three reasons. First, although a minority of people in Western society are able to live on income from capital and are likely to have inherited their wealth (Giddens, 1989), for most others inequalities in the distribution of wealth are a result of differences in earned income. Income is in turn related, albeit imperfectly (Jencks, 1972), to occupation. Thus, beliefs developed in childhood about the relation between income and occupation may be expected to have consequences for vocational aspirations. At the very least they will shape children's assumptions about the economic consequences of their occupational goals.

Second, the income–occupation relation raises issues of distributive justice: to what extent are inequalities of income regarded as fair and legitimate (Dahrendorf, 1959; Mann, 1970)? The beliefs children develop about the reasons for inequalities of wealth and income are also beliefs about the legitimacy of the prevailing social order.

Third, occupation is related, in the beliefs of most adults, to various other social differences (Hope, 1982). Jobs are perceived as differing not just in the material quality of life or relative standard of living they allow, but also in their social value – the relative contributions they make to society – and in the educational qualifications they require, as well as in the power and influence over the affairs of society with which they are associated. Ever since a division of labour emerged in human societies, its significance has extended far beyond the mere distribution of tasks. It has become the major axis upon which relative social honour, prestige, power and control over resources are distributed (Berry, 1976) so that knowledge about occupations is knowledge about the moral order of society.

7.2.2 Distributive justice

Children are not normally directly involved in employment relations, although they do directly experience the benefits or costs of their own family's socioeconomic position. And as we shall see, children do hold beliefs about the relative social status of different occupations, about differences in wealth and income, and about the reasons for such differences. In other words, thinking about social inequality is not simply postponed until one becomes an adult; on the contrary, what a person believes as an adult is very likely to reflect beliefs that person has developed over the course of childhood. If you take for granted the basic terms of employment relations, including the practice of paying people different salaries for different jobs, this is largely because beliefs assembled and constructed during your childhood have brought you to this point.

There are several theories concerning the kinds of connections people will perceive between status, occupation and income, and particularly about the judgements they will make concerning occupation-related income differences. Conflict theories (cf. Dahrendorf, 1959) take the view that people's attitudes to social inequalities will be conditioned by their own position in the socioeconomic structure. Those who benefit from the status quo will regard it as just, whereas those who are disadvantaged by it may not. What children believe, therefore, will depend on the social class in which they are raised.

Most other theories predict that everyone, whatever their own position in the system of inequalities, will regard inequalities as on the whole legitimate. Thus, Lerner's (1977) 'Just World' theory implies not that justice is at work in society, producing deserved inequalities, but that people have a need to *believe* that this is the case. He further argues that the need to believe in a just world has its origins in childhood.

Equity theory (Adams, 1965; Homans, 1974) implies, on the contrary, that a consensus about the legitimacy of inequalities could arise from people perceiving matters objectively. If individuals' contributions to society differ, then their outcomes or rewards should also differ. Therefore, if people believe that individuals generally get what they deserve, this may be because they are right and not because they have confused the operation of fate with the workings of justice (as the Just World theory assumes). Equity theory implies that commitment to a 'contributions rule' for distributing resources is a natural human inclination and thus one in which children, as members of this species, will naturally share.

Functionalist sociology (Parsons, 1952) assumes that the survival of any social system requires a broad consensus among its members about the legitimacy of the social arrangements it contains. If these arrangements include inequalities of wealth – and those of all human societies apart from semi-nomadic hunter-gatherers do – then this, too, should be widely accepted as justified. In other words, shared beliefs that inequalities are fair are a functional requirement of social systems rather than psychologically required distortions or objective deductions. This consensus is assumed to be produced by processes of socialization.

Cognitive constructivism (Piaget, 1953) deserves our particular attention because it gives a more complete account of the developmental process than any of the preceding theories. Its key idea is that intellectual development is the evolution of a set of problem-solving instruments; these are progressively constructed and perfected by individual children over the first fifteen or so years of their lives. It further assumes that the logical capacities which children gradually construct to make sense of the natural world are also applied in their representations of the social world. To paraphrase William Damon (1981), in reasoning about the social world, 'children call on their abilities to categorize the world, establish reciprocal relations between events in the world, to quantify goods and rewards' (p. 62). The underlying assumption, therefore, is that what individual adults think and believe, whether about natural phenomena or social arrangements, is a function of the capacities each has developed to reason about and make deductions from available evidence.

Let us now consider how these ideas have been applied in research on children's understanding of social structure.

7.3 Research on children's understanding of social structure

7.3.1 Perceptions of status

One of the basic ways in which adults in contemporary societies represent social stratification is in terms of the relative status or prestige of different occupations. Moreover, whatever their own position in the social structure, people tend to agree about the rank order of prestige of occupations. It turns out that this rank order is rapidly learned in childhood (Dickinson, 1986). It is likely that concepts of broad occupational strata (e.g. white-collar versus blue-collar) are gained first and then further differentiated in terms of the social standing of individual jobs. Jahoda (1959) found that Scottish children as young as 6 were sensitive to some visual cues to socioeconomic status such as clothing and housing, and they frequently described pictures of working-class and middle-class stereotypes in occupational terms: 'workman', 'painter', 'plumber', 'gentleman', 'businessman', 'doctor', etc. By early adolescence, ratings of occupational prestige are very similar to those of official measures of socioeconomic status (Dickinson, 1986; Himmelweit, Halsey and Oppenheim, 1952). Perceptions of occupational prestige are widely shared, and class differences are relatively minor. Thus working-class adolescents tend to overestimate the prestige of skilled manual jobs (Dickinson, 1986; Himmelweit *et al.*, 1952; Weinstein, 1958), while middle-class children generally are more conscious of occupational status (Dickinson, 1986; Simmons and Rosenberg, 1971). But how do children account for these status differences?

7.3.2 Explanations of inequalities

Connell (1977) observed a form of representation of inequalities among children up to the age of 8 which he described as a stage of 'dramatic contrasts'. During this period children recognize very salient and concrete contrasts in material wealth and poverty, but they articulate no clear explanations for these differences. However, Duveen and Shields (1985) found that even 3- to 5-year-olds recognize that some people – and particularly those who are apparently powerful: for example, the police or men as compared to women – are paid more for their work.

From the age of 7 or 8 children also begin to refer to jobs in value-laden terms such as 'important', 'good', 'dirty' or 'ordinary' (Dickinson, 1987; Jahoda, 1959). They are also likely to provide descriptions when asked to explain occupational status or income. So, for instance, bus drivers earn less than doctors because 'all they do is drive a bus', while doctors 'cure people' (Dickinson, 1987; Emler and Dickinson, 1985; Gunn, 1964; Siegal, 1981; Weinstein, 1958). Frequently the turn of phrase and tone of voice convey notions of value: 'it's a dirty job', 'it's a good job'. Explanations in the form of descriptions remain common well beyond 10 years of age and may reflect feelings that the reasons for inequality are somehow self-evident and an integral part of the job.

None the less, from the age of 7 or 8 children do also begin to provide more 'rational' explanations in terms of factors related to the individual or the job such as 'importance', 'effort' and, more rarely, 'brains' or 'training' (Dickinson, 1987; Gunn, 1964; Leahy, 1983a; Weinstein, 1958). This corresponds to Connell's stage of 'concrete realism'; representations of society now contain intermediate groups between the very rich and the very poor, and differences are linked to a number of concrete details connecting wealth, income and work.

The use of individualistic explanations of the earnings associated with different jobs, with the addition of further factors like 'responsibility', 'qualifications' and 'skills', gradually increases throughout later childhood and adolescence, and forms the predominant way of explaining inequality in adolescence and adulthood. Leahy (1983b) argues that the move from descriptive to individualistic or 'central' explanations reflects cognitive-developmental changes in person-perception – changes from reliance on observed, external characteristics to inferred, psychological characteristics.

During adolescence, explanations in terms of social forces begin to be reproduced. These may include references to the social structure and economic processes such as 'market forces', 'class' or 'political power', 'public opinion' and 'financial incentives' rather than individual characteristics to explain wage differentials (Dickinson, 1986; Leahy, 1983a). Again, there are cognitive-developmental arguments for the emergence of these 'sociocentric' explanations: Leahy (1983b) attributes their appearance to the development of more abstract thought and the ability to focus on relationships rather than single groups or individuals. These types of explanations, however, are rare in adolescence and even in adulthood (Dickinson, 1986) and do not seem to take over from the individualistic explanations.

Not all young people believe income differences are fair, and even the majority who favour inequality in general tend to have some quibbles about particular wage differentials. Interestingly, the criteria that are used to explain and justify wage differentials are also used to declare them illegitimate. Thus 'road sweepers should earn more money because they do hard, tiring work', or 'bus drivers should earn more because transport is important to the community'. Wage relations are based overwhelmingly on the existing structure of relations. Despite the prevalence of the Western democratic myth of equal opportunity, more prevalent in America than Britain, research by Simmons and Rosenberg (1971) has shown that American children and adolescents do not believe that everyone has the same chance to achieve economic success, and they are aware of socioeconomic and racial disadvantage.

To summarize: children's views about inequality change and develop with age. From quite early on they are aware that there are differences in wealth and status, and that these are linked in some way to the work people do. Their beliefs about these differences become more differentiated and detailed with age. Explanations and judgements also evolve with age. Connell (1977) has reported that young children are more likely to regard inequalities in wealth as unfair, whereas older children are more likely to argue that inequalities are justified, and commonly their justifications appeal to considerations of equity. Leahy (1983a) reported that judgements about wealth and poverty which appeal to *equality* show a curvilinear relation with age, while those which appeal to *equity* increase linearly with age at least up to 14. He concluded that explanations for wealth and poverty which reflect the idea of 'meritorious earning' (p. 116) do become more frequent with age, though at 17 they still accounted for less than 50 per cent of all explanations.

One straightforward explanation for these changes is that they reflect cognitive development. On the one hand, children progressively assemble a range of observations, insights and concepts which form the elements of their accounts of social structure and the inequalities it contains. On the other, the mental operations of which they are capable become increasingly sophisticated, with the result that their mental representations of social structure integrate the assembled elements into frameworks which are themselves progressively more abstract and complex. Thus early in life, social structure is understood in highly concrete and descriptive terms. By the time individuals reach adulthood they have become capable of abstract theorizing about social structure.

7.3.3 Cognitive elements in knowledge about social stratification

Let us look next at the elements of knowledge upon which children may be drawing to construct their interpretations of social structure.

In understanding the relation between work and income, one of the basic problems to be solved is where the money for work is to come from (Berti and Bombi, 1988; Dickinson, 1986). Perhaps the most basic requirement here is to understand that an exchange is involved: work for payment. This in turn requires that children understand something about the nature of money as a medium of exchange. Research by Danziger (1958) suggested that the work-for-money exchange is well understood by 7- to 8-year-olds. Berti and Bombi (1988) provide evidence for the ages at which children appreciate how payment for work is organized. At their first level – up to the age of 6 or 7 – children think in terms of direct exchanges between employees and consumers; thus, for example, people working in shops receive money from customers, bus drivers receive money from passengers, and so on. At a second level – between the ages of 7 and 9 – children recognize that payment may be made by a boss as well as directly by customers and consumers. At the third level – 9 to 11 – the idea that the exchange is between worker and boss is (inappropriately) generalized to all occupations, but only at the fourth level, which all children are likely to have reached by 13, do they show an appreciation of how bosses come by the money they use to pay employees.

Another kind of cognitive prerequisite relates to inputs and the capacity to distinguish between inputs – such as effort, time, skill or responsibility – in relevant ways. A key capacity here involves the comparison of intentions. Piaget (1932) observed that young children fail to consider intentions when apportioning praise and blame; they tend instead to focus on objective outcomes. Older children, by contrast, will argue that an individual can take credit for – and should be rewarded for – only those outcomes he or she intended. Studies relating this to children's judgements of task performance indicate that at 4 they give more weight to outcomes; they shift, by the age of 8 to 10, to giving more weight to effort in deciding rewards (Weiner and Peter, 1973; Wimmer, Wachter and Perner, 1982). However, Weiner and Peter (1973) also found that after the age of 12 objective outcomes were again given more credit than effort. Their conclusion – that society reinforces a 'more primitive' developmental stage (reward for outcome rather than effort) – implies that social influences can modify the effects of cognitive development, but it does not tell us why society's reinforcement has this effect on teenagers but not on younger children.

Next, what relation do children expect to obtain between people's inputs into their work, such as skill or effort, and the outcomes they enjoy? One body of research relating to this question has used quasi-experimental tasks which put the child in the position of paymaster. The typical task (e.g. Leventhal and Anderson, 1970) presents children with information about the work inputs of two or more people and asks them to distribute a fixed reward between them. The work inputs may be amount of work completed, amount of time worked, quality of work produced or amount of effort expended. The rewards may be money, sweets, or something else desirable. Note that in these studies the dependent variable is the allocation of rewards actually made rather than explanations of or justifications for allocations.

In a comprehensive review of this literature, Hook and Cook (1979) showed that when work inputs can be quantified, and when the allocator is not also one of the recipients, three distinct types of allocation emerge from these studies, which they labelled respectively equality, ordinal equity and proportional equity. Ordinal equity involves allocations that are in the same rank order of magnitude as the work inputs of the individuals concerned. Proportional equity involves allocations that are also in proportion to work inputs. Ordinal equity is the predominant type from 6 years of age onwards; proportional equity appears only after the age of 13. Hook and Cook link these age patterns to cognitive changes. Children between the ages of 6 and 12 will be capable of ordinal comparisons on two dimensions, but not of computing ratios. This latter requires formal operations (Inhelder and Piaget, 1958). Hook and Cook's analysis suggests, therefore, that children apply the principle of equity in so far as their cognitive skills allow them to do so.

Do children make judgements about distributive fairness which correspond to Hook and Cook's age-related pattern of allocation decisions? Research examining children's verbalization of justice principles has generally revealed qualitative differences associated with age. In this research children are asked to propose how a limited resource like candy bars or pizza (Damon, 1977) should be divided between two or more people, and to explain what makes their proposals fair. The recipients – usually children – between whom these benefits are to be divided differ in various ways, such as age, past behaviour, needs or prior deprivation. Piaget (1932) found that most children under 7 confuse fairness with obedience to the wishes of parents or other adults (the 'authority' stage). Between 7 and 10 the most frequently voiced definition of fairness interpreted it as strict equality of treatment. Beyond that age, children would often distinguish between claimants in terms of their relative merit. Piaget called this attitude 'equity', but it subsumed considerations of both deserts earned by past efforts or good behaviour and need.

Damon (1975), on the basis of studies with children aged 4 to 10, reported a slightly different sequence. He did not find an authority stage, but did find that some 4-year-olds equated justice with self-interest. Between the ages of 5 and 7, the equality principle seemed to be predominant, but after the age of 6 notions of merit and deserving appeared. After the age of 8, weight was also given to differing needs; the poor, for example, might get special consideration.

The relevance of considerations of need in expectations about the distribution of wealth or incomes is unclear. Siegal (1981) asked children more directly about pay. His study dealt with children's views of the economic needs of people in specific occupations. However, the finding that many 8- to 12-year-olds judged the fairness of incomes on the basis of need may reflect the fact that need is what these children were explicitly asked about. In other research in which children have been asked about the fairness of perceived income differentials (e.g. Emler and Dickinson, 1985), need is seldom – if ever – mentioned by them.

Despite variations in findings the above research indicates how conceptual developments over childhood could underlie the observed changes in children's accounts of social stratification described in the previous section: children progressively integrate their understandings of how wealth is acquired, how work varies in terms of inputs, and how inputs can be related to outcomes.

7.4 Theoretical accounts: cognitive development or social transmission?

Piaget's theory of cognitive development provides one possible account of the manner in which children develop beliefs about social stratification. What we have referred to as genetic social psychology provides an alternative account, based on the following propositions. The construction of knowledge in the child is a social process. In particular, knowledge is transmitted to children and derives from the cultures and social groups of which they are a part. What is assembled in the mind of any individual child will depend upon the society to which that child belongs, and the position occupied by that child within it. This is not to imply that children play an entirely passive role in the construction of knowledge: they are active participants in communicative exchanges with others. Through communication and interaction with both adults and other children, each child participates in a process of social influence, the effects of which are to construct and sustain particular interpretations of reality.

The contrasting implications of constructivism and genetic social psychology can be illustrated in two ways. The first concerns the part played by the principle of equity in explanations and evaluations of social inequalities; the second is in terms of the differing interpretations they provide of social class differences in beliefs and judgements. Let us take them in turn.

7.4.1 Equity as explanation and justification for inequality

We have seen that as they grow older children are increasingly likely to allocate hypothetical payments on an equitable basis – that is, in direct proportion to contributions (cf. Hook and Cook, 1979). We have also seen that the most common forms of both explanation and justification given by older children for inequalities of wealth and income are 'equity-like': they refer to differential contributions. So are children, as they grow older, acting increasingly like scrutineers guided by the principle of equity, examining the inputs and outcomes of different individuals in society, estimating what they deserve, and then comparing this with the status quo, with what they actually receive, and concluding that the status quo does, after all, agree with what is just? This does not seem likely.

Piaget (1932) made the following important point about children's understanding of social rules. Children must decide jointly what rules to apply when they play a game such as marbles together. In doing so they will more clearly appreciate the principles and procedures according to which rules ideally ought to be formulated. Piaget also observed that children are seldom in a position to make similar decisions about most of the other rules that govern social life, and only rarely will they have occasion to reflect on the adequacy of any of these rules. But when they do so, the cognitive resources they draw upon will be those that are apparent when they reason about their own games.

The argument might be applied to employment relations as follows. People only occasionally think – and need to think – about the relation between income and occupation. When they do so, they draw upon the principles of distributive justice they have constructed when faced with other, and perhaps simpler, allocation problems. If the most sophisticated solution they have evolved is that of equity, then it is this which they therefore apply. Thus, the system of employment relations as a method for distributing wealth secures support and acceptance amongst the population at large because on those occasions when members of the population do reflect upon it, they are inclined to perceive that its results are broadly consistent with the requirements of equity.

The difficulty is that estimates of what is equitable require a comparison not just of outcomes but also of inputs, even if only on an ordinal scale. In the research on allocation decisions, which seems most clearly to show processes of equity at work, the problems contain inputs which are precise, simple, quantified and known. For example, one 'employee' has painted six feet of fence while the other has painted four. In the case of real occupations inputs will be complex, imprecise mixes of task requirements and personal attributes which are difficult to quantify and only vaguely recognized by most people. Yet one must be able to decide at the very least whether the contributions made by A are greater than, equal to or less than those made by B.

The necessary comparisons are probably impossible, for three reasons. The first is the difficulty of knowing with any accuracy what the inputs are. Second, even if all inputs were known, the relevance or relative weight to be attached to each is in principle undecidable on logical grounds alone; all inputs cannot be translated on to a single scale. What is to count more – effort, skills, physical risk, level of responsibility, hours worked, training required, the social value of the work, the quality of the performance? Third, most of these different inputs cannot be quantified in any meaningful way, even if different levels of any one kind of input could be crudely ordered. If this were not so, agreement on performance indicators in the workplace would be relatively straightforward. But even within occupations and in the most quantifiable of work, it is notoriously difficult to quantify work input (cf. Bass and Barrett, 1981). It seems more probable, therefore, that any consensus about the pricing of different kinds of work is a product of negotiation and influence rather than one of logical deduction from a knowledge of inputs. In other words, consensus results from *social* rather than *logical* processes.

There is, however, a more fundamental point on which constructivism and genetic social psychology differ: it concerns the process by which children come to believe what they believe – about income–occupation relations, or anything else. Constructivism represents a line of thought – going back at least to Alfred Binet's (Binet and Simon, 1908) analysis of intellectual development – which rests on the premiss that the environment presents experience with problems – problems, moreover, which have single correct answers. These problems are universal, invariant and ubiquitous; they are inherent in nature and social life: Why do some objects, but not others, float on water? How can scarce resources best be divided amongst multiple claimants? Constructivists argue that the process by which these answers are discovered is the spontaneous problem-solving activity of the individual child.

From the perspective of genetic social psychology, this almost entirely ignores what it is to be a social animal. Social species – and humans above all – inhabit and, indeed, create environments which present the individual inhabitants not merely with problems but also – undoubtedly more regularly, and much more significantly – with *solutions*.

The experience of children in particular is to be presented with solutions and arguments for solutions, and in various ways, and to varying degrees, to be urged to accept them. Different solutions can be presented in different societies, and even within the same society children may be confronted with different and even conflicting solutions to the same problems. In this sense, existing income distributions represent solutions, not problems, but they remain inherently matters of controversy – that is, these solutions are open to dispute and reconsideration (cf. Billig, 1987).

Problems of social life are more akin to those of engineering than to those of physics; they admit of several viable solutions, each with its advantages and disadvantages. But even this analogy is suspect; engineering cannot escape the immutable laws of physics. It is not evident that there is an equivalent set of laws for social life.

Constructivists appear to disagree. We say 'appear', because it is not quite clear what kind of invariant properties constructivists attribute to the social environment. Or rather, there are at least two views. One is represented by theorists such as Furth and Jahoda, who seem to be saying that the child's problem is to arrive at a correct interpretation of certain objective processes or relations. Furth says of experience of society:

> Societal institutions . . . present themselves as objectively given, with some clear-cut rules of how they work. Adults could easily recognise a list of statements relative

to business, occupational roles, government or community. To understand societal institutions means precisely to understand this framework. (1978, p. 120)

Jahoda points to the social practices involved in buying and selling of commodities as instances which contain a necessary and discoverable logic (cf. Jahoda, 1984). Indeed, what the individual child supposedly discovers is this very necessity. The argument might be extended: labour markets are systems of relations (between a workforce, differentiated in talents and wants, and a market for various kinds of labour), just as a balance is a set of relations (between weights and lengths), and both can be correctly or incorrectly understood. This particular analogy is apposite because the same logic of ratios underlies the physical relations in the balance and the relations between inputs and outcomes in proportional equity (Hook and Cook, 1979).

But one can see immediately that there are some important differences between the two systems. The mechanical system of relations between weights and lengths in a balance is *necessary*; they hold whether or not anyone on the planet understands them (and many adults, in fact, do not understand them). When, in an economic system, the conditions for proportional equity hold between work and pay, these conditions are entirely optional. One might add that since they are produced by human behaviour, their occurrence may well be affected by whether the humans concerned understand the principle involved.

This brings us to the second view, represented by Lawrence Kohlberg. For Kohlberg, whereas the relations in a balance are physically necessary, those in equity are morally necessary. Moral necessity here refers to what is ideal in a conflict of interests (cf. Kohlberg, 1984). In this theory the invariants or universals of social life are moral 'issues' which arise in every human society – issues such as authority, the value of life, ties of affection, contracts and promises. Cognitive activity is directed towards finding solutions which are morally satisfying, given these social invariants. What changes over the course of development is the child's understanding of what is morally satisfying. So, in this species of theory, the developmental task or problem for the child is not to arrive at a correct understanding of an objective social reality, but to construct progressively more sophisticated moral theories which can generate increasingly adequate solutions to the problems of social – and that includes employment – relations.

Let us now return to the logic of equity in order to examine the idea that it represents an invariant. Organizational and industrial psychologists point out that the equity or contributions principle induces competition (Deutsch, 1986; Leventhal, 1976). In part the competition is for an inherently scarce resource, relative status. It seems at least plausible that members of a society orientated towards competition for individual status will support the contributions rule (equity) because differential reward or remuneration operates as a public marker of status. And as George Homans (1976) once observed, in the pursuit of status the public nature of the differential is everything. Thus children growing up in such a society may be expected to argue for application of the contributions rule when they are engaged in a competition for status. Where an equitable allocation would benefit them, they will want the rule applied as a public acknowledgement of their superiority over their rivals. Status competition is less appropriate between team members, so in this case the contributions rule would not be applied, as Lerner (1974) has shown.

But why might children apply the contributions rule when they are acting as disinterested third parties? Presumably they will do so when they think they are judging a competition, and when they believe that they and the claimants share the norms of status competition. When an individual is personally disadvantaged by application of the contributions rule (in the sense of losing status) he or she might be expected to favour an alternative, such as parity – as research carried out by Mikula (1980) indicates.

If the significance of equity lies in its role in the public marking of status differences, then we should expect a greater commitment to this principle in cultures that emphasize status competition. Both Nisan (1984) and Mann *et al.* (1985) report findings consistent with this expectation, as does Snarey (1985) with respect to the different forms of moral argument identified by Kohlberg (1984); in this latter case, moral arguments which emphasize the distribution of rewards according to relative merit are more commonplace among the adult members of competitive industrialized societies than in more cooperative and communally orientated societies.

7.4.2 Social knowledge and group membership

We have seen that the priority children give to a distribution principle like equity can depend upon the social or cultural groups to which they belong. This possibility is not excluded in cognitive-developmental theory, but it is interpreted in a particular way: the social environment of one culture may stimulate or facilitate more rapid cognitive growth than the social environment of another. Hence it might be argued that working-class children will develop intellectually at a slower rate than middle-class children if their environment presents them with less stimulation and is informationally less rich (cf. Jahoda, 1984). Enright *et al.* (1980) have reported, with respect to simple distributive justice problems, that middle-class children are more likely to apply the principle of equity than their working-class peers. They interpret this as a purely developmental difference: 'lower class children lag behind their middle class cohorts in distributive justice reasoning' (Enright *et al.*, 1980, p. 561).

Genetic social psychology takes the social group to be the origin of knowledge. In so far as social classes are distinct social groups, they may be expected to present the children who inhabit them with information that is different in both quantity and kind. Moreover, some of the crucial differences relate to social stratification itself. Children who grow up in middle-class environments are immersed in both more and different kinds of information about income inequalities. They will hear different kinds of explanations for these inequalities, and particularly a wider range of justifications. Dickinson (1986) has shown in two studies that middle-class, privately educated children, at all ages examined, produce more explanations for income differences than working-class, publicly educated children. Dickinson has argued that changes in explanations can be explained by social influence processes such as the learning of socially acceptable accounts or reasons which are widely available in everyday discourse. The belief in 'a fair day's work for a fair day's pay' is widely upheld in democratic society, and when workers are called upon to justify wage demands – as in disputes concerning wages – they tend to emphasize their personal contribution in terms of hours worked, productivity, commitment, importance to the economy, and so on.

Dickinson (1986) also suggests that education plays a major role in inculcating individualistic conceptions of wage relations at the expense of sociocentric ones. The qualifying and grading task of schools means that they are obliged to present a 'carrot and stick' image of society to children: effort leads to reward, qualifications justify high pay, responsibility entails personal sacrifice but financial compensations. To present any other image would risk deterring ambition and take away from schools what little power they have in promoting social mobility. The paradox of education in terms of its indoctrinating role and its liberating role is perhaps responsible for class differences observed by Dickinson (1986). Middle-class, privately educated children explained and justified wage inequalities by differences in qualifications far more often than working-class children, as would perhaps be predicted by their attendance at schools which stress the importance and necessity of academic qualifications and the desirability of professional jobs. Another class difference emerging in late adolescence, however, is the increased use of sociocentric explanations by middle-class pupils. These pupils were already prepared and motivated to sit exams and aim for high-ranking occupations; they could afford to be exposed to ideas contradicting the moral rule that rewards are based simply on effort.

If social class is important for the kind of informational environment in which it immerses children, it is also significant as a sociocognitive category which organizes experience as a function of class position. Tajfel (1984) provides a useful general model here. When social phenomena are grouped into categories, we tend to exaggerate the differences between the categories. Further, when we compare categories, we will often ourselves belong to one of them. Finally, when we compare our own category with any other, we tend to emphasize any difference that favours our own and deemphasize any that does not.

Social class is one potentially salient category membership. Moreover, it is defined largely in terms of occupation. Consequently, social classes differ on the dimension of income. So when children are asked about the incomes of different occupations, they are potentially being asked to compare social categories to which they do belong with those to which they do not belong. The conclusions they come to may therefore be influenced by their own social class position.

There are several indications that social class membership is more salient for middle- than for working-class children, so that the former are more likely to categorize themselves in terms of social class, and more likely to organize their knowledge of occupations in terms of social class categories. These effects should also be exaggerated in a more class-conscious society, and should be less evident in societies where class environments are less sharply divided, or where ideologies of equality are more prevalent.

This helps to make sense of certain other findings concerning children's beliefs about the links between income and occupation. Surprisingly, although researchers have frequently asked children what they think about inequalities of wealth or income, they have much less often explored what children actually believe the scale of these inequalities to be. It turns out that even if children and adults largely agree about the fairness of differences, many adults – let alone children – have very hazy ideas about what the inequalities involved actually are (Dickinson, 1986).

Emler and Dickinson (1985) asked Scottish 6- to 12-year-olds about the weekly earnings of people in four occupations: doctor, teacher, bus driver and road sweeper. Their sample included children from a state school with a working-class catchment area, and middle-class children from a private, fee-paying school. There was broad agreement between the two groups on the rank order of occupations by earnings, but not on the absolute levels of income. The middle-class children questioned estimated the income differences to be much greater than did the working-class children. One possibility is that differences in understanding of equity lie behind these different perceptions. Thus if middle-class children are more likely to have developed an understanding of the principle of equity than working-class children of the same age (cf. Enright *et al.*, 1980), these findings are as one would expect. But in this case, the perceived differentials should also increase with age. Emler and Dickinson (1985) found no such increase: estimates were unrelated to age. It is also difficult to see why children who have very different beliefs about the scale of inequalities should at the same time agree that these inequalities are fair. Intergroup comparisons could, however, produce this pattern. As income differences favour the middle class, the middle-class–working-class difference will be perceived as greater by middle-class than by working-class children. But middle-class children should emphasize this difference only if they also believe it is legitimate. Significantly, those middle-class children who regarded the income differences as unfair perceived the gap to be smaller than those who regarded them as fair.

Emler and Luce (1985) found that American children's perceptions of income differences similarly varied as a function of their own social class positions, and a similar pattern was obtained in France (Ohana, 1987). The one exception to the pattern was that French working-class children perceived a greater difference between the occupations of bus driver and road sweeper than did middle-class children. This too, however, may be consistent with social categorization effects. Road sweepers in Paris, where the children came from, are commonly North African, and the white working-class children in this sample may well have regarded North Africans as a subordinate group and so exaggerated the difference between this and the more proto-typically white working-class occupation of bus driver. The middle-class children would feel less need to make this distinction among working-class occupations.

Finally, we are suggesting that children's income estimates for different occupations are more widely dispersed to the extent that their knowledge of occupations is organized in terms of social class categories. If this is so, then categorizing occupations in some way should have the effect of dispersing estimates. We have completed two exploratory experimental studies which lend some support to this hypothesis. In one study, 12-year-olds were presented with six occupations which were either categorized (by printing the names on different colour cards) or uncategorized. Children presented with the categorized occupations perceived larger differences between the categories. The second study involved university students and produced the same effect.

Tajfel (1984) also argued that people react quite differently in deciding the justice of exchanges among individuals *within* a group and in deciding the justice of exchanges *between* groups. Individuals in relatively advantaged social groups will refer to powerful and dominant social myths to justify the privileged position of their own group. In Moscovici's (1984) terms, these myths are 'social representations', shared belief systems generated and sustained by social groups. In this context, we regard equity as part of such a myth – part of the ideology of status competition, its precise contents tailored to sustain a particular ordering of status and economic advantage – and not as an attempt to calculate justice according to objective standards. Thus in America, where the economic advantage of the middle class depends on their greater capacity to buy higher education, it is hardly surprising that the higher income of occupations like that of doctor is justified by reference to the investment in education which such occupations require (Emler and Luce, 1985). Similarly aged children in Britain are more likely to invoke skill or contribution to the community to justify doctors' income (though Dickinson, 1986, found class differences here – see above). In the same way, the inputs invoked to explain or justify the income of different occupations vary with the case: managers have a more responsible job than janitors, but doctors do more skilful work than road sweepers.

To conclude this section: we are proposing, therefore, that social myths are propagated to sustain particular patterns of economic advantage. Since they are not based on any ultimate, verifiable, objective truth, their precise content will probably vary between cultures and social groups, and they are open to and challenged by counter-myths and arguments. In other words, they remain, inherently matters of controversy, even if one view appears for a time to have the upper hand (Billig, 1987). The system of employment relations has become the dominant way of organizing work in twentieth-century Western society, and with it has arisen a set of myths and arguments to sustain it and the distribution of wealth and status it produces. Children who grow up in this society are exposed to the various myths, arguments and counter-positions which make up the ongoing debate about this system, and they progressively assimilate these sociocognitive entities, these social representations. So when we ask children why certain income levels or differences in wealth exist, it is unlikely that we are simply accessing their own self-constructed moral judgement capacities, structured according to universal laws of cognitive organization and discovered by us in this kind of research at varying stages of completion. It is more likely that we are accessing their understanding of their culture's framework of legitimations for and challenges to the status quo.

What children understand, however, will depend on their own position in the existing system of inequalities. Middle-class children, like middle-class adults (Mann, 1970), will have more extensive and detailed representations of income inequalities and more elaborated justifications for these inequalities, to which they will also be more committed.

7.4.3 Sociocognitive development as socialization

How are these beliefs acquired? Not through logical reconstruction, because there is no single logic that could be recovered. We suggest instead that the process is more probably social transmission, and specifically social influence. Piaget recognized that social transmission could be involved in the child's acquisition of forms of understanding which do involve a single logic. He recognized that each child need not completely reinvent every intellectual insight for itself, and that cultures provide a range of cognitive tools to support intellectual development. Beyond this, however, Piaget did little to explore the processes by which social transmission might operate. Later generations of constructivists have all but dismissed any role for social transmission, for three reasons.

First, 'equilibration', the idea that mental systems are intrinsically self-balancing, tending constantly to change in the direction of greater internal consistency and external adaptation, seemed a more plausible general mechanism of development than social transmission. It was possible to see how equilibration could operate to generate logical operations, so why could it not also generate social insights? And this interpretation was consistent with observations of apparently spontaneous discovery by children of intellectual principles.

Second, constructivists (e.g. Turiel, 1983) have objected that social transmission implies a passive child as the object of influence, when it is clear that children are active agents in their own intellectual development. Here it is true that certain versions of social influence theory fit the caricature (Moscovici, 1976). However, Moscovici himself has shown that social influence processes involve interaction and negotiation between active parties, not the shaping of passive targets; and it is hard to understand why such social influence processes should work between adult human beings but not between adults and younger members of the species. The major difference between the two cases is that there is more inequality between adults and children. Adults have more extensive cognitive resources than children, and hence more capacity to generate distinctive and consistent positions; so influence is more likely to flow from older to younger than in the reverse direction. This expectation is also borne out by studies of the effects of joint task performance by children differing in cognitive level (Doise and Mugny, 1984).

A final objection to social transmission is that it somehow implies lack of resistance by the child's mind, or 'the assertion that a child can directly absorb information from his social environment' (Damon, 1977, p. 8). It implies that children will believe anything their society chooses to present to them – an objection that has in the past been raised to explanations of cognitive development in terms of social learning processes. This objection confuses compliance with influence. Compliance is an overt behavioural response requested, demanded or expected by another; it need imply no change in underlying beliefs (Moscovici, 1980). Social influence involves a change in a person's cognitive system, in her system of knowledge and beliefs. Research with adult subjects shows that cognitive systems provide all kinds of resistance to influence, and there is no reason to expect children to be any different except, perhaps, in degree. We suspect that the true contribution of the Piagetian tradition will prove to be an appreciation of the kinds of resistance the child's mind provides to social influence.

7.5 Summary and conclusions: the child as sociologist

From quite early in life, it seems, children do have representations of social inequalities, and by adolescence they can provide detailed accounts of the distribution of wealth in society. In this sense, they have become lay sociologists; they have begun to reflect on social stratification and its causes. We have argued that there are two kinds of theoretical account for the development of this kind of knowledge. The more established and traditional interpretation is that the process is one of cognitive development. Individual children progressively construct interpretations of society; their constructions progress through an invariant sequence of changes as each individual works his or her way towards an adult understanding of societal phenomena.

The alternative view – that of genetic social psychology – is that social groups generate practices and institutions together with explanations and justifications for these social arrangements, and these explanations and justifications – these 'theories' of why society is the way it is – are assimilated by new members through processes of social influence. Moreover, knowledge will be unequally distributed in society, and the representations shared among the members of powerful groups will not necessarily be the same as those found among the members of less powerful groups. Thus, what children come to know and believe about social and economic inequalities depends on their own position in the stratification system. The most advantaged are also the most conscious of the scale of inequalities, and possess the most extensive arguments for their legitimacy. This is a matter not of having proceeded further along the same single developmental pathway, but of systematic structural differences in the distribution of knowledge within society. Children acquire those ideas which have currency and significance within the social environments they inhabit – ideas which are therefore collectively constructed and sustained, not individually discovered.

Finally, none of this is at all incompatible with the observations that development is gradual, that the ideas children are able to assimilate depend on what they have assimilated so far, or that these ideas are structured mental operations. After all, what children acquire through interaction and social influence is not the cognitive equivalent of a scrapheap, a collection of unconnected 'facts' and observations. Rather, it is a working intellectual system, a mental structure which allows understanding. The social group can no more build a working mental structure in children by heaping beliefs upon them willy-nilly than it could build a working airliner by throwing bits of metal into a pile. The structure must be built up, piece by piece. Hence, whatever kinds of social theorists children become, their progress will be gradual: from simple to complex.

There are three questions for future research, each of which is as yet only partially answered. The first concerns the content and organization of children's beliefs and knowledge about social structure. The second and related question concerns the distribution of knowledge across different social groups: to what extent do children who grow up in particular social categories have more detailed knowledge of social structure than others, and to what extent do they have different kinds of beliefs? Finally, how is knowledge about society generated and disseminated? Future research might profitably draw upon the work of Moscovici and others on social influence processes, and that of Doise and Mugny (1984) on the constructive effects of sociocognitive conflict to illuminate in more detail the processes by which children acquire knowledge about social structure.

References

Adams, J.S. (1965) 'Inequity in social exchange'. In L. Berkowitz (ed.) *Advances in Experimental Social Psychology*, vol. 2. New York: Academic Press.

Bass, B.M. and Barrett, G.V. (1981) *People, Work and Organisations: An introduction to industrial and organisational psychology*. Boston, MA: Alyn & Bacon.

Berry, J.W. (1976) *Human Ecology and Cognitive Style*. New York: Wiley.

Berti, A.E. and Bombi, A.S. (1988) *The Child's Construction of Economics*. Cambridge: Cambridge University Press.

Billig, M. (1987) *Arguing and Thinking: A rhetorical approach to social psychology*. Cambridge: Cambridge University Press.

Binet, A. and Simon, T. (1908) 'Le developpement de l'intelligence chez les enfants'. *L'Année Psychologique*, 14, 1–94.

Boissevain, J. (1974) *Friends of Friends: Networks, manipulators and coalitions*. Oxford: Blackwell.

Connell, R.W. (1977) *Ruling Class, Ruling Culture*. Cambridge: Cambridge University Press.

Dahrendorf, R. (1959) *Class and Conflict in Industrial Society*. Stanford, CA: Stanford University Press.

Damon, W. (1975) 'Early conceptions of positive justice as related to the development of logical operations'. *Child Development*, 46, 301–12.

Damon, W. (1977) *The Social World of the Child*. San Francisco, CA: Jossey-Bass.

Damon, W. (1981) 'The development of justice and self-interest during childhood'. In M.J. Lerner and S.C. Lerner (eds) *The Justice Motive in Social Behavior*. New York: Plenum Press.

Danziger, K. (1958) 'Children's earliest conceptions of economic relationships (Australia)'. *Journal of Social Psychology*, 47, 231–40.

Deutsch, M. (1986) *Distributive Justice: A social psychological perspective*. New Haven, CT: Yale University Press.

Dickinson, J. (1986) 'The development of representations of social inequality'. Unpublished Ph.D. thesis, Dundee University.

Dickinson, J. (1987) *The development of beliefs about socio-economic structure*. Paper given at the Conference of the Social Section of the British Psychological Society, Oxford.

Dickinson, J. (1990) 'Adolescent representations of socio-economic status'. *British Journal of Developmental Psychology*, 8, 351–71.

Doise, W. and Mugny, G. (1984) *The Social Development of the Intellect*. Oxford: Pergamon.

Duveen, G. and Shields, M.M. (1985) 'Children's ideas about work, wages and social rank'. *Cahiers de psychologie cognitif*, 5, 411–12.

Emler, N. and Dickinson, J. (1985) 'Children's representation of economic inequalities: The effects of social class'. *British Journal of Developmental Psychology*, 3, 191–8.

Emler, N. and Luce, T. (1985) 'Social class background and perception of occupation related income differences in middle childhood'. Unpublished MS., University of Dundee.

Enright, R., Enright, W., Manheim, L. and Harris, B.E. (1980) 'Distributive justice development and social class'. *Developmental Psychology*, 16, 555–63.

Furth, H.G. (1978) 'Young children's understanding of society'. In H. McGurk (ed.) *Issues in Childhood Social Development*. London: Methuen.

Giddens, A. (1989) *Sociology*. London: Polity Press.

Gunn, B. (1964) 'Children's conceptions of occupational prestige'. *Personnel and Guidance Journal*, 42, 558–63.

Himmelweit, H., Halsey, A.H. and Oppenheim, A.N. (1952) 'The views of adolescents on some aspects of the social class structure'. *British Journal of Sociology*, 3, 148–72.

Homans, G.C. (1974) *Social Behavior: Its elementary forms*. New York: Harcourt Brace Jovanovich.

Homans, G.C. (1976) 'Commentary'. In L. Berkowitz and E. Webster (eds) *Advances in Experimental Social Psychology*, vol. 9. New York: Academic Press.

Hook, J. and Cook, T. (1979) 'Equity theory and the cognitive ability of children'. *Psychological Bulletin*, 86, 429–45.

Hope, K. (1982) 'A liberal theory of prestige'. *American Journal of Sociology*, 87, 1011–31.

Inhelder, B. and Piaget, J. (1958) *The Growth of Logical Thinking from Childhood to Adolescence*. London: Routledge.

Jahoda, G. (1959) 'Development of the perception of social differences in children from six to ten'. *British Journal of Psychology*, 50, 158–96.

Jahoda, G. (1984) 'The development of thinking about socio-economic systems'. In H. Tajfel (ed.) *The Social Dimension: European developments in social psychology*, vol. 1. Cambridge: Cambridge University Press.

Jencks, C. (1972) *Inequality*. Harmondsworth: Penguin.

Kohlberg, L. (1984) *Essays on Moral Development, vol. 2: The Psychology of Moral Development*. New York: Harper.

Leahy, R.L. (1983a) 'Development of the conception of economic inequality: II. Explanations, justifications and concepts of social mobility and change'. *Developmental Psychology*, 19, 111–25.

Leahy, R.L. (1983b) 'The development of the conception of social class'. In R.L. Leahy (ed.) *The Child's Construction of Social Inequality*. New York: Academic Press.

Lerner, M. (1974) 'The justice motive: "Equity" and "parity" among children'. *Journal of Personality and Social Psychology*, 29, 539–50.

Lerner, M. (1977) 'The justice motive in social behavior: Some hypotheses as to its origins and forms'. *Journal of Personality*, 45, 1–52.

Leventhal, G. (1976) 'The distribution of rewards and resources in groups and organizations'. In L. Berkowitz and E. Walster (eds) *Advances in Experimental Social Psychology*, vol. 9. New York: Academic Press.

Leventhal, G. and Anderson, D. (1970) 'Self-interest and the maintenance of equity'. *Journal of Personality and Social Psychology*, 15, 312–16.

Leventhal, G. and Lane, D. (1970) 'Sex, age, and equity behavior'. *Journal of Personality and Social Psychology*, 15, 312–16.

Mann, M. (1970) 'The social cohesion of liberal democracy'. *American Sociological Review*, 35, 423–39.

Mann, L., Radford, M. and Kanagawa, C. (1985) 'Cross-cultural differences in children's use of decision rules: A comparison between Japan and Australia'. *Journal of Personality and Social Psychology*, 49, 1557–64.

Mikula, G. (1980) 'On the role of justice in allocation decisions'. In G. Mikula (ed.) *Justice and Social Interaction*. New York: Springer.

Moscovici, S. (1976) *Social Influence and Social Change*. London: Academic Press.

Moscovici, S. (1980) 'Toward a theory of conversion behavior'. In L. Berkowitz (ed.) *Advances in Experimental Social Psychology*, vol. 13. New York: Academic Press.

Moscovici, S. (1984) 'The phenomenon of social representations'. In R. Farr and S. Moscovici (eds) *Social Representations*. Cambridge: Cambridge University Press.

Nisan, M. (1984) 'Distributive justice and social norms'. *Child Development*, 55, 1020–9.

Ohana, J. (1987) 'Social knowledge and educational style'. Report to the Centre National de le Recherche Scientifique, Paris.

Parsons, T. (1952) *The Social System*. London: Tavistock.

Piaget, J. (1932) *The Moral Judgement of the Child*. London: Routledge & Kegan Paul.

Piaget, J. (1953) *The Origins of Intelligence in the Child*. London: Routledge & Kegan Paul.

Siegal, M. (1981) 'Children's perceptions of adult economic needs'. *Child Development*, 52, 379–82.

Simmons, R.G. and Rosenberg, M. (1971) 'Functions of children's perceptions of the stratification system'. *American Sociological Review*, 36, 235–49.

Snarey, J. (1985) 'Cross cultural universality of socio-moral development: A critical review of Kohlbergian research'. *Psychological Bulletin*, 97, 202–32.

Tajfel, H. (1984) 'Intergroup relations, social myths and social justice in social psychology'. In H. Tajfel (ed.) *The Social Dimension*, vol. 2. Cambridge: Cambridge University Press.

Turiel, E. (1983) *The Development of Social Knowledge*. Cambridge: Cambridge University Press.

Weiner, B. and Peter, N. (1973) 'A cognitive developmental analysis of achievement and moral judgments'. *Developmental Psychology*, 9, 290–309.

Weinstein, E.A. (1958) 'Children's conceptions of occupational stratification'. *Sociology and Social Research*, 42, 278–84.

Wimmer, H., Wachter, J. and Perner, J. (1982) 'Cognitive autonomy of the development of moral evaluation of achievement'. *Child Development*, 53, 668–76.

Chapter 8

Developing psychologies
Paul Light

8.1 The developmental significance of understanding others

Within psychology, the developmental significance of understanding other people has been construed in a number of ways. For some 'sociogenic' theories, such as those of Vygotsky or G.H. Mead, such understanding is the foundation of all mental life. These authors held that reflective thought in all domains depended upon the ability to take others' perspectives towards oneself. Language was seen as a crucial mediator of this socially mediated construction of selfhood.

Piagetian psychology, although it contains occasional echoes of this standpoint, offers a more universalistic cognitive analysis. Through inter-action with the world in all its aspects, the child constructs increasingly powerful and general cognitive tools ('mental operations'). These are at first limited to concrete situations, but become increasingly abstract in form. Scientific thinking (hypothetico-deductive reasoning, control of variables, etc.) is seen as representing in some sense the natural goal of cognitive development.

Piaget's child is thus in some sense a child scientist, but not particularly a child psychologist. From a Piagetian position, the development of understanding of other people parallels other aspects of understanding, reflecting the same general stages of the development of cognitive competence. And whereas Mead and Vygotsky saw development as a fundamentally social process through which individuality is constructed, Piagetian psychology sees the movement of development as being from the individual to the social: from a state of egocentrism towards a progressively differentiated awareness of others.

Contemporary developmental psychology shows new and different influences. Information-processing approaches have had a significant impact. These, like Piagetian psychology, typically grant no privileged position to 'understanding others'. Unlike Piagetian psychology, however, they do not presuppose that developing an understanding of others must necessarily be governed by the same cognitive-developmental stages and sequences which characterize other fields of understanding. On the contrary, researchers such as Carey (1985), Keil (1989) and Ceci (1990) see cognitive development not in terms of the acquisition of high-level general cognitive processes but rather as a set of much more local and circumscribed achievements relating to particular domains of knowledge (e.g. number, language, music).

Expertise in a particular domain depends first and foremost on the extent of the knowledge available within that domain. The cognitive representations and strategies that the child comes to use in one domain may bear little or no resemblance to those used in another. From this standpoint, we need to consider the possibility that the child's understanding of other people might constitute a distinct domain, and thus have a developmental agenda all its own.

Domains are held to relate to distinct classes of phenomena, and to embody explanatory theories in terms of which the child understands these phenomena. To this extent, there is some reason to expect them to correspond to the 'disciplines' of academic knowledge. Objects, forces and movements, for example, belong to the academic discipline of physics, but corresponding to this 'official' physics there are 'naive' theories. Naive theories of motion, for example, which are by no means exclusive to childhood, are seen to differ sharply from Newton's Laws of Motion (Viennot, 1979). In much the same way it can be supposed that naive theories of *mind* may subserve understanding of how and why people act as they do. These may be at variance not only with 'official' psychology, but also with understanding of phenomena in other domains.

Since domain boundaries act as constraints on learning, they cannot themselves be entirely the products of learning. Within this theoretical perspective, it is generally held that some degree of domain specificity (affecting perception, attention, and so on) must characterize even the newborn. As knowledge accumulates within a domain, it is subject to organization and reorganization through processes not unlike Piagetian 'equilibration'. However, whereas Piaget saw such progressive restructuring as global in its effects, the domain specificity view sees it as a more local phenomenon, occurring as a function of the increasing base of knowledge in a particular domain.

The final perspective that I want to introduce offers an altogether less cognitive and individualistic analysis, and contains strong echoes of Vygotsky and Mead. It is an approach which recognizes the 'particularity' of human understanding. Influenced by anthropologists and sociologists, it sees understanding as being typically embedded in the social practices which make up everyday life. Such understanding is practical rather than theoretical, acquired through more or less informal processes of apprenticeship to the various practices involved (see Walkerdine, 1988).

The units of such an analysis are 'situations' or 'practices' rather than fundamental ontological domains. Claims for universality are therefore much weaker. Also, it is less clear that 'understanding others' represents a unitary category of understanding. Rather, the various situations in which we interact with others will have their own ground rules, and will call out different kinds of 'understanding'. All knowledge, not only knowledge of others, is seen to be 'situated' – i.e. linked to the situations of everyday life and not readily transferable. To the extent that such situations are typically social, we can see here once again the idea that understanding others (or at least understanding with others) is basic to all understanding.

Thus the first and the last of our 'perspectives' have much in common, being merely aspects of a long tradition of research which has followed a social agenda, seeking the origins of understanding in the forms of social life. By contrast, the other approaches I have identified seem to reflect a cognitive agenda, concerned to understand social behaviour (along with other forms of behaviour) through an analysis of individual cognitive development. Such a classification is admittedly very crude, and the various chapters which make up the present volume cannot be slotted neatly into it. None the less, the distinction between cognitive and social agendas offers me a way of organizing my comments on issues that arise from this fascinating collection.

8.2 The cognitive agenda

It is noticeable that Mark Bennett, in his introduction, finds his starting points in the social-psychological literature. He notes, quite rightly, that social psychology has been much neglected by developmentalists. Indeed, the bringing together of social and developmental perspectives is one of the useful functions of this volume. One factor which helps to make this *rapprochement* possible is the increasing prevalence in both fields of essentially cognitive accounts of human development and behaviour. Under the influence of the 'information technology revolution' and the concomitant growth of the cognitive sciences, psychological work in many fields has become almost exclusively concerned with cognition.

This dominance of cognitive approaches is reflected in the fact that not only intellectual but also social behaviour and development have come to be conceived in largely cognitive terms. Perhaps the clearest reflection of this can be seen in current concern with children's 'theory of mind'. Much of this literature, well reflected in Sue Leekam's chapter, is framed within an information-processing (domain specificity) perspective, albeit with strong Piagetian overtones.

There is a great deal of argument over what it means to say that a child 'has' a theory of mind, what can be said to be the defining properties of such a theory, and what experimental 'litmus test' can be applied. The arguments seem as much epistemological (i.e. about the nature of knowledge) as psychological. The concept of theory and the allied concept of representation are problematic, and are used in several different senses in psychology. At the moment we seem to be some way away from sorting them out.

Meanwhile, the false-belief task has emerged as the main contender for a litmus test for theory of mind, and looks set to occupy a similar role in this literature to that occupied by the conservation task in Piaget's theory of operational thinking. Its results are important for what they show about representational competence; what they show about false beliefs *per se* is almost incidental. Interest centres on the age at which children can be said to have attained such competence rather than on, say, the factors which account for individual differences, or the relation between such attributes and the patterns of everyday social behaviour. Nor are group differences apparently of much interest, except those (as in the case of autism) which promise to offer other avenues to testing the existence of a theory of mind.

When they do address the question of how these cognitive developments might be related to everyday social behaviour, researchers in this field often seem to assume, rather uncritically, that behaviour will simply be a reflection (albeit, perhaps, a somewhat blurred one) of underlying cognitive development. A similar assumption was made by an earlier generation of Piagetian researchers – namely, that as children decentre their thinking in the transition from pre-operational to operational thinking, so their tendency to cooperate, to help others, and generally to behave 'pro-socially' will increase. Innumerable studies in the early 1970s investigated the correlation between perspective-taking tasks of various kinds and measures of helpfulness, friendliness, popularity, and so on. The results were not encouraging; the amounts of variance accounted for by such correlations are typically very low, and there is little convincing evidence of specificity in the relationships involved (see review by Light, 1987).

Although it may seem natural to treat cognitive competencies as causes and social behavioural tendencies as effects, it is possible to construe the relationship differently. Developments in understanding may be *born out of* social practices into which the child is inducted in quite other ways. Thus practical social competencies, supported by others, might be thought of as antedating the cognitive competencies to which they correspond. Such a course of development 'from the social to the individual' would, of course, be consonant with the sociogenic theories of Mead and Vygotsky.

There are a number of other problematic aspects of any simple assumption that developments in understanding cause developments in social behaviour.

Such an approach neglects emotional and motivational factors on the one hand, and temperamental and personality factors on the other. It also ignores wider considerations such as how individuals are positioned in relation to the social order. These are all factors which will affect social behaviour, and potentially also social understanding.

Emotional development, or at least the development of children's understanding of emotions, is addressed in Mark Meerum Terwogt and Paul Harris's chapter. Here cognitive elements and social elements in the account are explicitly separated. The relationship between cognition and emotionality is seen largely in terms of the development of cognitive strategies for monitoring, tempering or blocking the experience or the expression of emotion.

Children's emotional development and behaviour is seen as being constrained from the outset by an innate repertoire of basic emotions. Children's experience of these emotions is 'first-hand', while knowledge of other people's emotions is achieved via simulation and imaginative projection. Here the movement of development seems very much from the individual to the social.

The child's social environment is given a role in the engendering of new and more complex 'social emotions', such as pride, shame and guilt. Even here, however, general cognitive constraints on information processing are seen to dictate a predictable developmental sequence. Overall, development is seen in terms of decentring to take account of multiple inputs, and more generally in terms of gaining conscious control over internal bodily processes.

In her chapter on children's understanding of social rules, Judith Smetana attempts to qualify the cognitive universalism of Piaget and Kohlberg, for whom 'rules are rules'. She does this by attempting a partition of the territory, articulating a distinction between moral and social-conventional rules. Moral rules are supposed to have a high degree of cross-situational and cross-cultural constancy, being ultimately dependent on some kind of innate moral sense. Social-conventional rules, as their name suggests, are envisaged as being much more contingent affairs, dependent on social authority.

Such distinctions are generally hard to sustain. To take an example from Smetana's chapter: the Indian caste system is clearly social-conventional in origin, but in many Western eyes it appears morally offensive. This in turn may relate to a cultural difference in the very basis of moral reasoning. While American moral reasoning seems to centre upon equity, Indian morality bears chiefly on issues of duty and responsibility. Such differences may threaten to undercut any attempt at distinguishing between moral and social-conventional domains. In practice, many – if not most – everyday situations appear to involve tangled webs of prudential, conventional and moral considerations.

Here again the relationship between understanding and behaviour arises as an issue. Developing an understanding of social rules is held to be 'one of the major tasks of childhood', on the grounds that such understanding is necessary if one is to function competently in society. This may not be as obvious as it sounds, at least if it implies that 'rule-governed' social behaviour necessarily depends upon any explicit understanding of – or ability to articulate – the rules themselves. For example, first-language learning offers the classic example of acquisition of rule-governed behaviour through a process which appears to be almost entirely independent of any explicit understanding of the rules (in this case the rules of grammar): children can speak grammatically before they can articulate the rules of grammar.

Although the problem is to some extent an empirical one, interpretation of evidence is rarely straightforward. For example, the finding that disruptive children's orientation to socio-conventional rules is at a 'lower developmental level' than that of normal children is clearly relevant, but we should be alert to the risk in such cases that we might mistake dissident social attitudes for cognitive deficits.

Nicola Yuill's chapter on children's understanding of personality and dispositions is one of the most directly apposite to the topic of 'children as psychologists'. In focusing on the understanding of traits and states, the chapter addresses not so much the *existence* as the *contents* of children's 'theory of mind'. One concomitant of this is that the age range with which Yuill is concerned extends well beyond the 3- and 4-year-olds so beloved by 'theory-of-mind' researchers.

A concern not infrequently voiced about theories in developmental psychology, especially by anthropologists, is that they may be ethnocentric: offering Western theories of Western children, dressed up as universals. It is interesting to consider, therefore, how far children's 'naive' psychological theories actually vary as a function of cultural location and situation. Yuill makes it clear that she sees this not as a dichotomy – *either* universal cognitive development *or* enculturation – but rather as an intimate relationship between the two. She explores the extent to which 'trait psychology' is linked to the individualism of Western cultures, suggesting that the use of trait terms may be adaptive in social settings characterized by relatively large numbers of superficial relationships. It appears that young children growing up within the framework of a small number of intimate relationships do not typically think of others in terms of personality traits at all.

We can see this as a small example of the idea that children's development 'as psychologists' might be envisaged not in terms of an inexorable progression towards cognitive maturity, but rather as a process of adaptation to the social and interpersonal situations in which they find themselves. It is to this more socially orientated agenda that I shall now turn.

8.3 The social agenda

Judith Hudson's chapter about understanding events makes two important claims about scripts. One is that scripts can be considered as the basic building blocks of cognitive development, supporting the early emergence of fundamental cognitive processes and providing a representational foundation for the development of more complex conceptual systems. The other is that scripts are essentially *cultural* products, acquired through a process of 'guided participation'. The conjunction of these two assertions puts cultural and social experience at the very heart of cognitive development. Such development is seen as being grounded not in the vicissitudes of individual social experience but in the weave of social practices which make up the reality of everyday life.

Script knowledge, as Hudson envisages it, may consist in largely unconscious sets of expectations concerning 'what goes with what', or what people will do in a given situation. Action-in-context is primary. Conscious reflection is secondary, and indeed may be occasioned only (as Vygotsky suggested) by breaks in the flow of normal experience.

Scripts are content-rich; they constitute organized knowledge. Development can be understood in terms of the progressive organization and reorganization of such 'knowledge bases'. This, together with Hudson's emphasis on the temporal and causal structure embodied in scripts, raises the question of how the concept of script relates to that of 'domain' as we were using it above. One notable difference is that domains are typically construed as originating in individual cognitive systems and founded upon fundamental ontological distinctions. Scripts, by contrast, are thought of as being acquired in the course of social experience, and grounded in culturally situated practices.

The notion of children's cognition being tied to scripts links quite nicely with Margaret Donaldson's (1978) idea that pre-schoolers could demonstrate their understanding of the world only in socially intelligible contexts: contexts which make 'human sense'. Donaldson saw development as a process whereby cognition is progressively freed from its initial state of embeddedness. Likewise, Hudson talks about the progressive decontextualization of cognitive operations from event representations. Following Donaldson, we might see literacy and schooling as the principal instruments of this process.

There is, however, a counter-argument – ably voiced by Walkerdine (1988) – to the effect that development is more a matter of *re*contextualization than of decontextualization. Thinking in adulthood, including the kinds of thinking that go with educational accomplishment, can be seen in many respects as just as highly scripted and just as firmly rooted in particular social practices as those of childhood. Indeed, one of the lessons of much contemporary psychology seems to be that, qualitatively speaking, there is not nearly as much difference between the thinking of children and that of adults as we once supposed. Such differences as there are relate more to what they know and to the social worlds they inhabit than to any qualitative changes in the nature of their thinking and reasoning.

An important aspect of 'the social agenda' is that it embraces consideration of children's particular social experience and situation, and of their positioning in relation to the social order. The chapter by Nick Emler and Julie Dickinson addresses children's understanding of one aspect of that social order: the relation between occupation and income. Rather than seeing this as an essentially cognitive problem, grist to the mill of cognitive-developmental analysis, they argue that the relation between occupation and income is inherently ideological. The idea that it is susceptible to rational analysis on the basis of equity is, they suggest, part and parcel of a social myth: a shared belief system or 'social representation'.

Such social representations are seen as being generated and sustained by social groups, and as playing an important role in intergroup perceptions and relations. Children's perceptions of matters such as occupation and income, therefore, will inevitably be coloured by the standpoint of the social group to which they belong.

The important point to note about the social representations position is that whereas cognitive-developmental approaches characteristically universalize the child, looking for general cognitive constraints on children's understanding, analysis in terms of social representations typically retains a concern with the particularities of the perspectives involved. Children are initiated into the practices and traditions of their own social group, and it is through these very particular social experiences that they acquire the cognitive tools they need for participating in a wider society. At the beginning of this chapter I noted Bennett's observation about the neglect of social psychology by developmental psychologists. This volume has contributed significantly to remedying this neglect, but it seems to me that there is still much to be learned from social-psychological approaches.

8.4 The child as psychologist

In this final section, I shall just offer a few reflections on the title of the present volume. 'The Child as Psychologist' is certainly an interesting title. We might imagine a sequel: 'The Child as Physicist', perhaps. The series might not run to any great length, though. 'The Child as Chemist' or 'The Child as Archaeologist' begin to sound a bit improbable.

What could such a title mean? In the case of physics, it might catch at a lively aspect of the domain specificity literature referred to above. This suggests that the child develops naive theories of physics, bearing on concepts of object, force, movement, etc. These are supposed to be developed on the basis of innately given constraints or perceptual affordances, and then progressively structured and restructured through experience in the world. Such naive theories are thought of as developing independently of tuition, whether formal or informal. Indeed, they frequently conflict with the 'officially sanctioned' physics taught in school.

Such a perspective – essentially a modern version of the constructivist cognitive agenda – tends to split nature and culture. The naive theories of the child are conceived of as 'natural' properties of the individual, developing independently of any processes of transmission or enculturation. By contrast, 'scientific' physics is recognized as a historically elaborated system of knowledge, culturally transmitted via tuition. To put it crudely: there is an assumption that naive theories *develop*, where scientific theories are *learned*.

In a similar way, when we turn to psychology, we might be looking for naive psychologies whose development follows a fairly universal course, reflecting the general properties of human cognitive organization. Many of the accounts offered in this volume do indeed seem to have something of this quality about them – at least to the extent that they are more concerned with development than with learning, more concerned with 'naturally occurring theories' which inform social action than with the role of social and cultural processes in shaping the child's perception of others.

My own anxieties – which have probably come through clearly enough by now – is that such an approach neglects the extent to which children can be guided into participation in practices of which they have – at least initially – little or no analytic understanding. It ignores the way in which the structure of language and social relations which surrounds the child serves to frame reality in particular ways, offering ready-made ways of carving up experience. To the extent that these processes are involved, 'naive psychologies' may be just as much historically and culturally located phenomena as 'scientific psychology'.

Some of the evidence on universality and variability in children's 'developing psychologies' bears upon this issue, and much more such evidence will be needed before any informed judgement can be made. Fortunately, the recent convergence of interest between psychologists and cognitive anthropologists promises to provide just such evidence.

What happens to common-sense psychology when it meets 'real' psychology? Not much, it seems. Just as physicists, when they leave the laboratory, seem to lapse quite happily into common-sense ways of thinking about the world, so psychologists seem well able to separate their professional theories from their everyday lives. Academic psychology functions for the most part as 'special-purpose' knowledge, and naive or common-sense psychologies seem to sit quite happily alongside it. It would be nice to think that developmental psychologists, for example, make exceptionally good parents by virtue of their expertise, but I am not at all convinced that this is the case! Here again, it seems that it is not the unity of the domain ('understanding others', or whatever) but the particularity of purposes and practices that really counts.

Everyday forms of psychological understanding are clearly very robust, presumably because they are well adapted to their contexts of use. The present volume has offered many valuable insights into their development, and the psychology of developing psychologies looks set to be a lively field of inquiry for some time to come.

References

Carey, S. (1985) *Conceptual Change in Childhood*. Cambridge, MA: MIT Press.
Ceci, S. (1990) *On Intelligence . . . More or Less*. Englewood Cliffs, NJ: Prentice Hall.
Donaldson, M. (1978) *Children's Minds*. Glasgow: Fontana.
Keil, F. (1989) *Concepts, Kinds and Conceptual Development*. Cambridge, MA: MIT Press.
Light, P. (1987) 'Taking roles'. In J. Bruner and H. Haste (eds) *Making Sense*. London: Methuen.
Viennot, L. (1979) *Le Raisonnement spontane en dynamique élémentaire*. Paris: Hermann.
Walkerdine, V. (1988) *The Mastery of Reason*. London: Routledge.

Name index

Subject index